THE MILITARY BORDER
IN CROATIA, 1740-1881

THE
MILITARY BORDER
IN CROATIA
1740-1881

A Study of an Imperial Institution

Gunther E. Rothenberg

THE UNIVERSITY OF CHICAGO PRESS
Chicago and London

Library of Congress Catalog Card Number: 66–13887

THE UNIVERSITY OF CHICAGO PRESS, CHICAGO & LONDON
The University of Toronto Press, Toronto 5, Canada

—·—·—·—·—·—

PREFACE

This book is a continuation of my study dealing with the history of a singular military institution, the Military Border, *Militärgrenze* or *Vojna Krajina*, maintained by the Habsburgs along their frontier with the Ottoman Empire. My earlier study traced the development of the frontier establishment in Croatia from its origins under Ferdinand I to its reorganization under Maria Theresa. The present volume will carry the story of this institution to its ultimate end in the third quarter of the nineteenth century.

The account presented here is necessarily limited. The history of the Military Border was, of course, very much influenced by the wider considerations of Austrian policy and by general developments in southeastern Europe. Although these factors have been taken into consideration, I have focused on military and administrative aspects, but there are all too many points of interest that limitations of space have prevented me from discussing as fully as I should have liked. Among these inevitable omissions are details of economic, cultural, and religious developments. Even though after the middle of the eighteenth century Austria maintained a frontier establishment along its entire boundary with the Ottoman Empire, only the Croatian Military Border has been considered in detail. Finally, I have tried to steer free of nationalist prejudices and I hope to have avoided adding fresh fuel to the chauvinistic claims and counterclaims that have poisoned so much of the historiography of this region. Even so, I am well aware that my work is not

Preface

likely to escape attacks either for omissions or commissions. It is my hope, however, that controversy will provide a starting point for additional research in a field that, at least in this country, has long remained obscure.

Publication of this work has been greatly aided by generous assistance from many sources. Above all I am grateful for grants from the John Simon Guggenheim Memorial Foundation, the American Council of Learned Societies, and the American Philosophical Society. I am indebted to Southern Illinois University, the University of New Mexico, and the Historical Research and Evaluation Organization of Washington, D.C., for financial assistance in the completion of this study. At the same time it is my pleasant duty to express my appreciation to the scholars and archivists whose advice and courtesy greatly facilitated research at their institutions, especially to Dr. Ivan Ilić of the Yugoslav Academy of Arts and Sciences and Dr. Bernard Stulli, Director of the State Archives in Zagreb. Dr. Miroslava Despot has steered me to sources on the Illyrian period I might otherwise have missed. In Vienna I am obliged for aid to Hofrat Dr. Wilhelm Kraus and Dr. Walter Wagner of the Kriegsarchiv, and to Major General Hofrat Dr. Oskar Regele, the dean of Austrian military historians. In this country I have greatly profited from the suggestions, criticisms, and encouragement of Professors George Barany, Ivo J. Lederer, William H. McNeill, R. John Rath, Peter F. Sugar, and Wayne S. Vucinich. I am indebted to my friend Professor Raymond P. Stearns for wise counsel, and lastly, I wish to express my appreciation to my most helpful critic, copyist, typist, and wife, Eugenia Rothenberg.

Grateful acknowledgments are also made to the University of Illinois Press and to the publishers of the *Slavic Review*, *The Slavonic and East European Review*, and the *Austrian History Yearbook* for permission to reprint passages from my previous work cited in the bibliography.

Albuquerque, New Mexico   GUNTHER E. ROTHENBERG

CONTENTS

ABBREVIATIONS

ARCHIVAL AND MANUSCRIPT MATERIALS:

Austrian:

HHStA	Haus,-Hof-und Staatsarchiv, Wien
Hofdep.	Hofdeputation
Prov.	Provinzen
Ill.	Illyrien, Illyrische
KS	Kroatien-Slawonien
KA	Kriegsarchiv, Wien
FA	Feldakten
HKR	Hofkriegsrat-Hauptreihe
HKR Kanz. Arch.	Hofkriegsrat-Kanzlei-Archiv
HKR Präs.	Hofkriegsrat-Präsidialreihe
KM	Kriegsministerium
Nostitz-Rieneck	Hofkommission Nostitz-Rieneck
MKSM	Militärkanzlei Seiner Majestät
Mém.	Mémoires
Nachl.	Nachlässe
Schriftgut	Schriftgut über die Militärgrenze
Systemal-Verordnungen	Übersicht sämtlicher für die Militair-Gränzen erflossenen Systemal-Verordnungen

French:

AN	Archives Nationales, Paris
AG	Archives de la Guerre, Vincennes
Rec.	Reconnaissances militaires

United States:

Beauharnais Arch.	Beauharnais Archive, Princeton University

Abbreviations Used in the Notes

Yugoslav:

Arhiv JAZU	Arhiv Jugoslavenske Akademije Znanosti i Umjetnosti u Zagrebu
Cod.	Codices
Jelačić Papers	Ostavština Bana Jelačića
DAZ	Državni Arhiv u Zagrebu
Banska gkda.	Banska generalkomanda u Zagrebu
Bgda. Petrinja	Brigada Petrinja 1840–73
Karl. Varažd. kraj.	Karlovačka i Varaždinska krajina
Rak. buna	Rakovička buna
Slav. gkde.	Spisi i zapisnici Slavonske generalkomande
Spisi Hrv. Kraj.	Spisi Hrvatske Krajine
Varia	Varia Militaria
Zagr. gkda.	Zagrebačka generalkomanda

PRINTED SOURCES AND SERIALS:

AÖG	Archiv für Österreichische Geschichte
AV	Arhivski vjesnik
DR	Der Donauraum
FRA	Fontes rerum austriacarum
Godišnjak BH	Godišnjak Istoriskog društva Bosne i Hercegovine
HZ	Historijski zbornik
MIÖG	Mitteilungen des Instituts für österreichische Geschichtsforschung
MKA	Mitteilungen des k.k.Kriegsarchivs
MÖStA	Mitteilungen des österreichischen Staatsarchivs
MSHSM	Monumenta spectantia historiam Slavorum Meridionalium
ÖMZ	Österreichische Militärische Zeitschrift
SR	Slavic Review
SEER	Slavonic and East European Review
SMZ	Streffleurs österreichische militärische Zeitschrift
SOF	Südostforschungen, Südostdeutsche Forschungen
SOV	Südostdeutsche Vierteljahresblätter
Veröff. Kom. neu. Gesch. Öst.	Veröffentlichungen der Kommission für neuere Geschichte Österreichs
VDA	Vjesnik hrvatsko-slavonskog državnog arhiva
VZA	Vjesnik hrvatsko-slavonskog i dalmatinskog zemaljskog arhiva

Abbreviations Used in the Notes

ZIJK   *Zbornik za istoriju, jezik i književnost Srpske Akademije Nauke*
ZHIJA   *Zbornik historijskog instituta Jugoslavenske Akademije*

MILITARY RANKS AND OFFICES:

FM	Feldmarschall
FZM	Feldzeugmeister
GdC	General der Cavallerie
FML	Feldmarschall Leutnant
GM	Generalmajor
GQM	General Quartiermeister
GFWM	General Feldwachtmeister
GKdo.	Generalkommando

NOTE ON RANK:

The highest rank in the Habsburg armies was Feldmarschall followed either by Feldzeugmeister for officers of the infantry, artillery, and engineering branches, or General der Cavallerie. This was followed by Feldmarschall Leutnant and then by Generalmajor. A number of obsolete ranks survived until the reorganization of the Austrian army in the 1760's. Most important here was General Feldwachtmeister, about equivalent to Feldmarschall Leutnant. Otherwise, the lower commissioned and the enlisted ranks followed the general pattern of European armies and are always given in their English version.

Officers are mentioned with the rank they held at the respective time. Wherever possible, the first textual reference includes full name, title, and rank; thereafter a simplified form is used.

NOTE ON THE SPELLING OF PLACE AND PERSONAL NAMES:

The rendition of geographical and personal names is one of the difficulties in a study of a frontier region where so many languages overlap. During the period covered here, from 1740 to 1881, most localities were known under German, Serbo-Croat, Hungarian, and on occasion Italian names. The present work is a historical survey and not a philological study and therefore the author decided to adopt a rough and ready solution. In order to facilitate orientation, the current Serbo-Croatian version has been used and the other variants have been given whenever a name is introduced for the first time. There are, however, two exceptions. German was the official language of the Military Border administration and whenever a place name became part of the official designation of a military district or unit, the official version has been employed throughout. Also, familiarity has been the overriding rule and names that have become part of the common English usage are given as such.

The spelling of personal names also presented difficulties. It must be kept in mind that official documents as well as individuals and families often employed different versions of one name. The practice here has been to standardize all Serbo-Croatian names in accordance with present-day usage. German names have been rendered as they were spelled at that time, and again, exceptions have been made when the name formed part of a title or designation, or when it has become part of common English historical usage.

1

—·—·—·—·—

THE DEVELOPMENT OF THE CROATIAN MILITARY BORDER TO 1740

In the course of history the term border or frontier has had several meanings. In one sense it denoted a clearly defined line of demarcation, a boundary between the territories of different states. But this is a relatively restricted meaning, and more often the term described a geographic region whose exact limits fluctuated. Such a region could be either the outer reaches of established society — Turner's "hither edge of free land" — or a tract separating different civilizations and peoples. Sometimes this zone, perhaps because of its ruggedness or other difficulty, served as an effective buffer between two polities, but frequently it became the scene of hostile confrontations. When such confrontations were severe and protracted, they often changed the nature of frontier society. Entire districts and communities were specially organized for war: civil and military powers were combined in the hands of local commanders, and most aspects of life were subordinated to the needs of defense. In time such districts and communities developed a distinctive martial character, very different from that of the civilian hinterland. When such developments became fully institutionalized, a special military organization emerged: a military border. In this sense the term military border is used in this study.[1]

Military borders appeared in many different countries and in greatly varying circumstances. Nonetheless, there were some common features. Perhaps the most important was the utiliza-

---

[1] Dietrich Gerhard, "The Frontier in Comparative View," *Comparative Studies in Society and History*, 1 (1959), 205–29.

tion of soldier-colonists, men who in return for their services were granted certain privileges: usually land allotments to maintain themselves and their families. The reason for this was simple. Prolonged defense of an extended frontier against an active and determined enemy has always presented great difficulties. In the ancient world it usually was beyond the human and material resources of any state adequately to guard a long frontier with full-time soldiers. The introduction of peasant-soldiers who largely maintained themselves, at least in times of peace, was an answer to this vexing problem. To be sure, the solution was never entirely satisfactory. In their dual role the peasant-soldiers were often only indifferent troops, ill trained and poorly disciplined, neither good farmers nor good soldiers. Their deficiencies always plagued military borders, but, at least in Europe, the problem of finding manpower to guard frontiers and the perennial economic shortages besetting most states into the modern period admitted no other solution.[2]

Military colonists were already known in the ancient Near East, in Egypt, and in the Greco-Roman world. These early colonies were, however, not established exclusively for border watch, nor did they develop into separate military communities clearly apart from the rest of the armed forces. The first distinctive peasant-soldiers — the *limitanei* of the Roman Empire — appeared in the reign of Alexander Severus in the third century. The institution continued in the empire, reaching its greatest extent following the reforms of Diocletian and Constantine. In the fourth century the *limitanei* and *riparienses* — hereditary soldiers endowed with hereditary farmsteads — constituted a separate force clearly differentiated from the Roman field armies.

Very early in their history the Byzantines revived this institution, and during the seventh century greatly expanded it. Indeed, some authorities consider the *akritai* of the frontier districts a major factor in the strength and resilience of that empire. In medieval western Europe, too, peasant-soldiers were used, by the Merovingians and later by the Carolingians, to defend exposed frontiers. Charlemagne systematized the practice in his marches, concentrating all powers in the hands of margraves and giving special immunities to the peasant-soldiers. The

[2] Max Jähns, *Heeresverfassungen und Völkerleben* (Berlin, 1885), pp. 56–59; Ramsay MacMullen, *Soldier and Civilian in the Later Roman Empire* (Cambridge, Mass., 1963), pp. 21–222.

marches demonstrated another important aspect of the military border system. Although originally conceived for defense, a military border as such was not necessarily static but, as exemplified by Charlemagne's *limes Saxonicus*; it could also serve as the base for, and chief instrument in, the conquest and consolidation of new territory.[3]

During the later Middle Ages the progressive stabilization of state boundaries, the efforts of the feudal nobility to assert a monopoly of arms, and the steady rise in the use of mercenary troops combined to eclipse peasant-soldiers and military borders in western Europe. But they continued to be used in eastern and southeastern Europe, where military necessity required a constant frontier watch — a task for which the feudal levies were unsuitable — and where maintenance of a standing mercenary army of adequate size was prohibitively expensive. Here special groups, such as the Szeklers of Transylvania, continued to be used for frontier guards. Here also the existence of specially privileged groups of commoners provided the emerging dynastic absolutism with a useful tool to counterbalance the power of an arrogant and separatist-minded nobility. "The alliance between price and plebs" was to become an important aspect of the military border system.[4]

Conditions in Pontic and Danubic Europe — roughly the area of the modern Ukraine, Romania, Hungary, and the Croatian highlands — were particularly favorable for the continued existence and the development of new military borders. Here Christian Europe was locked in a protracted struggle against Moslem expansion. During the fifteenth century the Ottoman Turks consolidated their hold over the Balkans and established domination on the north shores of the Black Sea; early in the sixteenth century they overran most of Hungary. From these positions the Turks and their clients intensified their pressure on neighboring countries. These conquests, accomplished largely at the expense of incompetent and disintegrating polities, brought the Ottomans into conflict with new and more dangerous adversaries. On the Pontic steppe the Crim Tartars added their weight to the Turkish military potential, but farther north the decline of Tartar power enabled Ivan III of Moscow to as-

[3] Jähns, p. 59; Charles Diehl, *Byzantium: Greatness and Decline* (New Brunswick, N.J., 1957), pp. 48–50.

[4] William H. McNeill, *Europe's Steppe Frontier 1500–1800* (Chicago, 1964), pp. 90–91.

sert his independence in 1480. Within forty years Muscovy and Poland-Lithuania had annexed all the Russian principalities once subject to the Tartars and were pushing southward into the Ukraine. At the other extreme of the steppe frontier, north and northwest of the Hungarian plain, the Ottomans faced the rising Habsburg power. Moreover, changes in the art of war, the emergence of a strong infantry, and the general adoption of fire-arms favored the West. The traditionalist Turkish military establishment became increasingly obsolescent and no match for the veteran regiments of the Habsburg service.[5] Even the Muscovite and Polish-Lithuanian troops, backward as their state of the military art was compared with that of western Europe, rapidly assumed a stronger military position. But the full impact of the developments came slowly, and for the next hundred and fifty years the Moslems still retained the initiative. The Christian powers were so beset by domestic and foreign complications that they were unable to concentrate their first-line troops against the Turks and Tartars for any extended period. The Ottomans were equally distracted, but in the small border war that became the center of hostilities their cavalry held the advantage. Frequent Moslem raids struck deep into Christian territory and resulted in near depopulation of the frontier districts.

There was also opportunity amid this devastation, and in the frontier zone some of the hardiest individuals of the local population, joined by warlike refugees and escaped serfs from the hinterland, created their own rough-and-ready warrior communities free from the bonds of serfdom. These men met the Moslem raids by ambush, counterraid, and reprisals, and made their living by hunting, fishing, and expeditions into Turkish territory. In the east such warrior communities formed the nucleus for the Cossack hosts; similar groups, but on a much smaller scale, arose in the western Balkans. Neighboring Christian princes engaged such bands for frontier duty. On the southeastern frontiers of Poland-Lithuania, Cossacks were employed as early as 1530; in the west, warlike Balkan refugees entered the Habsburg service. These groups were not peasant-soldiers but at first served as freebooting auxiliaries, retaining a considerable autonomy under their elected leaders and occasionally plundering Christians as well as Moslems.[6]

[5] *Ibid.*, p. 13.

[6] Gunther E. Rothenberg, "Venice and the Uskoks of Senj: 1537–1618," *Journal of Modern History*, 33 (1961), 148–56.

The initial stage was shortlived. On the Austrian frontier the bands were soon placed under the overall command of officers appointed by the crown and integrated into the state service by 1553. The transformation of the Cossacks took more time, and until the end of the seventeenth century they intermittently aspired to an independent role. The Cossacks were always dependent on military supplies from the hinterland, and their struggle against the encroaching authority of Poland and Muscovy — and later, Russia — was fought on an uneven basis. By 1571 both states took steps to place the Cossacks in a more clearly defined and subservient military relationship, and established detachments of "registered" Cossacks — men who, in return for an annual grant, accepted a degree of discipline.[7]

The trend toward bringing the frontiersmen under the control of the state throughout the frontier zone of Danubic and Pontic Europe accelerated during the seventeenth century.[8] Two major developments, opposed in their aims, were detrimental to the continued autonomy of the frontiersmen. One was the bitter animosity of the landed nobility in the hinterland, who considered the special position of the frontiersmen, especially their independence from manorial jurisdiction, as a dangerous example to the docile peasantry. The constant Turkish-Tartar threat had prevented the removal of the special privileges enjoyed by the frontiersmen, but when the danger abated early in the seventeenth century the nobles demanded a change. A parallel development, aimed at curtailing the powers of the nobility but also at subordinating the frontiersmen to even greater controls, was the steady evolution of both the Habsburgs and the Romanovs toward centralized and absolute monarchies. Eventually, the frontiersmen had to choose complete submission to the state power and retention of a limited, highly regimented status as peasant-soldiers, or be reduced to the level of manorial serfs.

On the Austrian frontier there was only minor resistance, but in the Ukraine attempts to extend serfdom to the frontier led to a series of Cossack rebellions. After several decades of complicated maneuvering between Poland, Russia, and Turkey, the Orthodox Cossacks decided to submit to the Orthodox Tsar in 1681. Betrayed by their leaders, the rank-and-file Cossacks

[7] McNeill, pp. 90–91, 111–12.
[8] *Ibid.*, 126–69 passim.

were degraded into serfdom. The resulting bitter discontent manifested itself in a series of savage revolts during the final decades of the seventeenth century and during much of the eighteenth. Another result was a temporary decline in the effectiveness of the Cossacks as a barrier against incursions, especially when the Tartars renewed their raids in force between 1693 and 1713. Nevertheless, the system was considered sound, and during the second quarter of the eighteenth century was reorganized and greatly expanded by Empress Anna Ivanovna. In the Ukraine a line of Cossack stations between the Dnieper and the Donets protected the newly settled lands from incursions by the Tartars of the Crimea; new lines — the Orenburg line against the steppe Kazaks beyond the Urals, and the Caucasian line built first along the Terek — protected other Russian lands from raiders.[9]

At the same time the Cossacks were backed up with a more reliable border protection force. In 1727 a new border organization, the Ukranian Land Militia, was formed. From the outset this new establishment was subject to strict discipline. Army veterans were settled on state lands and organized to form five regiments of infantry. The scheme attracted few volunteers, and by 1750 attempts were made to recruit additional manpower among discontented Austrian frontiersmen of the Orthodox faith. In 1752 new volunteers permitted the establishment of four additional regiments. The institution did not flourish, and was strongly opposed by influential military officials. When the occupation of the Crimea by Russia eliminated the need for such a force on this frontier, it was discontinued by Catherine II.[10]

Meanwhile the Austrian Military Border — *Militärgrenze* or *Vojna Krajina* — underwent considerable expansion and change. After the middle of the eighteenth century the institution extended along the entire boundary with the Ottoman Empire, occupying an area a thousand miles long and from twenty to sixty miles wide.[11] In this region, from the Adriatic

[9] B. H. Sumner, *Peter the Great and the Ottoman Empire* (Oxford, 1949), pp. 15–16, and in general N. A. Smirnov, *Rossiya i Turtsiya v XVI–XVII vv.* (2 vols.; Moscow, 1946), *passim.*

[10] Alan D. Ferguson, "Russian Landmilitia and Austrian Militärgrenze," *Südost-Forschungen,* 13 (1954), 141–47.

[11] For a discussion of the history of the Croatian Military Border prior to 1740 see the author's *The Austrian Military Border in Croatia, 1522–1747* (Urbana, Ill., 1960).

coast to the northern end of the Moldavian Carpathians, there was no civil authority. The land was owned by the crown and assigned to military colonists, governed by military law and military officials. All men capable of bearing arms — *Grenzer* or *graničari* — were part of an ever-ready military force. The original purpose of this organization had been to ward off Turkish raids, but after the decline of the Turks, the function of the board changed: it became a source of cheap and reliable manpower in the wars of the Habsburgs. No longer a mere frontier militia, but an important component of the imperial army, the Grenzer showed their colors on almost all the battlefields of Europe, gaining the reputation of being tough and resourceful, if brutal and rapacious, fighting men. Austria's success in converting the institution was much admired by military experts throughout Europe. When Russia and other states undertook to organize new military settlements in the nineteenth century, they consciously imitated the Austrian pattern. Thus the Austrian Military Border can be considered as the most effective and representative example of such systems in modern times.

The Croatian Military Border was only part of this extensive frontier system, but it was the oldest, best-established, and strongest segment. It is with the Croatian Military Border, in the region south and west of the Drava, that this study is primarily concerned. Slavonia to the east also formed part of the historic Croatian kingdom, but the Croatian border, subdivided into several commands, always formed a separate administrative entity. Only during the last thirty years of its existence, from 1851 to 1881, were the western parts of the Slavonian Military Border joined to the Croatian command. To understand the operation of the Military Border, its special structure and singular character, a sketch of its historical evolution is necessary.

The Croatian Military Border was established early in the sixteenth century by Ferdinand I of Austria. At that time the decline of the once powerful Hungarian-Croatian kingdoms brought the Turks within striking distance of the Habsburg dominions. Year after year the Turkish advance came closer to the Austrian frontiers, and Turkish raids swept across the almost undefended Croatian uplands to ravage the adjoining Inner Austrian duchies: Carniola, Carinthia, and Styria. Attempts to improvise local defenses failed, and in 1522 the Inner

Austrian estates requested that their overlord Archduke Ferdinand, the younger brother of Emperor Charles V, establish a defended zone in northwestern Croatia. The Croatian nobility, despairing of getting any help from Hungary, supported this proposal, and the diet of the Holy Roman Empire promised financial aid. In the summer of 1522 Ferdinand moved mercenary troops to garrison a number of strong points in Croatia and temporarily blocked the enemy's invasion route.

In the following years, Ferdinand's financial position made it impossible to maintain an adequate force of mercenaries along the exposed frontier. Aid promised by the empire failed to materialize, and the disintegrating Hungarian-Croatian state could make no contributions. A remedy was found in the employment of military colonists. The Turkish advance on the Balkans had driven thousands of refugees, generally of the Orthodox faith, into northern Croatia. These warlike and hardy men were assigned land, abundantly available in the devastated frontier regions, on condition that they be ready for service in time of need. At first these arrangements were informal, but after his election as king of Hungary and Croatia in 1527 Ferdinand took steps to make these settlers a permanent and basic element of frontier defense. Further immigration was systematically encouraged, and the policy of colonization was extended to the remnants of the local, exclusively Roman Catholic, population. These military colonists received substantial privileges. They were endowed with small grants of land and relieved from the usual manorial obligations. They were to retain a share in all booty taken from the enemy and were authorized, subject to the ultimate control of appointed Habsburg officials, to elect their own leaders: captains (*vojvode*) and magistrates (*knezovi*). Most important, all settlers of the Orthodox faith were promised freedom of worship. These privileges attracted additional settlers, and by 1550 the Habsburg possessions in Croatia as well as in the Inner Austrian duchies proper were protected by a chain of fortified villages, blockhouses, and watchtowers, manned by some five thousand Grenzer, with only a small cadre of mercenaries to support them. This was the modest beginning of the military border.

During the first century of its existence the military border was hard-pressed by the Turks, and for generations there were constant small wars. In time, as the situation became more stable, the Habsburgs established a special administrative structure and created two military districts. The area between the coast and the Sava River was first called the *Krabatische Gränitz* (Croatian Border); later, after the name of its main fortress built in 1578, it became the Karlstadt (Karlovac) Border. The region between the Sava and the Drava was first called the *Windische Gränitz* (Slovinska Krajina, Slavonian Border); later, the Warasdin (Varaždin) Border, after the name of the major regional town.[12] In 1553 Ferdinand appointed a general officer to command both borders with full authority over civil as well as military affairs. Whatever the original intent, this appointment removed the border establishment from the jurisdiction of the Croatian civil authorities and effectively divided the kingdom into civil and military sectors. The Habsburgs continued to share the administration with the representatives of the privileged estates assembled in the Croatian diet (*Sabor*) and with their chief executive (*Ban*). On the military borders, however, administration was entirely in the hands of appointed Habsburg officials, and the will of the crown was supreme. This development did not go unchallenged. The special status of the borders and of the Grenzer constituted an unending cause for conflict between the Croatian estates and the Habsburg rulers, and there were repeated attempts to expand the power of Ban and Sabor into the military zone. Throughout the sixteenth century the constant Turkish menace prevented the Croatians from pressing their demands, and later the institution had become too well established to be disrupted.

Of outstanding importance during this period was the dynastic allegiance of the Grenzer. At a time when serfdom and subservience to feudal lords were still the general rule, the Grenzer regarded themselves as free tenants of the emperor who were far superior to ordinary peasants and looked to the Habsburgs as the guarantors of their privileged status. Incorporation into civil Croatia would have meant their reduction to peasant status; therefore the Grenzer aligned themselves with the dynasty against the aspirations of the Croatian estates. In 1627, for example, the Warasdiner Grenzer declared that they

[12] In the sixteenth century Slavonia referred roughly to the lands between the Sava, the Drava, and the Danube, including the region of Zagreb. After the Turks were pushed out of the greater part of Hungary-Croatia in the last decade of the seventeenth century, Slavonia came to denote the eastern part of that area.

"would rather be hacked into pieces than be separated from their officers and become subjects of the Croatian nobility."[13]

As long as the Habsburgs were able to exclude Ban and Sabor from the military border, they were obliged to share its administration and control with the Inner Austrian estates. Inner Austria had participated in the maintenance of the border from the start, and its support became even more important when after the death of Ferdinand I in 1564 the Austrian lands were divided into three family lines that held their own courts, made their own policy, and maintained their own military forces. Although the emperor in Vienna retained ultimate authority on the border, responsibility for the immediate administration fell on the ruler of Inner Austria, Archduke Charles of Styria. To carry out this responsibility, the archduke in 1578 negotiated a subsidy agreement with the Inner Austrian estates — the Brucker Libell — that established permanent quotas for the contributions made by the three duchies. Styria undertook to support the Warasdin Border; Carinthia and Carniola were jointly responsible for the maintenance of the Karlstadt Border. In return, the estates received important concessions, including the right to fill all positions in the border establishment except for that of commanding general, whose appointment remained an imperial prerogative. In addition, the estates obtained the right to furnish arms and supplies for the Grenzer on favorable terms, and were also given a strong voice in the separate Inner Austrian Hofkriegsrat established in Graz. The creation of a separate military organization in Graz was necessary because the affairs of the border required a certain degree of autonomy. In the long run, however, divided authority between Vienna and Graz became a serious hindrance to good administration.

This arrangement lasted for more than a hundred and fifty years, although Austria was reunited early in the seventeenth century by Ferdinand II of the Styrian line. The emperor initiated the process that was to move the Habsburg realm toward a centralized and absolute monarchy, although during his lifetime he had only limited success in this respect. On the military border he consolidated the various statutes, regulations, and privileges into one comprehensive administrative document. In

---

[13] Thus the report of the Duke of Sachsen-Hildburghausen, "Beytrag zur Geschichte der Warasdiner und Carlstädter Gränz Verfassung," KA HKR Kanz. Arch. VII-349.

October, 1630, he issued the *Statuta Valachorum*, which emphasized and confirmed the military character of the border establishment.[14] All Grenzer between the ages of sixteen and sixty were declared subject to military service not only against the Turks but against all enemies of the emperor. The statute made the *zadruga* — the large, joint-family household common among the southern Slavic peoples — the basis of the border's social and economic organization. The zadruga, not the individual, became the recipient of the land grant and was responsible for the families of men on military service. Under the circumstances then prevailing on the border, the zadruga enjoyed real advantages. Although a single-family farm might well be ruined by the death of one adult male, the zadruga could more easily absorb such a loss.

The new statute also clarified the chain of command on the border. Knezovi and vojvode continued to be elected by the Grenzer but were clearly subordinated to the appointed Austrian officers, headed by a commanding general with headquarters in Karlstadt fortress. Although the statute, originally issued for the Warasdin Border only but soon extended to the Karlstadt Grenzer, imposed increased military obligations, it was well received. The Grenzer considered the enumeration of their privileges a welcome protection against the continuing attempts by the Croatian nobility to abrogate their special status.[15]

After 1630, as a sign of the increased importance of the bor-

[14] The term *Wallach* was employed at this time to identify refugees from Turkish-occupied territories. Although it often referred to Orthodox Grenzer, it held no definite ethnographic or religious significance at this time, but was used along with other terms such as *Uscoc, pribeg,* or *predawetz.* In the nineteenth century the religious and ethnic status of the Grenzer in Croatia became the subject of heated polemics between Croatian and Serbian scholars. This arid controversy need not detain us here. The numerous Balkan migrations during the Turkish period brought about a complete admixture of people, and when stabilization occurred in the seventeenth century the only dividing line was religion. This became the convenient rule of thumb used by the Austrian authorities and still accepted by most scholars today. "The Catholic became a Croatian; the Orthodox became a Serb." Ludmil Hauptmann, *Die Kroaten im Wandel der Jahrhunderte* (Berlin, 1942), p. 52; Robert W. Seton-Watson, *The Southern Slav Question and the Habsburg Monarchy* (London, 1911), p. 2; and Rudolf Trofenik, "Über die rechtliche Stellung der Religionsgemeinschaften in Jugoslawien," *Schriften der Südosteuropa Gesellschaft,* 2 (Munich, 1961), 476. For the official Austrian attitude see Karl v. Czoernig, *Ethnographie der österreichischen Monarchie* (3 vols.; Vienna, 1857), II, 168.

[15] The most recent discussion of this in B. P. Sučević "Razvitak 'Vlaških prava' u Varaždinskom generalatu," *HZ,* 6 (1953), 33–70.

der establishment, the documents generally speak of the Karlstadt and Warasdin Generalcies. These developments created
considerable dissatisfaction in Croatia and were among the
main reasons leading Croatian feudatories to participate in
the Conspiracy of the Magnates in 1670. The Grenzer, however, could not be seduced from their personal attachment to
the Habsburgs. When the conspiracy collapsed, the Croatian
estates were left in a much weakened position but finally managed to gain a foothold on the border in the 1690's. When, following the repulse of the last Ottoman offensive against Vienna
in 1683, the Austrians advanced on the entire front against
the Turks, the line of the border moved southward to recover
parts of Croatia-Slavonia lost for nearly two hundred years.
Seizing this opportunity, the Sabor raised forces and actively
participated in the reconquest of the area between the Kupa
and Una Rivers. Croatian troops liberated the eastern part of
this region as far as the Sava, and here the Sabor organized a
new military district with the Ban as commander. At this time
Vienna needed Croatian support to fight a rebellion in Hungary;
therefore the emperor confirmed this arrangement, and a third
border district — the *Banal Gränitz* — came into existence.

In the last decade of the seventeenth century a large number of immigrants arrived from Serbia. In 1689 the Austrian
armies advanced to Pec, the seat of the Serbian patriarchate,
and encouraged a general uprising against Ottoman rule. In the
following year, a Turkish offensive drove the Austrians back
across the Danube and forced Patriarch Arsenius Crnojević to
flee with some thirty thousand families who feared Turkish reprisals. The imperial authorities settled the refugees in southern
Hungary and western Slavonia. After the Treaty of Karlovci
(Karlowitz) ended the war in 1699, many of the Serbs accepted
Grenzer status and were settled in new military colonies along
the lower Sava and along the lines of the Theiss, Maros, and
Danube. Still others were incorporated into the Warasdin and
Karlstadt Generalcies; the remainder settled in and around the
towns of Zemun (Semlin) and Karlovci.

From the point of view of this study, the importance of
this massive migration was that it greatly strengthened the
Serbian element of the Grenzer. Although there would be slight
fluctuations, Orthodox Serbs now predominated in the Karlstadt
Generalcy and in the Slavonian military districts. In the Banal

Border they constituted more than half of the population, and in the Warasdin Generalcy they formed a strong minority. Moreover, with the arrival of the patriarch, the Serbs also had a most effective leader. Crnojević immediately sought to secure privileges for his church and his people. In 1691 Emperor Leopold I granted the Orthodox Church special concessions far exceeding the religious rights offered by Ferdinand I. Not only did the Orthodox Church receive guarantees of religious autonomy, but the Leopoldine patents gave the patriarch authority to make laws "in spiritual as well as secular matters," for all followers of his faith, whether civilians or military. As a result, the patriarch became a very powerful figure among the Grenzer and Karlovci, where the patriarchate was established in 1712, became the national as well as the religious center of the Serbs in the Habsburg dominions.[16]

Although the religious privileges were repeatedly confirmed in the following years, the Inner Austrian as well as the Croatian and Hungarian authorities were much opposed; the Roman Catholic Church was of course openly hostile. Many attempts were made to abrogate the special rights of the Orthodox. On the Croatian borders, the Catholic hierarchy, especially the bishop of Zagreb (Agram), sought with the help of the Jesuits to convert the Orthodox to the Catholic faith or at least to coerce them into accepting the Uniat rites. On many occasions, especially in the Warasdin Generalcy, these efforts were aided by the military authorities and accompanied by the use of brute force. Moreover, the efficiency of the Inner Austrian administration sharply deteriorated with the lessening of the Turkish danger. All the duchies competed to obtain a greater share of patronage, and their appointees increasingly regarded their positions as convenient sinecures to exploit the Grenzer. Absenteeism among the officers, false musters, promotions of incompetents, fraud, and other peculations were common. Pay for the Grenzer was always in arrears, and officers often personally pocketed the money destined for their commands. It is not surprising that the Croatian borders simmered with discontent which sometimes flared up into violence.

[16] The withdrawal of Arsenius left the Serb patriarchate in a most vulnerable position. Although it continued for over fifty years, Phanariote and other Greek elements gained influence in Constantinople, and in 1766 the Porte abolished the patriarchate.

Open rebellion broke out in the Warasdin Generalcy in 1695, 1719, and 1728. There were disorders in the Karlstadt Generalcy in 1702, and open rebellions in 1714, 1728, and 1735. Similar incidents occurred in Slavonia in 1727, and in the Theiss-Maros military districts in 1735. There was much discontent in the Banal Border, where the rule of the Sabor was equally corrupt and inefficient.

In general Vienna turned a blind eye to the systematic violation of the religious rights of the Grenzer, but the evident deterioration of the morale of the border establishment did arouse the concern of the Hofkriegsrat. In the first three decades of the eighteenth century various commissions inspected the Croatian borders, deliberated at length, assembled reams of documents, resolved on administrative changes, and then departed without having achieved any great improvements. Similar efforts, with similar results, were made in Slavonia.

Eventually a more fundamental scheme of reorganization was developed and at least partly introduced. The author of this scheme was Duke Joseph of Sachsen-Hildburghausen, one of the many minor German princes seeking fame and fortune under the Habsburg banners. The duke, a mediocre fighting general but an able administrator, was commissioned in 1735 to investigate and if possible to correct the causes of an exceptionally severe revolt in the Warasdin Generalcy. Proceeding with considerable energy, he settled the mutiny by threatening the Grenzer with reduction to peasant status. Then, gaining approval of the Orthodox clergy, he introduced draconian articles of war and reestablished discipline, although he realized that more basic reform was necessary. In his final report, a lengthy document with more than a hundred enclosures, he surveyed the past history of the border institution, described the unsatisfactory conditions prevailing, and finally proposed a thoroughgoing overhaul of its antiquated military organization and administration.[17] He bluntly charged that the maladministration of the Inner Austrian authorities was at the root of the troubles and demanded the elimination of the political patronage and the nepotism associated with appointments to command on the border. The Inner Austrian estates, he said, should be

[17] The report in KA HKR Kanz. Arch. VII-349. Parts of the report printed in Radoslav Lopašić, ed., *Spomenici hrvatske krajine*, MSHSM 20 (Zagreb, 1889), 344–82.

closely supervised to make certain that they carried out their obligations.

Even more important was the duke's program for a complete transformation of the role of the institution that became the basis for the entire future development of the military border. He said that the Grenzer constituted one of the major military resources of the dynasty and proposed to convert them from a mere frontier militia into a nation under arms — "eine paleastra militia perpetui et ferrei" — usable against all enemies and subject to call at all times. He argued that the number of soldiers levied on the borders could be substantially increased, and estimated that as many as fifty thousand fighting men could be raised on the Croatian borders alone. Moreover, he suggested that with proper organization and leadership the Grenzer themselves could carry most of the expenses for the maintenance of such an establishment. Of course, the duke conceded, a complete reorganization of the military and political structure of the border was necessary to provide such a large body of troops, and he submitted a plan that, though specifically drafted for the Warasdin Generalcy, was with some small changes in detail applicable to all other Croatian borders where conditions were similar.

At that time the military establishment of the Warasdin Generalcy was comprised of both "German" — that is, Inner Austrian troops — and Grenzer levies. The Inner Austrian element, which absorbed the greatest part of the expenses of the generalcy, consisted of a staff of some thirty well-paid officials and four infantry companies stationed in Warasdin. Originally these units had been established in the sixteenth century to reinforce the Grenzer and to keep them in order, but by this time they were much too weak and much too far sunk in patronage to fulfill either purpose. Some forty-five hundred rank-and-file Grenzer were organized in thirty captaincies in the Warasdin Generalcy. Each captaincy raised one company of foot soldiers, who were supposed to have standard organization, equipment, and training. In reality their equipment, training, and discipline were lamentably deficient. Except for the captain and a small number of non-commissioned officers, the Grenzer received no pay but were supported by their zadruge. Each zadruga, regardless of size, furnished one armed man. In addition there were five under-strength squadrons of hussars, who received a modest fixed stipend to support their mounts. Altogether the Grenzer establishment was much below its potential capacity.

The duke's proposals aimed to augment the armed strength of the Grenzer. He suggested that the obsolete German companies be disbanded and their equipment used to arm additional Grenzer units. The old-fashioned captaincies should be abandoned. Instead, the generalcy should be divided into two infantry and one hussar regiments. Possibly influenced by the Prussian canton system then in the process of organization, the duke recommended that each regiment be assigned a definite territory with an approximately equal number of inhabitants. Each zadruga — or *Hauskommunion,* as it was called in the official documents — was to furnish a quota of men, fixed according to its size and the number of male members.

The regiments were administrative rather than tactical formations, supervising all details of civil and military life. Battalions and companies on the regular Austrian pattern were the tactical units. Normally the Grenzer were to work on their land and would be called in rotation for training and guard duty. In the event of mobilization, the entire force was to be divided into three levies. The first levy would form the active service battalions and march to join the field army; the second would man the frontier defenses; the remainder would continue with their normal occupations and act as a general reserve.

These, in outline, were the most important features of the plan submitted by Hildburghausen to Emperor Charles VI and the Hofkriegsrat. Although the scheme received surprisingly prompt imperial endorsement, its full implementation was delayed. In the summer of 1737 the emperor began an aggressive war against the Ottoman Empire, and the well-connected Hildburghausen at once obtained an important field command. In his absence, execution of his plans for the Warasdin Generalcy was entrusted to General Count Galler, a conservative officer who regarded the radical innovations with ill-concealed distaste. Also, as could have been safely predicted, the reform project encountered the determined opposition of the Inner Austrian estates. With the operations of war proceeding badly, the emperor lost his early enthusiasm, and in December, 1737, the Hildburghausen reforms were suspended until after the conclusion of hostilities.

Austria's military fortunes did not improve. The casual administrative habits that had long plagued the Habsburg armies and whose evil effects had been counteracted only by the genius of Prince Eugene were disastrously revealed in 1738. That year the Austrian armies suffered abject defeat, and after an interval of confused negotiations the emperor and his advisors hastily concluded peace on extremely disadvantageous terms. The reverses of the war highlighted the gross inadequacies of the military establishment. The army was demoralized; its equipment, training, and leadership were revealed as totally inadequate. Yet so parsimonious were the money-granting estates of the Austrian Empire that the army actually had to be reduced in 1739 and 1740.

In these circumstances little in the way of major reorganization and improvement could be expected on the border. General Galler in Warasdin made some half-hearted efforts to form Grenzer battalions on the regular pattern, and in Karlstadt General Stubenberg attempted to train his men for regular operations with the field army. Inner Austrian officials continued their peculations and no regiments were established at this time. Reform and reorganization on the scale necessary for the Militärgrenze to provide forces capable of holding their own in full-scale European warfare were achieved only in the course of another conflict, which nearly spelled the end of the Habsburg Empire.

2

_·—·—·—·—

THE MILITARY BORDER UNDER
MARIA THERESA: 1740–56

The reverses suffered during the War of the Austrian Succession, especially in the first Silesian campaign, disclosed grave shortcomings in the military and administrative structure of the Habsburg realm. Prussia's new style of warfare made demands that could be met only by new methods, new leadership, and new standards, and required assertion of the crown's overriding authority and increased centralization and control. "After I was forced to sign the Treaty of Dresden," wrote Maria Theresa, "I resolved to take all measures necessary to secure and protect my realm against my two main enemies: the Prussian and the Turk."[1] Out of this resolution grew the great series of Theresan reforms of which the reorganization of the military border system formed an integral part.

The war demonstrated the importance of the Grenzer as a reservoir of trained manpower. When in 1741 the hard-pressed queen appealed to the lands of St. Stephen's crown to redress the balance against the larger battalions of Frederick of Prussia, the Hungarian diet responded with the famous declaration: "Our lives and our blood for our queen!" The total Hungarian contribution was, however, only six regiments of foot and some light horse. In contrast, the military borders, the Croatian and Slavonian generalcies, as well as the Sava, Theiss-Maros, and Danubian military districts placed more

[1] Alfred v. Arneth, _Geschichte Maria Theresias_ (10 vols.; Vienna, 1863–79), IV, 9.

than forty-five thousand men under arms.[2] No such force ever took the field at one time — the land had to be worked, and the watch along the Turkish frontier maintained. By 1741 more than twenty thousand Grenzer fought in Silesia, and every year thereafter large contingents were levied to reinforce the queen's armies.[3] These troops — "the fierce Croatian and the wild Hussar" — fascinated and shocked contemporaries.[4] Only a few of the Grenzer units — primarily the "regulated" battalions of the Warasdin Generalcy — were uniformed, equipped, and disciplined to standards approaching those of western armies. The Warasdiner appeared in square-cut green coats, tight red breeches, and a black felt cap with a brass badge in front and a tassel in the regimental colors. Most of the Grenzer, however, dressed in their national costumes, with dirty white linen trousers tied at the ankle, sashes bristling with daggers and pistols, long Turkish muskets, and hooded red cloaks as worn by the Karlstadters and the Slavonians. Thus attired, they presented a sight not seen in western Europe for more than a century.[5]

During the course of the hostilities the Grenzer showed themselves most adept at small war — "a most useful light infantry."[6] They screened the Austrian main body from surprise attacks and, constantly hovering around the flanks and rear of the enemy, forced him to devote a considerable part of his forces to defending his depots and lines of communication.[7] The Grenzer fought against the Prussians in Bohemia

[2] At the outbreak of the war the total Austrian forces numbered 153,000 men. For data on the Grenzer mobilization see Kriegsgeschichtliche Abteilung des k. u. k. Kriegsarchivs, *Der österreichische Erbfolgekrieg* (9 vols.; Vienna, 1896–1914), I, 502. Documents on the mobilization of the Karlstadt Generalcy, DAZ Zagr. gkda. F-6.

[3] Figures compiled from Alphons v. Wrede, *Geschichte der K. und K. Wehrmacht*, Supplementary volumes to *MKA* (5 vols.; Vienna, 1893–1903), V, 212–14.

[4] Thus described by Samuel Johnson, *The Vanity of Human Wishes* (London, 1749), ll. 249–50.

[5] A series of colored prints by Martin Engelbrecht (1684–1756), showing the various Austrian irregular troops of the period is our best contemporary guide to their costume. For information concerning the uniforms of the regulated Grenzer, I am indebted to Dr. Liselotte Popelka of the Heeresgeschichtliches Museum, Wien.

[6] Hans Delbrück and others, *Geschichte der Kriegskunst im Rahmen der politischen Geschichte* (7 vols.; Berlin, 1900–37), IV, 321–23.

[7] John F. C. Fuller, *British Light Infantry in the Eighteenth Century* (London, 1925), pp. 46–48.

and Silesia and against the French and Bavarians in southern Germany, Alsace, and Italy. They took a prominent part in the operations of 1744, when the aged Field Marshal Count Traun maneuvered Frederick II out of Bohemia by threatening Prussian communications with a force of light troops — Grenzer, Hungarian, and Slavonian mounted volunteers, and some Hungarian light infantry called *tolpatsches*.[8] The effectiveness of Maria Theresa's light troops compelled the other powers to introduce or augment similar forces. "By the time the War of the Austrian Succession had been concluded, light infantry, chiefly on account of the Croats and Pandours, forced themselves, willy nilly, into recognition."[9] Prussia increased her light cavalry and raised free battalions, and France organized five light regiments; but these troops were no match for the Grenzer hardened in the recurring small wars of the Turkish frontier.[10]

Nonetheless, the use of the Grenzer in western European warfare created serious command problems. Officers were unable to restrain the Grenzer, whose passion for drink and plunder was ungovernable and who, even in friendly territory, were a terror to the inhabitants. In enemy territory they were given to every species of rapine. Indeed, their brutality became proverbial and the term "Croat" an epithet.[11] The most infamous and bloody excesses were committed by the Pandour free corps of Baron Trenck, recruited in large part from the cutthroats and ruffians of the Slavonian Border. In fact their conduct became so outrageous that Trenck was removed from his post and court-martialed in 1744.[12] Other Grenzer units were not much better, and despite the efforts of the authorities their excesses occasionally went as far as those of the marauding bands that had terrorized Europe during the Thirty Years' War.

Even more unsatisfactory, from the point of view of the Austrian command, was the Grenzer predilection toward mutiny and desertion. In 1741, for instance, Field Marshal Count

[8] Charles E.P. de Roche-Aymon, *Des Troupes Légères* (Paris, 1817), pp. 53–56. Cf. KA FA 1744, Böhmen 23-9/6.

[9] Fuller, pp. 56–57.

[10] Delbrück, IV, 323; Roche-Aymon, pp. 56–57.

[11] Max Bertling, *Die Kroaten und Panduren in der Mitte des XVIII. Jahrhunderts* (Berlin, 1912), pp. 14–22; Franz Vaniček, *Specialgeschichte der Militärgrenze* (4 vols.; Vienna, 1875), II, 329, 369–71.

[12] On Trenck's corps see KA HKR 1744-I-849/561. A summary of his trial in KA Mém. XXVIII-1118.

Khevenhüller reported that the regulated Warasdiner battalions had done well but that the irregular detachments from the Sava had deserted en masse.[13] In 1742 more than seven hundred of a thousand Grenzer deserted from the Banal contingent in Italy.[14] The same year there was a serious revolt among the Karlstadter, and the following summer the Hofkriegsrat was much disturbed by reports of unrest among the Slavonian Grenzer.[15]

These shortcomings of the Grenzer were in part the legacy of many decades of merciless frontier warfare, but they were aggravated by the obsolete system of administration and command. The three districts of the Croatian Military Border — Karlstadt, Warasdin, and Banal — still remained under the control of the Inner Austrian and Croatian estates with little actual supervision from Vienna. Although these arrangements had long been unsatisfactory, they became intolerable under the stress of war. The Inner Austrians again proved unable — or unwilling — to supply their Grenzer with any degree of regularity, and the pay and rations of the Banal troops was also usually in arrears.[16] Little improvement could be expected until unification, standardization, and regimentation were imposed on the entire border establishment. This was clearly recognized by the queen, who regarded the matter as so urgent that reforms were actually begun while hostilities were still in progress.

In October, 1743, Maria Theresa dissolved the Inner Austrian Hofkriegsrat in Graz and transferred its functions to a new agency, the *Militär-Direktorium*.[17] Hildburghausen was entrusted with the control of this office and instructed to proceed with the reorganization of the Warasdin and Karlstadt Generalcies along the lines he had already suggested in 1737.[18] His chief objective was to convert an irregular frontier militia

---

[13] Wrede, V, 213.

[14] Reports of June 1742, in DAZ Karl.-Var. kraj. F-6/83-86.

[15] Nikolaus v. Preradovich, "Deutsche und Südslawen," *SOV* 8 (1960), 24–25; Vaniček, I, 485–86.

[16] Hofkriegsrat complaint, Vienna, Feb. 13, 1743, DAZ Zagr. gkda. F-6. Also entries for July 5, Aug. 28, and Sept. 4, 1747, in KA Mém. XXIII-90.

[17] Entry for Oct. 16, 1743, KA Systemal Verordnungen. Cf. Victor Thiel, "Die Inner-österreichische Zentralverwaltung, 1564–1749," *AÖG*, 111 (1930), 614–15.

[18] "Instruction für den FM. Prinzen zu Sachsen-Hildburghausen," KA HKR Kanz. Arch. VII-283.

into a rigidly disciplined and ever-ready military force, maintained at little or no cost to the state in times of peace. Such
a sweeping change of course took time, and the process of reorganization was slow and extremely complex. In fact, the
problem of supporting large military forces from the proceeds
of the Grenzer land allotments alone was never satisfactorily
solved. Nonetheless, during his five years in office, from 1744
to 1749, the duke made considerable progress toward a complete overhaul of the border establishment.

Hildburghausen immediately abolished the obsolete captaincies and organized the two generalcies into territorial regiments.
The Warasdin Generalcy was subdivided into two regiments of
infantry and one of hussars; four foot regiments and one hussar
regiment were established in the Karlstadt Generalcy. Until
1753 the foot regiments were known by the name of their
colonel-proprietors, though these never received the customary emoluments; later the regiments took their permanent appellations from their home stations or districts.[19] The St. Georg
and the Kreutz (Križevci) Regiments comprised the Warasdin
Generalcy; the Lika, Ottoschatz (Otočac), Ogulin, and Szluin (Slunj) Regiments formed the Karlstadt Generalcy. The
cavalry regiments were recruited from the two generalcies at
large and were designated as the Warasdin and Karlstadt Hussars. In theory each infantry regiment was to consist of twenty
companies, a total of some four thousand rank and file recruited and supported from regimental districts of approximately equal numbers of inhabitants. In practice the pressing
need for ready field units was paramount, and the time-consum-
ing tasks of land survey and the taking of an accurate census
were deferred. As a result the infantry regiments were of uneven size, resulting in considerable hardships for the weaker
units.[20] The situation was also difficult in the hussar regiments.
Because of the expense of maintaining a mounted trooper, the
strength of the Warasdin Hussars was set at five hundred, and
that of the Karlstadt Hussars at eight hundred, but even this
modest establishment was seldom achieved.[21]

With the reorganization came changes in the judicial system. Hitherto justice on the border was in the hands partly of

[19] Wrede, V, 214–216.
[20] Vaniček, II, 73-74.
[21] Rosters and strength returns, 1746-53, KA Schriftgut F-29/5.

military officials, partly of elected judges — the knezovi. In 1737, however, Hildburghausen, convinced that only the most draconian measures could control the "savage and wild Grenzer," obtained royal sanction to introduce a most severe judicial code.[22] This code had fallen into disuse, but it was reproclaimed in 1745. Even by the standards of the age, the code was severe. The block and the gallows, impalement and quartering, mutilation, branding, the whip, hard labor, and exile were threatened for a wide variety of offenses. In addition, the code abolished the knezovi in the Karlstadt Generalcy, though they continued to function, albeit with reduced powers in the Warasdin. Finally, Hildburghausen curtailed certain of the immunities of the Grenzer, introduced a land tax, and burdened them with heavier *corvée* duties.[23]

During these years Maria Theresa took steps to assert the direct control of the throne over the Grenzer. In 1746 she deprived the Inner Austrian estates of their cherished privilege to make patronage appointments in the two generalcies. "It is Our exclusive right," the queen informed the estates, "to appoint all officers from ensign to commanding general."[24] The next year, after some Grenzer officers complained that they were still treated as militia and discriminated against in allowances and promotions, Maria Theresa ruled that the Grenzer units in Croatia "shall in all matters be treated as regulars, except that in order of precedence they shall forever follow the regiments of the line." The edict, continued, however, in view of their "ancient habits and customs" the Grenzer should always be employed as light troops.[25] The Inner Austrians, needless to say, resented the diminution of their influence, especially since they were expected to continue their contributions for the upkeep of the border establishment. Styria, responsible for the Warasdin Generalcy, did not prove difficult, but Carniola and Carinthia, jointly responsible for the support of the Karlstadt Generalcy, were most obstinate and attempted to

[22] Hildburghausen, "Beytrag zur Geschichte der Warasdiner und Carlstadter Gränz Verfassung," KA HKR Kanz. Arch. VII-I-349.

[23] "Artikelsbrief," encl. 38, *ibid.* Cf. B. P. Sučević, "Razvitak 'Vlaških prava' u Varaždinskom generalatu," *HZ*, 6 (1953), 46–54.

[24] Letter, Vienna, March 18, 1746, in KA Systemal-Verordnungen. Also the draft "Vorschläge zur Abstellung einiger Missbräuche im Carlstädter Generalat," KA HKR Kanz. Arch. VII-239.

[25] Resolution, Apr. 23, and decree, June 13, 1747, in KA Systemal-Verordnungen.

withhold their contributions. In September, 1745, Maria Theresa sent strong letters to the lieutenant governors of the two duchies demanding immediate compliance. No delay was to be tolerated, and the queen announced that it was her "firm intent to proceed with the long overdue reorganization." [26] The estates continued to procrastinate, and in March, 1746, Maria Theresa applied more pressure.[27] Carniola finally paid its share later that year, but the Carinthians held out until 1747. In the end, however, these dilatory tactics were of no avail. The general reorganization of state finances undertaken in 1748 by Chancellor Haugwitz severed the last financial link between the military border and Inner Austria. Subsequently, all expenditures for the Karlstadt and Warasdin regiments were met out of the general army budget and the Grenzer units formed part of the regular imperial army.[28]

By this time the ambitious Hildburghausen had become restive in office. He had made important enemies, and he was interested in obtaining a more attractive command. In March, 1749, he submitted his resignation "for the good of the state." [29] In the reshuffle of commands that followed, the Militärdirektorium was discontinued.[30] The Karlstadt and Warasdin regiments were grouped into separate commands, each reporting directly to the Hofkriegsrat. For the time being, General Feldwachtmeister Leopold Baron Scherzer was appointed to command the Karlstadt regiments, with headquarters in fortress Karlstadt; Obrist Feldwachtmeister Count Benevenuto Petazzi went to the Warasdin, with headquarters at Koprivnica (Kopreinitz).[31]

There still remained the Banal Border, administered and maintained by the Ban and Sabor. Since 1704 ultimate control

[26] Letter, Vienna, Sept. 15, 1745, KA Mém. XXIII-110.
[27] "An den Prinzen von Sachsen-Hildburghausen, Commission und Vollmacht zur neueren Einrichtung des Carlstädter Generalats mit Zuthun beider Länder Kärnthen und Krain," Vienna, March 19, 1746. Also "Nachdruckschreiben" of the same date (copy), KA Mém. XXIII-111.
[28] Various documents concerning the negotiations with Carinthia and Carniola, Sept., 1746, through Feb., 1747, KA Mém. XXIII-112; Vaniček, I, 514–15.
[29] Entry for March 12, 1749, in "Chronologischer Aktenauszug über die Organisierung der Militärgrenze," KA Mém. XXIII-90; letter of resignation, Graz, March 12, 1749, in Radoslav Lopašić, ed., *Spomenici hrvatske krajine,* MSHSM 20 (Zagreb, 1889), 386.
[30] Thiel, p. 615.
[31] Vaniček, I, 581–82.

over this region was vested in the Hofkriegsrat, but actual supervision had been extremely lax. Conditions were as bad as they had been in the districts administered by Inner Austria. Military efficiency was low; neglect and corruption were common; and the discrimination practiced by Roman Catholic Croatian officers against Orthodox enlisted men caused much dissension.[32] During the Silesian Wars the Hofkriegsrat attempted to halt the worst abuses, but these efforts were denounced by the Croatian estates as gross interference. In 1749, perturbed over the developments in the neighboring generalcies, the Sabor once again strongly asserted its position on the Banal Border.[33] Maria Theresa was reluctant to precipitate open conflict with the Croatian estates, closely allied with the powerful and ever-suspicious Hungarian nobility. She proceeded carefully and, employing cajolery, judicious flattery, and concessions, gained in 1750 the support of the Ban, Field Marshal Count Batthyany, for a mutually acceptable solution. The organization of the Banal Border was made to conform to that of the two other Croatian generalcies. Two Banal infantry regiments and one hussar regiment were established. The Ban retained nominal command as well as the colonel-proprietorship of the two foot regiments. His powers of appointment were limited to the subaltern officers; the Hofkriegsrat received the right to choose all higher ranks. Moreover, the troops were to swear obedience to the throne and not to the Croatian kingdom, and the Ban was to render monthly reports to Vienna on the state of the regiments.[34] In the final analysis, the arrangement favored Maria Theresa; but it was accepted by the Sabor, and implementation of the new regime started at once.[35]

By 1750 the military border in Croatia was organized on a uniform pattern, but there still remained vexatious differences among the individual regiments. Land allotments were not standardized, and subsidies and allowances varied greatly. The Warasdin Grenzer, for instance, had to purchase their uniforms

---

[32] See the report of an investigation by Baron Scherzer, Karlstadt, Aug. 1, 1746 (copy), DAZ Zagr. gkda. F-6.

[33] Resolution, Joannes Kukuljević, ed., *Jura regni Croatiae, Dalmatiae, et Slavoniae* (3 vols. in 2; Zagreb, 1861–62), II, 150–58.

[34] *Ibid.*, pp. 431–38. Also the "Allerhöchste Resolution die Einrichtung zweyer Banal Inf. Regt. und eines Cavallerie Regimentes betreffend," Vienna, Feb. 7, 1750, KA HKR Kanz. Arch. VII-295.

[35] Regulations for the Banal regiments, KA HKR 1750-I-229, and 1750-II-206, 208, and 358.

and equipment; only the muskets were furnished by the state. The Karlstadt and Banal units, on the other hand, received free issue of arms, equipment, and uniforms, although they were obliged to maintain these items out of their own pockets.[36] Another serious complaint concerned the unequal size of the regiments, which placed heavy burdens on the smaller units. In 1752 the Hofkriegsrat ordered that efforts be made to "place all regiments as far as possible on the same footing," and a number of villages, especially in the Karlstadt Generalcy, were reallocated. At the same time all regiments were standardized on the pattern of the German line regiments, each with four battalions of four companies, each two hundred forty men strong. Finally, the new regulations reconfirmed the practice of dividing the Grenzer into three levies and decreed that "at no time shall more than one third of a regiment be called for active service." When actually serving with the field army, the Grenzer were to receive regular pay rates.[37]

Similar arrangements were made in the neighboring Slavonian Border. On June 29, 1747, an edict announced the formation of three infantry regiments and one hussar regiment, to "be treated just like all regulars and to serve by land and by sea."[38] Field Marshal Baron Engelshofen organized the Brod, Gradiska, and Peterwardein Infantry Regiments, as well as a regiment of Slavonian Hussars.[39] The organization of these regiments also needed considerable readjustment, and in 1753 Field Marshal Count Serbelloni reorganized the regiments on the pattern set up in Croatia.[40]

The culmination of Maria Theresa's early reforms on the border was the promulgation of a new administrative and judicial code, the *Militär-Gränitz-Rechten*, of 1754.[41] An extraordinary mixture of public and private law, the code subordinated all activities in the border region to military considerations. The

[36] Wrede, V, 215–19.

[37] Hofkriegsrat instructions, Vienna, May 24, 1752, DAZ Zagr. gkda. F-7. Also Hofkriegsrat instructions to the Ban, Vienna, June 22, 1752, KA IIKR 1752-VI-431.

[38] Edict, Vienna, June 29, 1747, DAZ Slav. gkda. 1747-50.

[39] "Kurtze Auskunft über die Eintheilung und Gebrauch der Sclawonischen Gränitz infanterie," KA Mém. XXIII-145.

[40] Vaniček, I, 561–63.

[41] *Militär-Gränitz-Rechten Von Ihro Kaiserl. Königl. Majestät für das Carlstädter und Varasdiner-Generalat Vorgeschrieben im Jahr 1754* (Vienna, n.d.), no pagination. Copy in KA Schriftgut.

document was divided into seven major titles with numerous paragraphs. Titles I, II, and III reviewed and summarized the existing laws, established a system of military courts, and elaborated on the civil statutes applicable on the border. Judicial proceedings were to be handled by military judges — *Auditore* — basing their decisions on the code and on "natural law and the ten commandments."[42] On active service and when under arms for the performance of internal duties, the Grenzer were subject to the articles of war, reinforced by special regulations for the border service. Off-duty offenses and civil delicts were to be handled according to the Austrian civil code, modified to suit local customs and usages.

The land regulations — Title IV — were the very heart of the code, aimed primarily at preserving the communal households — the *Hauskommunitäten*. The code proclaimed the land held by the Grenzer crown property, granted to each household as long as it met its military obligations. Land was the Grenzer's primary compensation, and the size of the grant depended on the quality of the soil and on the type of service, mounted or unmounted, required. In the Karlstadt regiments, for instance, the basic homestead allotment for one communal household supporting one foot soldier consisted of eight yokes of good land, ten of mediocre, or twelve of poor. Hussar homesteads were larger, rating a minimum of twelve yokes. There were also double — even triple — homesteads, and in some instances smaller allotments of three-quarter or even one-half homesteads were made. The basic allotment could not be sold, leased, mortgaged, or given away. Only when a household possessed land over and above its basic homestead — a rather rare occurrence — could this surplus be disposed of. Even then it could be transferred only to another Grenzer family, and the transaction had to be approved by the proper military authorities.[43] The restrictions against traffic in land were reinforced by Title V — regulating inheritance — which specified that the Grenzer could freely dispose of their movable goods, but the homestead had to be passed on to heirs capable of meeting the military obligations.[44]

[42] *Ibid.*, "Preamble."

[43] Title IV, paras. 14–18. A yoke was a rectangle, 220 paces in length and 50 paces wide. In 1807 it was standardized as six-tenths of one hectare.

[44] Vaniček, I, 30–31.

The land regulations aimed also at preserving the exclusive military character of the border population, and all persons not serving the needs of the military establishment had to leave. There were exceptions for the inhabitants of a few military townships — the *Militär-Communitäten* — where a few essential trades were permitted, for the clergy (Orthodox as well as Roman Catholic), and for the families of regular officers and imperial officials; but these classes were barred from owning land, except for houses and small garden plots.[45] Orthodox priests could hold a homestead, provided that their sons undertook the usual military obligations.

Title VI dealt with the criminal procedure and the penal system. It did away with the most barbaric methods of execution, introduced in part by Hildburghausen, and limited punishments in peacetime to flogging, running the gauntlet, prison with or without forced labor, and capital punishment by either hanging or the firing squad. Torture to gain confessions was still permissible, but it was finally abolished in 1776. Moreover, the code introduced the principle of communal responsibility. In cases of murder or highway robbery — banditry was endemic, especially in the Karlstadt Generalcy — it made the nearest village, even if it was not implicated, subject to a heavy fine.[46]

Originally promulgated for the Karlstadt and Warasdin Borders only, the code was soon extended to the Banal and later to all other military borders except the Transylvanian, which always occupied a special position. Together with all the other reforms and innovations, the code contributed additional strength for the Austrian central authorities on the military border. Indeed, it was a measure of the success and the skill displayed by Maria Theresa in her dealings with the Austrian, Croatian, and Hungarian estates that the changes would be made with little opposition from these usually so obstreperous and particularist-minded bodies. But the story was far different with the Grenzer. Here the transformation of the border into an integral part of the Austrian military establishment encountered violent resistance, riots, mutinies, and rebellions, culminating in the great Warasdin revolt of 1755.

The causes of these outbreaks were complex, but basically

[45] *Militär-Gränitz-Rechten*, para. 38.
[46] *Ibid.*, Title VI, and Vaniček, II, 246-49.

the Grenzer feared that the new organizations, regulations, and codes were part of a deliberate plan to curtail their special status. There was justification for such fears, since the Grenzer were increasingly burdened with new obligations. The Hildburghausen statutes, as well as the Border Law of 1754, imposed a host of new duties and at the same time reduced the competence of the elected Grenzer leadership.[47] Native leaders were replaced by foreigners, usually not attuned to the customs, habits, and religion of their subordinates. The regulations of 1752 standardized the regimental organization and also reserved most commissions as well as non-commissioned appointments for regular, mainly German and Roman Catholic, soldiers.[48] Finally, the introduction of new uniforms — tight, uncomfortable, expensive, and all too frequently changed to keep up with the fads of military fashion — was a grievous vexation.[49]

These matters were serious enough to cause considerable unrest among the Grenzer, but they were aggravated by the constant pressure exerted against the rights and privileges of the Orthodox Church in Croatia and Slavonia. The attitude of the Habsburgs, always closely allied with the Catholic Church, toward their Orthodox subjects was thoroughly opportunistic, and concessions granted to the "non-Uniat Greek rite," as it was officially called, were determined solely by reasons of state. As long as the services of the Orthodox Grenzer were needed, their religion was respected; but when the need had passed, the throne did nothing to restrain the efforts of the Catholic hierarchy, which, with the zealous collaboration of the military, attempted forcibly to convert the Orthodox or at least to coerce them to accept the Uniat rites. Thus it had been under Leopold I and under Charles VI, and Maria Theresa continued this seesaw policy.[50] Statesmanlike and tolerant in many ways, the queen was a most zealous Catholic, and the hope of "saving

[47] Sučević, pp. 64–66.

[48] Rudolf Kiszling, *Die Kroaten* (Graz-Cologne, 1956), pp. 41–42; Johann H. Schwicker, *Geschichte der österreichischen Militärgrenze* (Vienna-Teschen, 1883), pp. 90–91; and copy of regulations in KA HKR 1752-VI-432.

[49] For illustrations of the uniforms see Rudolf v. Ottenfels and Oscar Teuber, *Die österreichische Armee von 1700–1867* (Vienna, 1895), pp. 85–105. On the dislike of the Grenzer for the new uniforms see Karlo Horvat, ed., "Zapisci od 1752–1759. Ivana Josipovića župnika križevačkoga," *Starine*, 34 (1913), 315.

[50] Gunther E. Rothenberg, *The Austrian Military Border*, pp. 106–107, 111.

thousands of souls" led her to endorse measures against her Orthodox subjects that clearly violated both the letter and the spirit of the border privileges.[51] The requirements of state occasionally overrode Maria Theresa's religious fervor, but on the whole she heartily approved of the anti-Orthodox activities.

This opportunistic pattern of Habsburg religious policy was once again revealed in 1741 when the Hungarian diet, at the request of the Croatian delegation, abrogated the jurisdiction of the Orthodox metropolitan over the clergy and laity of his faith in Croatia. Maria Theresa, desperately in need of Hungarian-Croatian support, sanctioned the resolution. But, as a shrewd contemporary remarked, "she also needed the services of the Grenzer for the war, and for this reason she hesitated to deprive them of their rights."[52] Although she endorsed the resolution, she negated it just as promptly. Reports about the intentions of the Hungarian diet, combined with continued religious persecution by Catholic zealots in the Inner Austrian administration, were responsible for a mutiny of the Karlstadt contingent in Bavaria in the summer of 1742. The lesson was not lost on Maria Theresa, and the following year she prudently reconfirmed the privileges of the Orthodox Church and the competence of the metropolitan over all Orthodox dioceses in Croatia and Slavonia.[53] Dissension on the military borders gained added impetus by Hildburghausen's abolition of the voivode and knezovi. The Grenzer were ready to believe the worst. In 1744 rumors circulated in the Warasdin regiments that the newly "regulated" units would be treated as troops of the line and stationed for long periods, perhaps for life, in faraway countries. In their absence, so the word went, their families were going to be forcibly converted to Catholicism and reduced to peasant status. The rumors were widely believed, and when the Warasdin levy was ordered to Germany the men mutinied and refused to depart until the authorities had solemnly reconfirmed their special rights and privileges.[54]

[51] Johann H. Schwicker, "Zur Geschichte der kirchlichen Union in der croatischen Militärgrenze," *AÖG*, 52 (1875), 342–43.

[52] Johann Christoph v. Bartenstein, *Kurzer Bericht von der Beschaffenheit der zerstreuten zahlreichen Illyrischen Nation in den kaiserl. königl. Erblanden* (Leipzig, 1802), p. 75. Printed version of a memorandum of 1761.

[53] Friedrich Walter, ed., *Die Geschichte der österreichischen Zentralverwaltung in der Zeit Maria Theresias (1740–1780) Veröff. Kom. neu. Gesch. Öst.*, XXXII (Vienna, 1938), 84–87.

[54] Vaniček, I, 487.

Two years later, in 1746, there was a serious revolt in the Karlstadt Generalcy. The exact circumstances of this affair remain obscure because most of the documents have disappeared. The rebellious Grenzer seem to have acted with the connivance of certain regular officers who were frustrated in their demands for promotion and higher pay and with the support of the former knezovi. After being ordered to Italy, some five thousand Grenzer mutinied, demanding additional safeguards for their faith and their families.[55] At first the local authorities were confused and intimidated. Hildburghausen sent word from Graz to the rebels that the queen had more than enough soldiers to smash the mutiny. If this had to be done, continued the duke, the Grenzer would most certainly be reduced to mere peasants; but if they promptly abandoned their rebellion, the duke promised them an impartial investigation of their grievances and "much glory and booty in the service of the queen."[56] At the same time Hildburghausen instructed Baron Scherzer to reassure the Orthodox by a public proclamation of their privileges "with military pomp, drums, and trumpets."[57] The duke's tactics were most effective, and the mutiny collapsed. Several compromised officers committed suicide, about a dozen ringleaders were executed, and others were sentenced to long terms at hard labor.[58]

On the Banal Border too the introduction of the new regulations triggered an Orthodox revolt. Settled by the Sabor near the end of the seventeenth century, the Banal Grenzer did not enjoy the special privileges granted to other settlers, although the Leopoldine patents guaranteeing freedom of worship to all Orthodox immigrants certainly applied here too.[59] Croatian rule had always been harsh, and now the Orthodox feared further religious discrimination. In the summer of 1750 they took up arms and drove out all Catholic officers. The rebels tried to establish contact with the other Grenzer regiments, sent emissaries to look for aid from Slavonia, and laid plans for a retreat into Bosnia. Clearly this was a dangerous development, and the Hofkriegsrat dispatched a strong body of regulars accompanied by loyal detachments from Karlstadt to restore

[55] *Ibid.*, pp. 500–502.
[56] Letter from Graz, December, 1746, DAZ Zagr. gkda. F-6.
[57] *Ibid.*, instructions to Scherzer, Graz, Dec. 26, 1746.
[58] Vaniček, I, 505–6.
[59] Rothenberg, p. 92.

order.[60] But unrest continued in all regiments: a steady trickle of deserters made their way across the frontier into Turkish territory,[61] and in 1751 there was a minor revolt in the Lika Regiment.[62]

The spirit of revolt also manifested itself farther east in Slavonian and Hungarian military districts. The rebellions had the usual causes: government corruption, heavy burdens, and failure to give just rewards and punishments. Here too Austria's opportunistic policies had left the Serb Grenzer bitter and disillusioned. In 1741 Maria Theresa promised the Hungarian diet that the Theiss-Maros districts would be turned over to Hungarian administration. When this transfer actually took place in 1750, there were riots and near mutiny. The Grenzer opposed becoming mere peasants, and in the end Vienna had to resettle them on the new military border then being formed in the Banat of Temesvar.[63] Many of the Orthodox turned from Vienna to Moscow. Russian agents, active in all the Orthodox regiments during this period, recruited several thousand families for emigration to southern Russia.[64] The open pro-Russian sentiments among the Orthodox Grenzer, the Orthodox clergy, and civilian elements disturbed the Austrian government. Orders were issued to apprehend all Russian agents, especially Orthodox priests, and to deport them at once.[65] A high-level conference was called in Vienna to discuss measures to prevent further emigration.[66]

By this time Austria's relations with the Orthodox were in large part managed by a special agency, the *Hofdeputation in Banaticis, Transylvanicis, et Illyricis,* originally established in 1745 as a mere *Hofkommission* and elevated to *Deputation* sta-

[60] Documents on the Banal revolt in KA HKR 1750-IX-100.

[61] On the desertions see the "Vorschläge zur Abstellung einiger Missbräuche im Carlstädter-Generalat" (n.d.), KA Kanz. Arch. VII-293.

[62] A contemporary description of this revolt in T. Smičiklas, ed., *Balthasari Adami Kercselich: Annuae 1748–1767, MSHSM,* 30 (Zagreb, 1901), 67–69. Also Vaniček, I, 575–77.

[63] On the disturbances in the Theiss-Maros districts see KA HKR 1750-VII-450, and 409-12. Also the memorandum "Betrachtungen über die Wiederherstellung deren ehemalig bestandenen Confinien und Untersuchung des 24^en Art. vom Jahre 1754" (n.d.), KA Mém. XXIII-7.

[64] Schwicker, *Geschichte,* pp. 75–76.

[65] Orders of May 25, 1751, in DAZ Zagr. gkda F-7; Arneth, IX, 84–85.

[66] "Protocolle und Vorsichtsmittlen um den raitzischen Volck den Hang und die Auswanderung nach Ruszland zu benehmen," KA HKR 1752-VII-513-14.

tus two years later.[67] The exact competence of this new agency
was never closely defined. Originally it was not concerned with
the military or economic affairs of the southeastern frontier
areas, but was to handle the affairs of the "Rascian nation" —
one of the many names then used for the Serbs.[68] In practice,
however, it proved impossible strictly to delimit the activities of
the deputation and especially to determine what exactly constituted "Illyricis." "Illyrian affairs," expounded Count König-
segg-Erps, chairman of the agency in 1753, "include not only
relations with the Ottoman and Russian Empires, but also the
lands of the Hungarian-Croatian crown, including the Warasdin and Karlstadt Generalcies, as well as the military districts in
Slavonia and Syrmia." [69] This wide interpretation brought the
deputation into frequent conflict with the Hungarian-Croatian
as well as the military authorities. The deputation usually defended the interests of the Orthodox, and this attitude became
even more pronounced after 1755 when Transylvanian and
Banat affairs were returned to the treasury (*Hofkammer*). The
truncated deputation came under the chairmanship of Johann
Christoph von Bartenstein, an Austrian expert on southeastern
affairs and long a champion of the Grenzer.[70]

The Orthodox Grenzer were indeed lucky to find a friend
at court. Maria Theresa, extremely perturbed about the tumults
and the mass emigration to Russia, resolved to curtail drastically the position of the Orthodox Church on the military borders. Although she still resisted Hungarian-Croatian pressure
for the dissolution of the Orthodox bishoprics, she countenanced schemes to force the Orthodox Grenzer to accept the
Uniat rite. In Croatia developments centered on the Sichelburg (Žumberak) district in the Karlstadt Generalcy and the
Orthodox monastery at Marcsa (Severin) in the Warasdin
Generalcy.

The Sichelburg district, one of the earliest settlement areas of
the military border, belonged to the Szluin Regiment. It was

[67] Walter, pp. 87–88.

[68] Karl v. Czoernig, *Ethnographie der österreichischen Monarchie* (3 vols.;
Vienna, 1857), II, 157–71.

[69] Report of July 28, 1753, in Joseph Kallbrunner and Melitta Winkler,
eds., *Die Zeit des Directorium in publicis et cameralibus. Aktenstücke, Veröff.
Kom. neu. Gesch. Öst.*, XVIII (Vienna, 1925), 117.

[70] Josef Hrazky, "Johann Christoph Bartenstein, der Staatsmann und
Erzieher," *MÖStA*, 11 (1958), 248–49.

surrounded on the north, west, and southwest by Carniola and the southeast by civil Croatia, forming a small military enclave in civil territory with a total population of only six thousand.[71] Here pressure against the Orthodox Church could be brought with relative impunity, and in 1750 Baron Scherzer began a systematic campaign to oust the Orthodox clergy and to establish in their place a Uniat bishopric.[72] Although this was a flagrant violation of ancient privileges, Maria Theresa permitted the military to proceed. Under severe pressure the Sichelburger Grenzer had by the mid-1760's largely accepted the Uniat rite.[73] Only the weakness and the isolation of the district made this conversion possible; attempts to spread the rite in the remainder of the Karlstadt Generalcy failed completely.[74]

During the same period efforts were made to install the Uniats at Marcsa but failed. Although the Warasdin regiments had a Roman Catholic majority, the monastery at Marcsa was the main religious center for the Orthodox Grenzer before the establishment of the patriarchate at Karlovci. Even more important perhaps, it also served as the repository for the original charters of privilege granted to the military border. For several decades Orthodox and Uniat monks, the latter usually supported by the Inner Austrian military authorities, had contested possession of the monastery.[75] Since 1739 the Orthodox had been in control, and in 1741 Maria Theresa refused to permit their forcible eviction.[76] A decade later, circumstances had changed. In the Warasdin Generalcy too there had been disturbances and occasionally near mutiny, largely because of poor administration. Maria Theresa was only too ready to blame

[71] Franz J. Fras, *Vollständige Topographie der Karlstädter Militärgrenze* (Zagreb, 1835), p. 379; Schwicker, "Zur Geschichte der kirchlichen Union," pp. 287–88.

[72] Order to deport all itinerant Orthodox monks, Sichelburg, Nov. 24, 1750, Schwicker, pp. 375–76. Also Smičiklas, p. 59.

[73] Schwicker, "Zur Geschichte der kirchlichen Union," pp. 347–50. Although Maria Theresa decreed draconic penalties, there was occasional backsliding. This caused much resentment and on July 4, 1752, the Hofdeputation in Illyricis requested the queen to soften her stand. HHStA Ill. Hofdeput. F-192.

[74] Schwicker, "Zur Geschichte der kirchlichen Union," p. 366. See also Johann C. v. Engel, *Staatskunde und Geschichte von Dalmatien, Croatien, und Slawonien* (Halle, 1798), p. 308, and Lazo Kostić, *Sporni predeli Srba i Hrvata* (Chicago, 1957), pp. 298–99.

[75] Rothenberg, pp. 106–7, 111.

[76] Schwicker, "Zur Geschichte der kirchlichen Union," p. 293.

the influence of Orthodox clergy. Therefore, when in 1753 and again in 1754 the Sabor urged that the monastery be turned over to the Uniats, a request strongly endorsed by Baron Petazzi, the queen agreed.[77] Orders were issued to oust the Orthodox monks and to install the Uniats in their place. On September 12, 1754, Petazzi reported that the Uniat Bishop Gabriel Palković had been installed at Marcsa amid "great jubilation and rejoicing of all the people."[78]

Petazzi's report was wide of the truth. The military action against Marcsa was widely resented not only by the Orthodox but also by the Catholic Grenzer, who suspected a threat to their cherished privileges.[79] Added to the various other irritations arising out of the reorganization of the border service, these fears and suspicions provided the most important factor behind the outbreak of the largest and potentially most dangerous border revolt. Matters were only slightly improved when late in the year Petazzi was transferred to Karlstadt, to be succeeded in the Warasdin by General Count Kheul, with Colonel Guiccardi, a brutal bigot, as his second in command. Petazzi had not been popular, but Guiccardi was soon detested.[80] Conditions were now ripe for an outbreak. The immediate occasion — though hardly the cause, as some historians maintain — was an order issued in December, 1754, requiring that the Warasdin Grenzer purchase new uniforms and equipment, in order to make a good impression during an expected royal review.[81] When in January, 1755, attempts were made to collect payment by force, the Grenzer reacted violently. In the Kreutz Regiment a score of unpopular officers, natives as well as foreigners, were killed; others saved themselves by hasty flight. A veteran Grenzer, Captain Petar Ljubović, long suspected by the authorities, assumed leadership and was joined

[77] Resolutions of the Sabor, Nov., 1753, and May, 1754, in Kukuljević, 2, 163-66, and 170-71. Petazzi's memorandum constitutes enclosure 6 of a compendium, Karlstadt, Apr. 13, 1754, KA Mém. XXIII-162.

[78] KA Mém. XXIII-164.

[79] See Kercselich's exposition "Qual causae et motiva tumultus," in Smičiklas, pp. 158–59.

[80] "Hinc universorum fuit de Petacci suspirium, Guiccardii detestatio," *ibid.*, p. 135.

[81] This view held by Arneth, IV, 96–97, and accepted by all German-Austrian writers, has most recently been restated by Kiszling, p. 39. It reveals the unwillingness of these writers to concede the justice of the Grenzer demands.

by a number of knezovi. The revolt spread rapidly, and by the end of January more than seventeen thousand armed Grenzer had assembled in and around Marcsa.[82] At the same time, but without any collusion with the military insurgents, the peasants of upper Slavonia rose against their manorial lords.[83]

With skill and good fortune the Austrian government prevented the revolt from spreading and succeeded in crushing it without bloodshed. Several companies of the St. Georg Regiment remained loyal. A small uprising in the Karlstadt Generalcy collapsed almost at once.[84] The Slavonian regiments remained quiet. The revolt was directed against the government's underlings and not against the government itself. Meanwhile the Grenzer leadership proved most inept. The Grenzer did not attempt to seize Warasdin or other centers but, considering themselves merely in a state of armed protest, spent much time formulating a detailed list of their demands for submission to the authorities in Vienna. On the whole, their demands were moderate. The main grievances were the recent expulsion of the Orthodox monks from Marcsa; the heavy labor service, often for private gain, exacted by certain officers; and the frequent abuses, beatings, and other brutalities inflicted on the enlisted men. Finally, the Grenzer complained about the forced purchases of new uniforms and about the preponderance of foreign officers that limited the opportunities of the Grenzer to rise in the service.[85]

The uprising came at a most inopportune time for Maria Theresa. Once again the international situation was tense, and conflict with Prussia was a distinct possibility. After some hasty consultation with the Illyrian Court Deputation, the Hofkriegsrat decided to play for time — to try negotiations first and to employ force only as a last resort. Lieutenant-Colonel Baron Philip Levin von Beck, a popular officer from the Slavonian Border, was sent to parley with the mutineers. He was in-

[82] Horvat, pp. 341–52; Smičiklas, pp. 153–59. A general discussion based on archival evidence in Ljudevit Ivančan, "Buna varaždinskog generalata i pograničnih kmetova god. 1755," *VZA*, 4 (1902), 151–73, 240–59, and also his "Iztraga proti buntovnim krajišnikom varaždinskoga generalata g. 1755," *ibid.*, 5 (1903), 65–88.

[83] Ivančan, "Iztraga proti . . . ," pp. 76–85; Horvat, pp. 348–49.

[84] Smičiklas, pp. 195–97. Order to pay special gratuities to the noncommissioned officers and men of the St. Georg Regiment in recognition for their fidelity during the revolt, Vienna, Feb. 26, 1755, KA Mém. XXIII-90.

[85] Sučević, pp. 54–62.

structed to persuade them against further violence and to ask them to submit their grievances directly to the throne.[86] Meanwhile, Field Marshal Count Neipperg was ordered to concentrate sixteen thousand regulars, supported by several batteries of artillery, at nearby Kanisza across the Drava in Hungary. Backed by this overwhelming force, Neipperg confronted the mutineers with the choice of either submitting and handing over their ringleaders, to whom he promised a fair hearing, or being conquered by force and reduced to peasant status.[87] The formula used in the past by Hildburghausen succeeded once again. The intimidated Grenzer submitted without resistance, handed over their leaders, and dispersed to their homes.[88]

For the next several months a special commission was convened in Kanisza to mete out punishment and to inquire into the causes of the revolt. On the whole, considering the practices of the times, reprisals were moderate. This was due in large part to the intervention of Bartenstein, the chairman of the Illyrian Court Deputation, who in a number of memoranda pleaded the Grenzer case. Bartenstein argued that the religious rights of the Orthodox had been violated and that the grievances of the rebels should be carefully investigated before the entire population was punished. Despite the pretenses of the Hungarian-Croatian nobility, he declared, the ancient rights of the Grenzer had not lapsed but were still in force and should be respected.[89] Apparently the authorities listened to Bartenstein. In all, 222 suspects were brought before the commission. There were a dozen executions, about double that number were sentenced to long prison terms, and others were sentenced to loss of rank and confiscation of property.[90] The Orthodox monks were not returned to Marcsa, but the much hated Uniats had to leave and the monastery was turned over to the Catholic order of Piarists.[91] On July 21, 1755, Maria Theresa issued an amnesty patent for the Warasdin Gener-

---

[86] Instructions to General Kheul to support Levin v. Beck and to allow Grenzer delegates to proceed to Graz. Feb. 11, 1751, KA Mém. XXIII-90.

[87] HKR to Neipperg, March 14 and 15, 1755, *ibid.*

[88] Vaniček, II, 60–62.

[89] Memoranda, dated March 13, 18, 20, 24, Apr. 16, and 25, 1755, KA Mém. XXIII-191.

[90] Courtmartial verdicts, July 20, 1755, in Ivančan, "Iztraga proti buntovnim krajišnikom," pp. 70–74.

[91] Horvat, p. 532; Smičiklas, p. 156.

alcy,[92] and on October 11 new regulations were promulgated which met some of the major Grenzer grievances.[93]

The new *Regulament*, designed to supplement the code of 1754, strictly prohibited the use of the Grenzer for private labor; it forbade all punishments without proper and recorded judicial proceedings; it made minor concessions regarding the procurement of uniforms, arms, and equipment. In the future all firearms were to be issued, but bayonets, sabers, and uniforms were to be purchased by the Grenzer. The regulations provided safeguards to ensure that these purchases were made for the best quality at the best possible price and that the officers would not defraud the men.[94] Additional relief was given through the introduction of the *Beihelfer* system, already in use for several years in Slavonia, under which more prosperous households were to assist their needy neighbors. The new regulations ended the ancient offices of the knezovi and concentrated all powers in the hand of the military. The new regulations stipulated that two-thirds of all commissions in the border regiments should be reserved for Grenzer, with preference to be given to Catholics or Uniats. Thus there arose an indigenous officer class to replace the knezovi and voivode. These officers did not usually attain high preferment but remained regimental officers. In this group of Grenzer the Austrian state found its most loyal supporters.

The Warasdin revolt marked the definite end of the old irregular frontier establishment. Introduction of the new regulations was supervised by Colonel Beck who, as a reward for his services during the rebellion, was promoted to major general in September and appointed acting commander of the generalcy in October. With Beck a new breed of officer-administrator entered the picture. Hardworking, honest, efficient, although perhaps given too much to paperwork, these men prevented any new eruptions even though, by order of the queen, there was continued pressure on the Grenzer to adopt the Uniat rites.[95] The next fifty years saw no such succession

[92] Patent, July 21, 1755, KA HKR Kanz. Arch. VII-307.

[93] These regulations, enclosed in the instructions to Baron Beck, *ibid.*, VII-309. Guiccardi was transferred to Italy.

[94] *Ibid.*

[95] See the complaints submitted by the Orthodox Metropolitan Paul Nenadović to the throne, Dec., 1763, copy in DAZ Zagr. gkda. F 7-8. Cf. Vaniček, II, 519-20, *passim*.

of riots and revolts as the preceding generation, but the problem of providing a sound economic base and a modest degree of prosperity for the Grenzer remained unsolved. Modest efforts in this direction were undertaken, but before they could yield any results the military borders were called upon to play an important part in the Seven Years' War.

3

—.—.—.—.—

THE MILITARY BORDER UNDER
MARIA THERESA AND
JOSEPH II: 1756–80

When, within a year after the suppression of the great
Warasdin revolt, the fortunes of the Habsburgs were once
again put to the test of war, Maria Theresa's forces were
stronger, better prepared, and better equipped. Now organized
on the regimental system, the Croatian and Slavonian Grenzer
constituted an important part of the Austrian armament. At
the opening of the Seven Years' War they mustered 34,000
foot and 6,000 horse, slightly more than a quarter of the army.[1]
The battalions of the Lika and Ogulin Regiments took the field
in 1756, followed during the next years by strong bodies from
all the other regiments. In all, about 88,000 Grenzer participated in the various campaigns of the war.[2]

Commonly described as "Croatians" by contemporary writers, the Grenzer performed valuable services under leaders such
as Baron Beck and Ernst Gideon Baron Laudon. Their discipline was much improved and the reformed Austrian commis-
sariat furnished adequate rations and regular pay.[3] To be sure,
it was impossible to repress their lust for loot and plunder,
but there were no repetitions of the mutinies that had marred the
Grenzer record during the previous conflicts.[4] This time the

[1] Estimate in Franz Vaniček, *Specialgeschichte der Militärgrenze* (4 vols.;
Vienna, 1875), II, 403.

[2] *Ibid.*, p. 488, and Alphons v. Wrede, *Geschichte der K. u. k. Wehrmacht*,
supplementary volumes to *MKA* (5 vols.; Vienna, 1893–1903), V, 257–98.

[3] HKR to Maria Theresa, Vienna, March 2, 1758 (copy), KA HKR
1758-3-64.

[4] Edith Kotasek, *Feldmarschall Graf Lacy* (Horn, 1956), p. 52.

40

Grenzer were employed not only for scouting and raiding duties, but also for the standard tasks of regular troops, especially in situations where the line might be handicapped — in woods and hills and in the defense of villages. They became an important part of the Austrian battle line, pouring devastating fire from the flanks into the advancing Prussian lines at Lobositz (1756) and at Kolin (1757).[5] But, at the same time, they preserved their effectiveness as light troops. They threw a nearly impenetrable screen around their main forces, and they participated in a number of daring enterprises against the rear of the enemy. Grenzer from the Szluin and Gradiska Regiments and from the Karlstadt Hussars constituted over half of the thirty-five hundred men accompanying Count Hadik on his raid on Berlin in 1757.[6] Their fighting qualities were recognized by friend and foe. Indeed, one contemporary asserted that Austria owed the greatest part of her military stature to her Croats and hussars, and a leading military historian speculated that "the absence of the Croatians at Leuthen may have materially contributed to the Prussian victory."[7]

The lesson was not lost on Maria Theresa and her military advisers, and as soon as peace was restored steps were taken to extend the military border system along the entire southern frontier of Hungary. This was done as much for economic as for military reasons. At the close of the Seven Years' War the Habsburg lands were exhausted and burdened with an ever-increasing public debt. Reduction of military expenditures appeared necessary, but the continued rivalry among the major powers demanded the maintenance of a large and effective army. The military border system, which provided a large num-

---

[5] Hans Delbrück and others, *Geschichte der Kriegskunst in Rahmen der politischen Geschichte* (7 vols.; Berlin, 1900–1937), IV, 322–23; John F. C. Fuller, *British Light Infantry in the Eighteenth Century* (London, 1925), p. 68; Charles E. P. de Roche-Aymon, *Troupes Légères* (Paris, 1817), p. 10. In his "Pensées generales pour la guerre," of 1755, Frederick II gave special attention to measures designed to counter the light troops of the "Queen of Hungary." W. v. Taysen, ed., *Friedrich der Grosse. Militärische Schriften* (Berlin, 1882), pp. 153–56.

[6] Kriegsgeschichtliche Abteilung des Generalstabes, *Zur Geschichte der Einnahme von Berlin im October 1757*, ("Urkundliche Beiträge und Forschungen zur Geschichte des preussischen Heeres"), IV (Berlin, 1903), 52–61.

[7] F. v. Blankenburg, *Schilderungen des preussischen Kriegsheeres* (Leipzig, 1795), p. 31; Delbrück, IV, 323.

ber of trained troops at little cost to the state, provided a solution. Foremost among the supporters of a strong military establishment was Joseph II, who after the death of his father in 1765 assumed the dignity of Holy Roman Emperor and the position of co-regent in the Austrian lands. Although the queen jealously guarded her ascendancy in this unprecedented arrangement, she did grant her son a free hand in military affairs. As co-regent, as well as sole ruler after 1780, Joseph II displayed a strong interest in the affairs of the military border, and under his aegis the spirit of Austrian cameralism penetrated the establishment. Major emphasis, however, continued to be placed on strengthening the fighting potential of the Grenzer, but there were attempts to improve their deplorable economic conditions.

In May, 1763, the Karlstadt and Warasdin Generalcies were combined under the command of Baron Beck, who had been promoted to Feldzeugmeister for his services in the field.[8] Largely to pacify the Sabor, which was once again pressing for the return of all Croatian territories, the Banal Border remained outside this arrangement.[9] When Beck arrived in the summer of 1763 he found his Grenzer nearly destitute. The war years, with their heavy drain on manpower, had ruined agriculture on which the regiments depended almost completely. The Karlstadt regiments, especially, were hard hit, and in 1764 and again in 1765 there was much misery and actual famine. In the Ogulin Regiment they ground cornstalks for bread; in the Lika, tree bark and roots.[10] To improve conditions, Beck permitted the establishment of grain markets at Karlstadt, Gospić (Gospich), Ottoschatz, Bjelovar, and Koprivnica. He also attempted to reduce the burden of military service. There existed serious inequalities in the sizes of regiments and Beck transferred a number of company districts from the oversized Lika to the hard-pressed Ottoschatz and Ogulin Regiments. Finally, he dissolved two squadrons of Karlstadt Hussars and assigned them as reinforcements to the foot regiments.[11] Even so, conditions in the Karlstadt regiments re-

[8] Appointment and instructions for Beck, Vienna, May 20, 1763, KA HKR Kanz. Arch. VII-315.

[9] Rudolf Kiszling, Die Kroaten (Graz-Cologne, 1956), p. 43.

[10] Vaniček, II, 611.

[11] HKR to Beck, Vienna, Oct. 15, 1765, DAZ Zagr. gkda. F 7-8.

mained very hard and a considerable number of Grenzer joined the bandits in the hills or deserted into Turkish territory.[12]

While Beck was struggling with the problems in Croatia, the Hofkriegsrat proceeded to establish new military borders. In 1763 the *Tschaikisten*, a unit of rivermen formed during the Turkish wars to patrol the Sava, Danube, and Theiss with small gunboats, were reorganized and established as a battalion on lands at the confluence of Sava and Danube.[13] Farther east, the irregular frontier militia of the Banat of Temesvar was regulated. After numerous changes of location, organization, and designation, two infantry regiments were established there. One, the Deutsch-Banater Grenzer Regiment, was recruited from German settlers; the other, the Walachisch-Illyrisches Grenzer Regiment, was raised from the Orthodox Serb and Vlach population. Attempts to form a Banat cavalry regiment met with great difficulties and were eventually abandoned.[14] During the same period, between 1762 and 1765, the military border system was also introduced in Transylvania. Here two Vlach and two Szekler infantry regiments were organized. In addition there were plans for a Vlach dragoon regiment as well as a Szekler Hussar Regiment. The introduction of the military system was opposed by the Szeklers in eastern Transylvania, who had long enjoyed a special privileged status and who had to be forced to assume Grenzer obligations. Under these circumstances the organizations of the military border in Transylvania was not completed until the 1780's. From 1770 on, however, there existed the basic framework of a frontier establishment from the Adriatic to the Carpathians.[15]

The increased importance of the military borders within the Austrian army was confirmed in 1765 when, as part of the overall reorganization and the quest for greater military and eco-

[12] Proclamation promising pardon to deserters, KA HKR Kanz. Arch. VII-321.

[13] Vaniček, II, 114–21, and also "Tschaikisten-Regulament," KA Schriftgut F-29.

[14] Wrede, V, 224–27. Also Francesco Griselini, *Versuch einer politischen und natürlichen Geschichte des Temeswarer Bannats* (Vienna, 1780), and Felix Miller, *Istorija banatske vojničke granice 1764–1873* (Pančevo, 1926).

[15] Wrede, V, 221–23. Cf. J. H. Benigni, Edler v. Mildenberg, "Pragmatische Geschichte der siebenbürgischen Militärgrenze," KA HKR 1813 B-7-9; and Mathias Bernath, "Die Errichtung der Siebenbürgischen Militärgrenze und die Wiener Rumänenpolitik in der frühjosephinischen Zeit," *SOF*, 19 (1960), 164–92.

nomic efficiency, three inspectors general were named. General Franz Moritz Count Lacy became inspector general for the infantry, Feldmarschall Leutnant Joseph Count d'Ayasassa for the cavalry, while Baron Beck was appointed inspector general of the Military Border. In this new capacity, Beck was to supervise the Grenzer regiments in Croatia, Slavonia, and Syrmia. The Banat and Transylvanian regiments, still in the process of formation, were for the time being excluded from his jurisdiction. Beck was instructed to conduct inspections at least twice a year, to direct and develop standard procedures for training, guard, and field service, and to report on the state of discipline, equipment, and economy, and on all other matters affecting efficiency. Essentially a staff appointment, the inspector reported directly to the Hofkriegsrat and was advised not to "interfere, prejudice, or reduce the authority of the commandants of the various generalcies."[16] The influence of this new position was so great, however, that it inevitably led to further centralization in the command structure of the military border. When in 1768 Beck was transferred to command in Bohemia, his successor Feldmarschall Leutnant Josef Baron Sisković, a member of the war council, did not move his headquarters to Croatia-Slavonia, but remained in Vienna and, aided by a small staff, carried on his duties from there.[17] This practice continued under succeeding inspectors general and was the origin of the special Military Border Department within the Hofkriegsrat.[18]

The immediate result of these developments was a striking increase in the attention paid to military details of all kinds. The border administration became more highly organized, more self-conscious, and involved in an ever-growing amount of paper work. All conceivable and inconceivable matters were regulated, prescribed, and ordered from above. By 1771 every company was required to maintain seventy-two separate files and render in minute detail two weekly, ten monthly, and two quarterly reports and one consolidated semiannual return. In addition there were thirty-five enumerated incidents that re-

[16] Appointment and instructions for Beck, Oct. 13, 1765, DAZ Zagr. gkda. F 7–8.
[17] Appointment and instructions for Sisković, copy, Vienna, Apr. 15, 1768, KA HKR Kanz. Arch. VII-330.
[18] Vaniček, II, 160–61.

quired separate and immediate reporting.[19] Higher formations, regiments, and generalcies, were similarly inundated with paper work that, so an order of 1772 reminded all commanding generals, had to be forwarded in proper form and through proper channels to Vienna.[20] And in this process the needs and the wishes of the Grenzer were often lost in the slow-moving mass of paper and official procedure.

There were frequent modifications in the organization and equipment of the regiments. Beck reduced the regiments from four to three battalions, a total of 3,600 effectives. Sisković in turn increased the infantry regiments to 4,080 men, augmented by special detachments of cannoneers and sharpshooters.[21] The increase, however, remained largely on paper, and the Croatian regiments never reached their projected strength levels during this period.[22] Considerable attention was given to the training of the gunners and the sharpshooters. In general the Grenzer gunners remained unsatisfactory. Their training, conducted for the most part with wooden dummy pieces, was decidedly inadequate. But there was slow improvement and by 1780 each infantry regiment had one howitzer and three six-pounders, handled by a detachment of about 250.[23] The specially selected sharpshooters were armed with a rather complicated and expensive double-barreled carbine. The upper barrel was rifled, and the lower barrel was smooth to allow more rapid fire.[24] These special detachments created special problems. In 1786 the Hofskriegsrat advised all commanders to be especially careful in the selection of sharpshooters and gunners "so that the first will not desert with their expensive weapons, and the second after having received their expensive training."[25] Finally, there was a continual decrease in the cavalry arm. As early as 1763 Beck reduced the strength of the Karlstadt and Warasdin Hussars, and this process, largely motivated by reasons of

[19] Lacy to Warasdin Gkdo. specifying returns and reports required, Vienna, March 27, 1768, DAZ Zagr. gkda. F 9-10.

[20] HKR to FML Kleefeld, Warasdin Gkdo., Vienna, May 8, 1768, *ibid.*

[21] Johann H. Schwicker, *Geschichte der österreichischen Militärgrenze* (Vienna-Teschen, 1883), pp. 121–23.

[22] Reports on the peace establishment of the Warasdin, Karlstadt, and Banal Borders, 1774-75, KA Nostitz-Rieneck IX-2, 3, 5.

[23] Vaniček, II, 271–74, gives the figure of 1,119 cannoneers per regiment. This number, accepted by Wrede, V, 229, appears absurdly high.

[24] Vaniček, II, 170–72.

[25] HKR instructions of July 12, 1782, DAZ Varia, Ogulin bgda., folder 1.

economy, continued until 1786 when all border cavalry regiments, except for the Szekler Hussars, were disbanded.[26]

During this period, the military border assumed an additional function. From 1770 on, the regiments were also charged with the maintenance of a permanent quarantine line, the *Sanitäts Kordon*, along the Turkish frontier.[27] Although by the middle of the eighteenth century the dreaded bubonic plague had almost disappeared in western Europe, it still remained endemic in the Ottoman Empire and from there threatened Austria and southeastern Europe. There was very little confidence in the efficacy of the medical arts against the plague, and the common method of dealing with the disease was to prevent, if at all possible, all contacts with the infected area.[28] Such quarantine measures were temporary and were lifted when the danger of contagion was over. For the Habsburg Empire, however, with over one thousand miles of common frontier with the Turks, the danger was permanent and required permanent measures. Given the military and financial situation of the Habsburgs, it clearly was impossible to maintain a quarantine cordon with troops of the line. In Transylvania attempts were made to utilize a corps of semicivilian frontier guards, the *Plajaschen*, but these proved unreliable.[29] The Grenzer provided the answer.

As early as 1710, at the request of the *Sanitäts Hof Kommission*, the commanding officers on the military border were instructed to assist in guarding the frontier line against suspected disease carriers.[30] But this was only a temporary expedient and after the Treaty of Passarowitz (Požarevac) in 1718, when the Turkish military menace disappeared and a greater amount of trade between Austria and the Ottoman Empire was expected, more permanent precautions were deemed necessary. In 1728 Emperor Charles VI decreed that because of the "ever-present

[26] Collection of documents concerning the disbandment of the Grenz hussars, HKR 1786-16-272.

[27] Except where indicated, information on the cordon is based on the informative article by Erna Lesky, "Die österreichische Pestfront an der k.k. Militärgrenze," *Saeculum*, 8 (1957), 82–105.

[28] Adam Chenot, *Tractatus de Peste* (Vienna, 1766), pp. 12–14; Georg Sticker, *Abhandlungen aus der Seuchengeschichte und Seuchenlehre* (2 vols. in 3; Giessen, 1908–10), I, 252–58.

[29] Lesky, p. 88, maintains that the expansion of the military border to Transylvania was primarily conceived as an antiplague measure.

[30] Vaniček, I, 162–63.

danger of contagion from the Turkish Empire" continual vigilance and permanent countermeasures were necessary, and in 1737 an imperial edict declared that "long experience has shown that a military quarantine line provides the best defense."[31] But the Turkish War of 1736–38 prevented the establishment of such a cordon, although a number of checkpoints and sanitary control stations were operated in the 1740's, especially when an outbreak of the plague was reported. Even so, the cordon was not established formally until 1770, when Maria Theresa issued the *Pest Contumaz Patent*.[32]

Along the entire frontier with the Ottoman Empire, from the Adriatic to the Carpathians, a chain of fortified lookout posts, the so-called *Tschardaken*, were constructed. On the Croatian Military Borders, which faced the ever-turbulent Bosnian provinces, the Tschardaken consisted of a wooden blockhouse placed on piles, with an observation gallery all around and a ladder to be drawn up in times of danger.[33] Regulations prescribed that these posts be placed within musket-shot distance of each other. Usually they were manned by a section under a corporal or a sergeant, and a senior officer, responsible for the entire regimental sector, was stationed at one of the small forts, sometimes provided with cannon, situated at strategic points. Roving patrols moved among the posts and standing orders prohibited unauthorized traffic across the frontier.

For authorized traffic a number of special frontier crossing points were designated. These were of two kinds. The larger ones, called *Contumaz Anstalten*, served as quarantine stations for travelers as well as inspection points for imports.[34] The smaller stations, called *Rastelle*, were merely enclosed areas where, under the guards' watchful eyes, goods, money, and letters could be exchanged. Goods were classified as contagious or non-contagious matter and were disinfected by fumigation, washing in vinegar, or by exposure to the air. Letters, including those from the Austrian diplomatic representative in Constantinople, were pierced with needles and fumigated.

[31] *Supplementum Codices Austriaci* (6 vols.; Vienna, 1777), IV, 449, 1009–10.

[32] KA Mém. XXVII-11.

[33] Plans for a typical Tschardake, dated Feb. 1752, in KA Schriftgut F-38, folder 22.

[34] Descriptions of a Kontumaz Anstalt, KA Mém. XXVII-26.

Money was immersed in a vinegar bath. As for travelers, their treatment depended on the degree of danger suspected. The Austrian government maintained an extensive pest intelligence service in the Ottoman Empire, and when an outbreak of the plague was reported, the vigilance of the cordon was stepped up. Posts were stationed at closer intervals, and sentries had orders to shoot to kill. Normally, travelers were detained for twenty-one days, later reduced to ten, but in times of danger they might be detained for as long as forty-two days.[35]

The actual handling of the sanitary inspection was carried out by employees of the Sanitäts Kommission, with the Grenzer furnishing the armed guards to enforce the regulations. Until 1776 the Sanitäts Hof Kommission exercised supervisory functions over the inspection, but after that the entire operation came under the control of the generals commanding the various military borders. The inspection and customs personnel, however, did not belong to the military border establishment, but were separately enumerated.[36]

On the Croatian Military Border there existed but one Contumaz Anstalt, at Kostajnica in the 2d Banal Regiment, as well as eight Rastelle. In Croatia, the quarantine line was divided into the "wet" and the "dry" cordon sectors. The wet sector, along the Una, was manned by the Banal regiments, and the dry sector, across the mountains of the Velebit range, was maintained by the Karlstadt regiments. The Warasdin Generalcy, having no common boundary with Turkish territory, was not obliged to furnish cordon guards. Duty was usually for a week. The frequency of this duty, however, varied. In the Karlstadt regiments it came about every six weeks, but in the Banal regiments it came as often as every three weeks.[37] Clearly this constituted a very heavy additional burden on the Grenzer. In 1777 Feldzeugmeister Count Colloredo, who had replaced Sisković as inspector general in 1775, proposed that in order to lighten this burden "all grown men in the generalcies, whether they

---

[35] Sticker, I, 316–17.
[36] Instructions, KA HKR 1776-79-38, 57.
[37] Johann C. v. Engel, *Staatskunde, und Geschichte von Dalmatien, Croatien, und Slawonien* (Halle, 1798), p. 263; Franz Bach, *Otočaner Regimentsgeschichte* (Karlstadt, 1853), p. 52. According to calculations made early in the nineteenth century the average Grenzer performed fifty-two days cordon duty every year. Carl B. v. Hietzinger, *Statistik der Militärgrenze des österreichischen Kaiserthums* (3 vols.; Vienna, 1817–23), III, 362–64.

were actually enrolled and on active service or merely supernumerary, should take their turn on the cordon." [38]

Cordon watch, the numerous regimental duties, and the periodic military training imposed, even in times of peace, very onerous demands on the Grenzer and greatly interfered with the agricultural economy of the region. This was especially true on the Croatian Military Border where poor soil yielded but little return for much labor and where conditions of life remained little above the subsistence level. Repeatedly Colloredo urged that alleviations be granted to the Grenzer, and he suggested a reduction in the number of men actually serving under arms. Joseph II, who had personally become familiar with the misery of the Grenzer during an inspection tour early in 1755, was sympathetic, but as so often before, military necessity prevented any improvement.[39]

When the Elector Maximilian Joseph of Bavaria died in 1777, he was succeeded by a distant relative, the Elector Palatine, who, in return for certain financial inducements, agreed to surrender more than a third of Bavaria to Austria. Such an accession of strength was opposed by Prussia, supported this time by the Elector of Saxony who also had claims to part of the Bavarian inheritance. Although Maria Theresa was anxious to avoid war, she gave in to her son and early in 1778 Austria mobilized and moved into Bavaria. Under these circumstances the emperor decided that no reduction in the number of the Grenzer was possible, but that on the contrary "all companies and regiments ought to be kept as strong as possible." [40] Even so, when the Grenzer were actually mobilized, the Hofkriegsrat ordered that only those men ought to be mobilized who could be spared without damage to the economy.[41] The Karlstadt and Banal regiments furnished only one battalion each, whereas Warasdin regiments, which did not have the additional burden of the cordon, mobilized two battalions. In addition, the Grenzer hussars were called out. The three Slavonian regiments also

---

[38] Colloredo to Joseph II, Vienna, Sept. 4, 1777, KA Nostitz-Rieneck, IX-7.

[39] Joseph's letters to his mother, May, 1775, cited in Alfred v. Arneth, *Geschichte Maria Theresias* (10 vols.; Vienna, 1863–79), IX, 464–66. Cf. Bach, pp. 34, 48.

[40] "Votum des Kaisers Josef II," Vienna, Jan. 4, 1778, KA Nostitz-Rieneck IX, 8.

[41] HKR to Karlstadt Gkdo., May 16, 1778, DAZ Zagr. gkda. F-13. For arrangements made to recompense Grenzer for wear and tear on their equipment, KA HKR 1778-9-629.

provided one battalion each, but no troops were called from the newly organized Banat and Transylvanian borders.[42]

War was declared in July. From the military point of view it was one of the most futile campaigns of the century. Neither side dared to come to grips with the opponent. Therefore, the main hostilities consisted of a series of small actions, raids, and ambuscades in which the Grenzer excelled, while the main armies wearily maneuvered to gain a strategic advantage.[43] Winter came and the armies retired to their winter quarters. Before operations could be resumed in the following year, mediation by France and Russia led to the conclusion of peace at Teschen in May, 1779. The Grenzer returned home, having suffered substantial casualties, but carrying with them eight captured Prussian flags that were put on public display to "encourage the people." [44]

Once hostilities ended, Joseph II took immediate steps to alleviate conditions on the borders. All units were returned at once to their ordinary peacetime establishment. The Karlstadt, Warasdin, and Banal Hussars were reduced from three to two squadrons each, the released men and their land going to reinforce the infantry regiments. At the same time the emperor ordered reduction of cordon and internal guards to the bare minimum and sharply reminded the Hofkriegsrat that "all the alleviations ordered be put into effect without fail, and that all harassment and pressure on the Grenzer, both in regard to military duties and to the performance of robot, will cease at once." [45]

The problems of the military border continued to occupy the emperor, and in December, 1779, he sent a lengthy memorandum to Field Marshal Count Hadik, President of the Hofkriegsrat. The memorandum pointed out that the Grenzer once again had proved their value during the recent war and that it was of the greatest importance to retain their services. Hadik was instructed to submit complete data on all Grenzer regiments, their actual strength, and to make a detailed survey of their efficiency, with particular attention to the sharpshooters

[42] Wrede, V.
[43] Vaniček, II, 488–513.
[44] HKR to Karlstadt Gkdo., Oct. 22, 1778, DAZ Zagr. gkda. F-13.
[45] New peace establishment, KA HKR 1779-23-19; instructions Joseph II to HKR, Vienna, May 15, 1779, and orders from HKR to the Karlstadt and Banal Gkdos., May 22, 1779, KA HKR 1779-23-20.

and the artillery detachments.[46] The training of the Grenzer, Joseph II observed, should not strive for perfection of linear evolutions, but rather concentrate on the essential movements required for fighting in open order.

Then, turning to the economic issues, the emperor noted that each generalcy required different treatment. The Karlstadt Border was the most impoverished and would require the most support; the Banal Border was but little better off, while the Warasdin and the Slavonian Borders were fairly prosperous.

Finally, the memorandum turned to the question of education on the military border. Here Joseph II, for all his pretensions, regarded the military border primarily as a great reservation furnishing cheap military manpower. As far as schools existed, he declared they might continue and receive support. The curriculum ought to be restricted, however, to a little reading, writing, and arithmetic. More knowledge, the memorandum warned, might well cause harm to the natural aptitudes of the population. The emperor was talking about the official schools maintained in the regiments by the state. There also existed schools maintained out of the voluntary offerings of the Orthodox Grenzer. The emperor did not intend to support these "national" schools at all, and when some years later Archbishop Putnik of the Karlstadt Orthodox diocese requested that at least two such schools ought to be maintained in every regiment, the emperor flatly refused.[47] Under these circumstances the Orthodox schools in the Croatian borders remained poor and had but few pupils.[48]

Joseph II was determined to continue and strengthen the military border institution, and to this end he strongly supported efforts, already started during Beck's tenure as inspector general, to separate civilian and military territories clearly and to establish a definite boundary between civil Croatia and the military border. In practice, this proved most difficult. During the irregular period, military settlement by necessity had been sporadic and unsystematic. Grenzer had been settled wherever land had been available. At the same time, local feudatories, especially the Catholic bishop of Zagreb, retained extensive

---

[46] Joseph II to FM Hadik, Vienna, Dec. 9, 1779, KA Mém. XXIII-57.
[47] Notation by Joseph II, KA HKR 1783-53-36. Cf. Vaniček, II, 580–82.
[48] Johann A. Demian, *Statistische Beschreibung der Militärgrenze* (2 vols.; Vienna, 1806), I, 184–85.

properties and feudal claims in the border region. In the 1740's this led to considerable trouble between the military and ecclesiastic authorities. The church, supported by the Sabor, accused the military of interference in manorial affairs; the military countered with charges that the civilian landowners were encroaching on the territories of the regiments. Ill-feeling reached new heights in 1751 when a dispute about forest rights in the Warasdin Generalcy led to bloody encounters between the Grenzer and the armed retainers of the Zagreb bishopric.[49]

Clearly something had to be done to provide better and more uniform delineations of property lines. Moreover, land was urgently required to provide more adequate allotments for the growing Grenzer population. Therefore, after the close of the Seven Years' War, the Vienna government sought to extinguish all ecclesiastic and feudal holdings on the Croatian Military Border and to transfer the land to the various regiments.

As a first step, a number of mixed civil-military commissions were formed in 1767 and charged with the demarcation of the boundary between civil and military Croatia. Their efforts, however, were frustrated by armed bands that, instigated by certain Croatian nobles, tore down the new boundary markers.[50] This became so serious that in 1769 a royal edict threatened ten years at hard labor for any commoner found destroying the markers, and noblemen were threatened with a very heavy fine.[51] Moreover, in order to conciliate the Croatian nobility, to whom the military status of the Grenzer was a constant irritant, the Hofkriegsrat in 1771 issued directives limiting military jurisdiction to persons actually enrolled or serving with the regiments.[52] After that the demarcation of the Warasdin Generalcy boundary proceeded without further incident and was completed in 1775.[53] In the Karlstadt Generalcy, however, the disputes continued. Negotiations continued for more than six years, from 1778 to 1784, and agreement was reached only

[49] Report from Koprivnica, May 7, 1751, DAZ Zagr. gkda. F-7; report by GFWM Scherzer, Apr. 13, 1754, KA Mém. XXIII-162; Vaniček, II, 127–31.

[50] Reports dated May, 1767; September, 1767; and June, 1768, DAZ Zagr. gkda. F-9.

[51] Edict, Vienna, Sept. 27, 1769, *ibid.*, F 9-10.

[52] HKR to Karlstadt-Warasdin and Banal Gkdos., March 9, 1771, DAZ Banska gkda. F-1.

[53] Vaniček, II, 239.

after direct imperial intervention.[54] Even then, agreement on the line of demarcation between the Karlstadt Generalcy and civil Croatia (the Banal Border had no common boundary with civil Croatia) did not solve the problem of actually transferring the civilian properties to the military. Negotiations on this matter continued for many years. As late as 1796 an observer remarked that "the map of the military border is as colorful as a patchwork quilt; strips of military land alternate with civilian domains."[55] Not until the first decade of the nineteenth century were all the differences resolved and all the land within the limits of the Croatian Military Border actually brought under military control.[56]

In line with the overall reorganization and systematization of the military border the authorities also attempted to consolidate the widely dispersed habitations of the Grenzer into a more compact pattern of settlement. Except on the Warasdin Border, where the nature of the terrain favored larger villages, the houses of the Grenzer were widely scattered. Especially in the hills and mountains of the Karlstadt and the Banal Borders, villages usually were mere hamlets with fewer than a dozen buildings. Many Grenzer homesteads were completely isolated.[57] This situation not only posed great difficulties for the maintenance of public security, but also interfered with the supervision, training, and rapid mobilization of the Grenzer. Regrouping of settlements had been suggested as early as 1740, and the proposal came up again in 1753.[58] It was not until after the Seven Years' War, however, that actual steps were taken to implement these ideas.

In 1767 Beck ordered a preliminary survey, and by 1773 definite plans had been drawn up not only to relocate certain households, but also to provide them with better dwellings

---

[54] Various "Excorporierungs Kommission Protocolle," DAZ Zagr. gkda. F-13. For the imperial intervention see the communication from HKR to Karlstadt Gkdo., Vienna, March 9, 1784: "Ist von Sr. Majest. der allerhöchste Befehl erflossem dieses Geschaft dergestalten zu beschleunigen, dass . . . die Gränz-Scheidung zwischen dem Militari und Provinziali mit 11 April dieses Jahres vorgenommen." DAZ Zagr. gkda. F-13.

[55] Engel, p. 259.

[56] Various documents in KA HKR 1800-30-20, 26, 31, and 32.

[57] André Blanc, *La Croatie Occidentale* (Paris, 1957), pp. 176–77; Engel, pp. 277, 328–29.

[58] Proposal by GQM Geller, Apr. 7, 1740, KA Mém. XIII-90; Bach, pp. 24–25.

"which among other benefits will raise the morals and the customs of the people."[59] But such schemes were expensive and Vienna was never willing to spend much on the military borders. Therefore these plans were never executed except along the Bosnian frontier, which was most exposed to the marauding bands still making periodic incursions. Here a number of more compact villages were established, although some senior officers, including Field Marshal Lacy, grumbled at the expense.[60] An additional difficulty was that there was very little free land available. When in 1780 some thousand Catholic refugee families from the Herzegovina entered the military border, the commanders were hard pressed to find room for them.[61] Matters dragged on in this manner for several years, and only when another war with the Turks appeared imminent did Vienna finally allot thirty-four thousand florins for regrouping exposed border settlements.[62] The outbreak of hostilities halted progress in this direction, however, and when the matter was taken up again after the Peace of Sistova, the new demands of the French wars, the poverty of the Grenzer, and the nature of the terrain precluded any large-scale resettlement.

Faced with a perennial shortage of funds and well aware of the grinding poverty existing on the military border in Croatia, the Austrian government sought additional means to sustain the military border system and, at the same time, to make it more self-sufficient. After the middle of the eighteenth century certain attempts were made to encourage a limited amount of commerce and manufacturing in this region. The emperor and many of the Austrian administrators were strongly influenced by cameralist ideas. "After population," Joseph wrote to his mother in 1765, "commerce contributes the most to the power and the wealth of the state."[63] He believed that a measure of industrialization and commerce would contribute greatly to the wealth of the region, providing a good tax base, which in turn could be used for the support of the Grenzer regiments. Such

[59] Report of FML Sisković, March 21, 1773, DAZ Banska gkda. F-1.

[60] Lacy's opinion, March 6, 1783, KA Nostitz-Rieneck IX-11.

[61] Hadik, Pres. HKR to Karlstadt-Warasdin Gkdo., Vienna, Apr. 18, 1780, DAZ Zagr. gkda. F-14.

[62] KA HKR 1787-5-3.

[63] Alfred v. Arneth, ed., *Maria Theresia und Joseph II. Ihre Correspondenz sammt Briefen Joseph's an seinen Bruder Leopold* (3 vols.; Vienna, 1867–68), III, 344.

developments, however, required the creation of a middle class, largely urban, and the military authorities were afraid that urban influences might corrupt the Grenzer. Moreover, the rise of such a *"purgarija"* was also opposed by the Croatian nobility and prelates, who feared a diminution of their exclusive powers in civil Croatia; therefore, despite directives from Vienna, efforts to develop urban commercial and manufacturing centers were halfhearted and largely unsuccessful.[64]

Towns in Croatia remained small throughout the eighteenth century. Warasdin, with some 4,800 inhabitants, was the largest, followed by Zagreb with 2,800, and Karlstadt with 2,700.[65] In any case, none of these towns were actually located within the boundaries of the military borders. Warasdin, a market town with a charter dating back to the fourteenth century, never had been included in the generalcy bearing its name. Headquarters for the Warasdin regiments were first at Koprivnica and after 1758 at Bjelovar.[66] Karlstadt had been founded in 1578 as the chief fortress of the military border, and although it remained the major military administrative center until 1786, it was considered part of civil Croatia and in 1778 received a charter as a royal free city.[67] The exception was Petrinja, located on military territory and headquarters for the Banal Border.[68]

Other villages on the military borders served as administrative centers for individual regiments. Headquarters for the 1st Banal were at Glina, while Petrinja also served as the center for the 2d Banal. The Karlstadt regiments, except for the Lika Regiment with headquarters at Gospić, had their headquarters in the villages from which they derived their regimental designations. When it was decided to encourage manufacturing and commerce, a number of these small communities were given special status as *Militär Communitäten*, although they usually remained headquarters for their respective regiments. The establishment of privileged military townships began in Slavonia where in 1748 Feldmarschall Leutnant Baron Engelshofen granted special rights to the inhabitants of Peterwardein, con-

[64] Blanc, p. 239.

[65] Anton Kugelmayer, "Topographisch-historische Beschreybung d. Königreiches Kroatien," Arhiv. JAZU Cod., 1-d-39.

[66] Wrede, V, 221.

[67] Engel, p. 308; Rudolf Strohal, *Grad Karlovac* (Karlovac, 1906), pp. 14–16.

[68] Wrede, V, 219.

firmed in 1751.[69] Within the next few years Zemun, Brod, Karlovci, and Gradiska received similar rights.[70] On the Croatian borders proper, Beck in 1764 gave limited trading privileges to Gospić, Ottoschatz, Brindl, Ogulin, Bjelovar, Kostajnica, Koprivnica, and Ivanić, which later were expanded to full Militär Communitäten status.[71] By 1785 there existed some twenty privileged military townships, including the ports of Senj (Zengg) and Karlobag (Carlopago) on the Adriatic, which until 1776 had been administered by the Trieste civil governor.[72]

The military authorities kept extremely close control over these new townships and issued numerous administrative regulations, consolidated in 1779 in the *Communitäten-Regulativ*.[73] Inhabitants were divided into two classes, *Bürger* and *Contribuenten*, and, if the town was also the location of a military center, there were Grenzer as well. Only the first class, always strictly limited in number, could hold the major municipal offices, and their appointments were subject to the approval of the commanding officer. Townsmen were not obliged to perform any military service, either in the field or on the cordon, although some of the larger communities raised a free company for local defense.[74]

Even so, Joseph II reported to Maria Theresa in 1775 that trade and industry were not making any great advances and suggested that some Jewish families be allowed to settle on the Croatian Military Border.[75] A similar proposal already had been submitted by Beck in 1758, requesting permission for Jewish merchants to reside in Bjelovar in order to supply cheaper uniforms for the Grenzer. This scheme, however, had aroused the opposition of the Sabor and was vetoed by Maria Theresa, always implacably hostile to non-Catholic elements.[76] Except

---

[69] In Slavonia regimental stations and designations did not coincide except in the case of the Gradiska Regiment. The Broder had their headquarters at Vinkovci and the Peterwardeiner at Srijemska Mitrovica. For the development of the privileged townships, see the documents in DAZ Slavon. gkda. 1747–50, 1751–62.

[70] Vaniček, I, 566–71.

[71] Entry for Oct. 14, 1790, KA Mém. 23-90.

[72] Hietzinger, II, 403.

[73] KA Schriftgut, MS vol. 33.

[74] Details in Vaniček, I, 567–70. Engelshofen's instructions to the Peterwardein "Freyschützen" company, Oct. 31, 1748, DAZ Slavon. gkda. 1747-51.

[75] Arneth, *Geschichte Maria Theresias*, IX, 466.

[76] Gavro Schwarz, "Prilozi k povjesti židova u Hrvatskoj u XVIII. stoljeću," *VZA*, 3 (1901), 186–87.

for a few Jewish families residing under strict controls at Zemun, Jews were excluded from the Croatian and Slavonian borders until the middle of the nineteenth century.[77]

During the entire period, military obstruction, tight control, and the paucity of natural resources prevented any substantial expansion of trade and industry on the military border. Manufacturing did not progress beyond production for purely local consumption, and commerce remained in the barter stage.[78]

Another important aspect of the reorganization of the border establishment was the regulation of the Orthodox Church. Although after the middle of the eighteenth century it was no longer as influential as it had been, it still remained "the center of life and the unchallenged leader of the community," for the civilian Serbs of southern Hungary as well as for the Orthodox Grenzer.[79] Although Joseph II did not share his mother's bitter aversion to the Orthodox "schismatics," he was convinced that the state needed obedient subjects above all, and to this end he set about to make the Orthodox patriarchate in Karlovci into a servile tool of the government.

For many years the Habsburgs had whittled away at the very extensive privileges bestowed on the patriarchate, and by 1749 they had established their right to confirm the election of the patriarch.[80] Even more important, they began to influence the Serb national church congress, which elected the patriarch and also dealt with the administrative problems of the Orthodox Church within the Austrian domains. In 1769 the Hofkriegsrat issued detailed instructions to General Count Hadik serving as royal commissioner at the national congress to be held that year in Karlovci. Hadik was told to see that the meeting was conducted with proper decorum and that unauthorized topics were not broached. He was to inspect the credentials of all delegates, make sure that the clergy did not exceed its authorized quota of one-third, and take care that no foreign priests attended the meetings.[81] Hadik in turn issued directives to the Croatian,

[77] Kiszling, p. 41; Vaniček, II, 519, 534–35.

[78] Blanc, pp. 236–40; Hietzinger, II, 260–73.

[79] Charles Jelavich, "Some Aspects of Serbian Religious Development in the Eighteenth Century," *Church History*, 23 (1954), 144–45.

[80] Confirmation for Paul Nenadović, Sept., 1749, in KA HKR Kanz. Arch. VII-284.

[81] Gen. Lacy to Gen. Hadik, Vienna, July 25, 1768; also "Nachtragsinstruction," Feb. 19, 1769, *ibid.*, 331.

Slavonian, and Banat border commands regarding the careful selection of the twenty-five delegates allotted to the Grenzer. Only loyal, well-reputed, and thoroughly reliable individuals were to be selected.[82] With these precautions, the congress elected Johann Georgević patriarch, and the election was duly confirmed in October, 1769.[83] After some discussion the congress also accepted the provisions of a new "Illyrian Regulation," officially proclaimed in September, 1770.[84]

The new regulation, which superseded all previous patents, assured the Orthodox of the continued undisturbed exercise of their faith. At the same time, the regulation reduced the functions of the hierarchy and limited it to the performance of purely religious duties. The regulation fixed salaries and fees for the clergy and established procedures for the convocation and conduct of church congresses and elections. The printing of religious materials and the conduct of religious schools were strictly controlled. Continued use of the Julian calendar was permitted, but fifty-six religious feast days were eliminated. Finally, all clerical appointments in the military border had to be made with the approval of the military authorities and were limited to Austrian subjects.[85]

The new regulations were none too well received and when after the death of Patriarch Georgević in 1773 it became necessary to convene a new congress in 1774, there was considerable sentiment for modification. The royal commissioner, Feldmarschall Leutnant Baron Mathesen, commanding general of the Slavonian Border, however, prevented any major changes. Vincent Ivanović-Vidak was elected patriarch, the number of religious feast days was further reduced, and the Orthodox monasteries were given new administrative rules.[86]

Two years later, in 1776, another church congress met in Karlovci. Again the results were further diminution of the privileges of the Orthodox hierarchy. This time the families of Orthodox priests on the military border, except for one male in each household besides the priest, were made subject to mili-

[82] Hadik to the commanding officers, March 11, 1769, DAZ Zagr. gkda. F 9-10.

[83] HKR to all commands, confirming election of Georgević, Vienna, Oct. 24, 1769, *ibid.*

[84] Copy of the "Illyrisches Regulament," *ibid.*

[85] Discussion in Vaniček, II, 540–47.

[86] Report on congress, HKR to Banal Gkdo., Vienna, Jan. 25, 1775, DAZ Banska gkda. F-1.

tary service. Priests, so the new regulation ordered, could be installed only in the presence of a properly designated officer, and the control of the church over its own funds was rigidly restricted.[87] Perhaps these measures were necessary because of the laxity, even corruption, of the patriarchate in financial affairs.[88] But the regulations were resented, and in 1778 Patriarch Ivanović submitted a seventy-eight point protest to Vienna.[89]

The Orthodox were especially apprehensive because the previous year Maria Theresa had dissolved the Illyrian Hofdeputation and divided its functions among the Hofkriegsrat, the Hungarian Court Chancery, and the administrative officers of the Banat of Temesvar. Despite assurances that this step would not prejudice the position of the Orthodox faith, there was considerable unrest and even some minor riots in Slavonia.[90] The government answered with an edict that again assured the Grenzer that there was no intention whatever to interfere with their cherished faith, but at the same time the edict sharply rejected all claims to secular jurisdiction made by the patriarch.[91] Finally, to settle matters, there was issued yet another Illyrian regulation, the *Erläuterungs-Rescript* of July 16, 1779.[92] This edict repealed the legislations of 1770 and 1777 and bluntly announced the intention of the Habsburgs to control the church. All privileges granted to the Orthodox Church, the document declared, were subject to interpretation and amendment. The government rejected all pretensions by the patriarch to secular jurisdiction and asserted that it had the right to nominate as well as confirm appointees for all major offices within the Orthodox hierarchy. The authority of the patriarch was only religious, while in secular matters, he, as well as all Orthodox priests, was subject to the proper military and civilian officials.[93] The new order was a strong assertion of the government's power against the Orthodox Church, but

---

[87] Regulation, Vienna, Jan. 2, 1777, KA Schriftgut F-32.

[88] Jelavich, pp. 149–50.

[89] "Beschwerde des Illyrischen Cleri und Natzion," Karlovci, Jan. 11, 1778, KA HKR 1778-17-133.

[90] HKR to Patriarch Ivanović, Vienna, Jan. 21, 1778, *ibid.*, 1778-32-38; Friedrich Walter, ed., *Die Geschichte der österreichischen Zentralverwaltung in der Zeit Maria Theresias (1740–1780) Veröff. Kom. neu. Gesch. Öst.*, XXXII (Vienna, 1938), 236–37.

[91] HKR to Karlstadter, Warasdin, and Banal Gkdo., Vienna, April 30, 1778, KA HKR 1778-17-133.

[92] Rescript, July 16, 1779, *ibid.*

[93] Discussion in Vaniček, II, 556–69.

there was no resistance this time. Patriarch Ivanović was a sick man and died within two years. After this, the Austrian authorities were able to place accommodating men in the office for the next seventy years.

The declaratory rescript of 1779 was the last great measure affecting the military border issued during the joint reign of Maria Theresa and Joseph II. This period, from 1765 to 1780, was above all characterized by an enormous growth in the administrative structure of the border establishment. The additional duties imposed on the regiments created additional burdens, and the beneficial effects of the increased centralization on military efficiency were counterbalanced by increased economic hardships. Indeed, it soon became questionable whether economic conditions would permit the continued existence of the border institution.

4

—.—.—.—.—

THE MILITARY BORDER AND
JOSEPH II: 1780–90

On November 29, 1780, Empress Maria Theresa died
and Joseph II became sole ruler of the Habsburg Empire. Freed
from the restraints and the prejudices of his mother, the emperor
struggled throughout the next decade to impose some of the
political ideas of the Enlightenment on the Habsburg lands.
Rigid and dogmatic, Joseph II strove to establish an absolute,
centralized state, and in the end this aroused so much opposition
that almost all of his measures had to be repealed by his suc-
cessors. A humanitarian, physiocrat, and cameralist at the same
time, he wanted to build a powerful army on the Prussian model.
Influenced by the then fashionable doctrine of the separation
of powers, he unsuccessfully tried to resolve the perennial conflict between maximum military utilization of the Grenzer and
amelioration of their economic circumstances by dividing the
military border administration into separate civil-economic
and military branches. At the same time, he played throughout
his reign with schemes for the conquest of new provinces, and
abandoning Maria Theresa's hostile attitude toward the Orthodox Church, and in alliance with Orthodox Russia, he tried to
make the military border the base for an expansive Balkan
policy.

After the conclusion of the War of the Bavarian Succession,
during the years 1780 to 1782, the Hofkriegsrat, frequently
prodded by the emperor, carried out another reorganization in
the tactical framework of the border regiments. The object of
the new arrangements, originally proposed by Wenzel Count

Colloredo, Inspector General of the Military Borders since 1778, was a reduction of the heavy burdens laid on the Grenzer by the maintenance of an overly large active establishment.[1] While the entire male population remained liable for service, it was now divided into "enrolled" and "supernumerary" Grenzer. Selection for enrollment or assignment to supernumerary status was governed as much by the needs of the economy as by military considerations. "The guiding principle," so an imperial directive ordered, "is that the selection be made with the least damage to the economy."[2] The number of men on active duty was materially reduced, for now only one man out of three was actually enrolled.[3] The enrolled Grenzer were divided into three categories. The first category performed cordon guard and other routine duties and received a basic annual allowance of twelve gulden, the so-called *Dienstconstitutivium*, which normally was credited against the landtax owed by the families. The second group, considered temporarily on furlough, was available as reinforcement whenever needed and received an allowance of four florins. The third group received no pay, but was trained in the use of arms and expected to take over local defense and other duties after the first two categories had departed on active service with the field army.[4] In addition, provisions were made to arm all supernumerary Grenzer with obsolete muskets for home defense.[5]

There was also a reform of the field service regulations. The cumbersome three levy system, under which one levy marched out in the early spring and having completed its tour of duty returned in late fall, was scrapped. Instead, each infantry regiment was required to provide a field contingent of two battalions, six companies each, accompanied by artillery and sharpshooter detachments. The total, about twenty-nine hundred rank and file to be selected from the households which could spare them best, were to serve for the duration of hostilities.[6] The emperor

---

[1] Franz Vaniček, *Specialgeschichte der Militärgrenze* (4 vols.; Vienna, 1875), II, 274-75.

[2] "Circularverordnung" to all border commands, Vienna, Nov. 2, 1782, DAZ Slavon. gkda. 1780-82.

[3] Estimates based on the muster lists for 1775 in KA Nostitz-Rieneck, IX-2, 4.

[4] HKR to Karlstadt Gkdo., Sept. 9, 1780, DAZ Zagr. gkda. F-14.

[5] Imperial instructions, March 26, 1780, circulated to all commands, KA HKR 1780-6-163.

[6] HKR directive to all commands concerning the organization, composi-

also took a great interest in the training and efficiency of the border troops, especially of the cannoneers and sharpshooters.[7] Realizing the importance of good non-commissioned officers, he ordered that promising young Grenzer were to be sent on temporary duty with line regiments and promoted on their return.[8]

At the same time, the emperor streamlined the command structure and reduced the number of major headquarters. In 1783, much to the displeasure of the Croatian estates, the Warasdin and Banal Borders were combined,[9] joined three years later by the Karlstadt Border. The new command, designated the Croatisches General Commando, had its headquarters in Zagreb and Feldmarschall Leutnant De Vins was appointed as its first commanding officer.[10]

This purely military reorganization, however, failed to improve the economic circumstances of the Grenzer. Especially in the Karlstadt and Banal regiments, the authorities were faced with the problem of a subsistence economy that always hovered on the margin of acute want and abject poverty. In 1783 and again in 1784 crops failed entirely in the Lika and Ottoschatz Regiments, and there was a poor harvest in all of Croatia. In the districts hit the hardest famine stalked the population, which, so travelers related with awe, had been reduced to eating tree bark mixed with earth.[11] These conditions precluded any serious military employment, and when late in 1784 trouble with the United Provinces over the navigation of the Scheldt River led to the dispatch of substantial reinforcements to the Austrian Netherlands, the contribution of the Croatian command was but two battalions of Warasdiner[12] and a combined cavalry-infantry free corps raised by voluntary enlistments.[13]

tion, and training of field battalions, Vienna, June 12, 1781 (copy), DAZ Zagr. gkda. F-14.

[7] Imperial instructions concerning recruitment and training of Grenzer specialists, Vienna, July 12, 1782, transmitted by the HKR to all border commands (copy), *ibid.*, Varia, Ogulinska bgda. F-1.

[8] "Circularverordnung" to all commands, Sept. 21, 1782, KA HKR 1782-7-355.

[9] HKR instructions, KA HKR 1783-3-382.

[10] Appointment, Aug. 23, 1786, DAZ Zagr. gkda. F-16.

[11] Thus the report of Hofrat Kraus, Aug. 20, 1785, KA HKR 1785-40-502. Cf. Franz Bach, *Otočaner Regimentsgeschichte* (Karlstadt, 1853), pp. 64–65.

[12] Mobilization orders, Oct. 28, 1784, DAZ Zagr. gkda. F-16.

[13] Instructions regarding organization of free corps, HKR to the Banal-Warasdiner Gkdo., Nov. 25, 1784, *ibid.*

For some time the emperor, keenly aware of the miserable economic conditions prevailing in the Croatian regiments and also cognizant of the many abuses to which the Grenzer were subject, had been casting around for an entirely new scheme to administer the military border. For many years he had been a keen admirer of the Prussian military system, especially its canton organization. The Prussian monarchy was divided into so-called cantons, districts of five thousand hearths for infantry regiments, or fifteen hundred for cavalry regiments, and the regiments drew their recruits from these districts. In the cantons a systematic census of the male inhabitants was taken, and although wide social groups and indeed whole areas were exempted, the regiments could call up the required number of new recruits each year. In many ways similar to the organization prevailing on the military borders, this system differed in that no land grants were provided in Prussia and also that the normal civilian administration continued to operate in the civil and economic affairs of the districts.

As early as 1770, Joseph II, together with General Lacy, then President of the Hofkriegsrat, had despite his mother's opposition introduced a systematic census, a general *Conscription*, of all male inhabitants in the Austrian lands. Liberal exemptions were granted to individuals, occupations, towns, and even whole provinces, but definite recruiting districts for the German regiments of the Austrian line had been established.[14] In these districts, however, civil authority continued to operate and the emperor now decided to extend a similar arrangement to the regiments of the military border. He wished to eliminate the exclusive military jurisdiction which, in his opinion, constituted an economic liability; the land suffered because the officers often ignored the needs of agriculture.[15]

In the spring of 1782 Joseph II instructed Colonel Geneyne, commanding officer of the German Banat Regiment, to undertake a survey of the various regiments and to submit a report on their conditions. In addition, the colonel was instructed to formulate proposals for improvements. During his extended tour of the border, from Karlstadt to the Banat, Geneyne came to the conclusion that the establishment required fundamental

---

[14] Edith Kotasek, *Feldmarschall Graf Lacy* (Horn, 1956), pp. 77–83.

[15] Emperor Joseph II to FML Gyulay, Karlstadt, asking for suggestions, KA Nostitz-Rieneck IX-12 (n.d.).

changes.[16] He contended that the border establishment lacked uniformity in organization, procedure, training, and discipline. There were wide variations in the economic management as well as in the service obligations of the Grenzer. The military commanders, Geneyne conceded, were well meaning, but the average officer neither had the time nor the experience and knowledge to deal with the economic and other essentially civilian aspects of life in the regiments. Geneyne suggested the organization of a completely separate administrative and civil affairs branch. Cantons, equivalent to the regimental districts, would constitute the major unit of administration and specially trained administrative officers, assisted by selected senior non-commissioned officers, would supervise all essentially civilian affairs. Moreover, in order to insure independence from interference, the administrative officers were to belong to a special service and to be in no way dependent on the regimental commanders for promotions and other career matters.

The emperor, always attracted by new schemes and systems, was highly impressed, but military opinion on the worth of such a radical innovation was sharply divided. Field Marshal Hadik, then President of the Hofkriegsrat, supported it with certain reservations, but many of the most senior generals in the Austrian service were strongly opposed. The best statement for the opposition, and in many ways the sharpest formulation of the fundamental problem facing the military border institution, was delivered by Field Marshal Lacy, who, in a memorial dated December 5, 1782, raised the question whether the military strength or the economic welfare of the border inhabitants was to be the major consideration. "It must be decided once and for all," Lacy declared, "whether the Grenzer are to be considered regular troops or whether they are to constitute a mere militia. If they are considered regulars, then they must be properly trained and exercised, and this will give them very little time to devote to agriculture. On the other hand, if they are to become nothing more than an ill-trained militia, the entire military border system will no longer be a major military resource for the state." [17] The memorial was not without effect. The emperor asked Geneyne to make another study of the

[16] "Relation des Obersten Geneyne," with extensive marginal annotations by Joseph II, KA Schriftgut F-40, folder 30.

[17] Memorial (copy), KA Nostitz-Rieneck IX-9.

regiments, and in the meantime the advice of the various commanding officers as well as the opinion of the Orthodox
Patriarch, Mojsije Putnik, was solicited.[18] Even before their
recommendations had been received, in February, 1783, Lacy,
evidently anxious about the proposed changes, again brought
up the question of the ultimate purpose of the military border.
He conceded that in the past perhaps too little attention had
been devoted to economic and civil affairs, but he maintained
that the Geneyne scheme went too far in the other direction
and considered economic progress as the primary objective of
the institution. This, he earnestly advised, would ruin the military character and the efficiency of the Grenzer. Lacy concluded that the emperor should realize that he could not have
both prosperous peasants and an ever-ready, cheap regular
soldiery.[19]

In his two authoritative memorials Lacy posed a fundamental question not to be solved until the dissolution of the
border institution. Lacy conceived the question of military efficiency not in terms of light infantry, but within the framework
of the rigid linear tactics so successfully employed by Frederick
II. He shared with most other Austrian generals a failure to
understand that the essential strength of the Grenzer lay in
their ability to operate in small war, but within these limits his
argument was sound. Joseph's desires were contradictory and
could not be met. Lacy, however, failed to convince the emperor. It is not entirely clear why the emperor decided to back
the Geneyne scheme. Perhaps he was genuinely influenced by
the deplorable economic circumstances and the misery of the
Grenzer; perhaps he was influenced by the then fashionable
doctrine of the separation of powers.[20] In any case, on April 9,
1783, by imperial command, the Hofkriegsrat informed all
border commands that the entire establishment would be re-
vamped and that Colonel Geneyne would begin by making the
necessary changes in the German Banat Regiment.[21]

Geneyne was advanced to major general and given charge

[18] Geneyne's second report, March 13, 1783, with enclosures containing
the responses of various officers as well as of Patriarch Putnik, KA HKR
1783-23-10.
[19] Memorial, Vienna, March 6, 1783, KA Nostitz-Rieneck IX-11.
[20] A. Klein, "Militär-Statistische Beschreibung der k.k. Grenzländer,"
ÖMZ, 12 (1871), 126–27.
[21] "Circularverordnung," KA HKR 1783-23-19.

of the entire organization. An exception, however, was made for the Transylvanian regiments where civilian and military land and authority intermingled.[22] The prospects of the new reform aroused considerable opposition and throughout the next year the Croatian commands, the Banal-Warasdiner as well as the Karlstadter, repeatedly submitted memorials urging a slow down, if not the complete suspension, of Geneyne's program.[23] A final attempt to halt the change was made early in 1786 by Inspector General Colloredo, supported by the commanding officers of all the Croatian and Slavonian regiments. The group submitted a joint memorial to the emperor, urgently pleading against the introduction of the Geneyne proposals.[24] Joseph II, however, would brook no further delay and, overriding all opposition, ordered on March 28, 1786, that the new system be implemented at once.[25] Nonetheless there were some modifications worked out by Feldmarschall Leutnant De Vins, and final details were determined in a series of high-level conferences held in Vienna during the summer and fall of 1786.[26] On February 14, 1787, the new regulations, the *Canton Regulativ*, were put into effect.[27]

The basic feature of the canton system was the creation of a dichotomy within the regimental framework. The heretofore unrestricted competence of the commander was limited to purely military affairs. For tactical purposes each regiment retained its two field battalions, six companies each, as well as the local reserve, organized in two *Landes-Defensions Divisionen*. The peace establishment of a border infantry regiment was set at 2,789, including a headquarters detachment of 28, and including 256 sharpshooters and 343 artillerymen. The local defense units mustered approximately 400 men each. In addition, the four Karlstadt and two Banal regiments each had small elite detachments of scouts, the so-called *Seressaner*. These units, dating back to the days of the irregular establish-

[22] Instructions to Maj. Gen. Geneyne, Vienna, Dec. 10, 1783, *ibid.*, 1783-23-19.

[23] Assorted memorials enclosed with an overall report on the conditions of the Karlstadt and Banal-Warasdin Borders, Jan. 24, 1784, *ibid.*, 1784-23-38.

[24] Colloredo's memorial with enclosures, *ibid.*, 1786-23-7.

[25] *Ibid.* 1786-26-272, and also the imperial instructions to the HKR, Vienna, April 8, 1786, *ibid.*, 1786-16-172.

[26] Conference records, *ibid.*, 1786-23-19.

[27] *Canton Regulativ* (copy), *ibid.*, 1787-23-6; discussed in Vaniček, III, 12–31.

ment, were recruited from the wealthier and best reputed zadruge. Numbering about 200 rank and file in each regiment, the Seressaner did not wear the regulation uniform but the colorful national costume, with red hooded cloaks and sashes bristling with arms. Usually mounted, they were used to patrol behind the cordon, to apprehend criminals, to intercept smuggler convoys, and on occasion to carrying out confidential missions beyond the Turkish frontier. Except for the non-commissioned officers — the *Harambassi, Unter-Bassi,* and *Vice-Bassi* — the Seressaners received no pay or allowances, but their households were freed from all taxes and robot duties.[28]

The regularly enrolled Grenzer too did not always wear their uniforms. In general the white regulation uniforms now provided free by the government were worn only for formal parades or when the field battalions went on active service outside the border area. For cordon and other local duties the Grenzer customarily wore an undress uniform, the *Haus Montur,* consisting of a homespun brown coat, homemade pants, and native soft boots.[29] The new regulations also brought order in the training procedures. The infantry underwent two annual training camps, two weeks in the late spring and another two weeks in the fall after the harvest; the sharpshooters did not go to camp but fired at the mark every second Sunday, and the artillery was instructed in a series of training courses at Petrinja and Karlstadt.[30] Similar provisions, varying only in detail, were made in all regiments.

Under the Canton Regulativ the civil, economic, judicial, and other routine non-military affairs of the border population came under the direction of a separate administration. Every regimental district was constituted a canton, looked after by officers selected for their interest and experience in directing an agricultural economy, fluency in the local language, and administrative ability. Of course, much of this was and always remained theory. In practice it proved hard to find enough qualified men to fill the posts.[31]

[28] Ignaz F. Bergmayr, *Verfassung der k.k. Militär-Gränze und Oesterreichischen Kriegs-Marine* (Vienna, 1845), pp. 89–94.

[29] For the frequent uniform changes which are only of antiquarian interest see Rudolf v. Ottenfels and Oscar Teuber, *Die österreichische Armee von 1700–1867* (Vienna, 1895), *passim.*

[30] Alphons v. Wrede, *Geschichte der K. und K. Wehrmacht,* Supplementary volume to *MKA* (5 vols.; Vienna, 1893–1903), V, 5, 232–33.

[31] *Canton Regulativ,* KA HKR 1787-23-6; Vaniček, III, 17–30.

At the head of each canton, in a hierarchy roughly parallel-
ing that of the regiment, stood a major, while battalion and
company districts were administered by subalterns, until finally each village and hamlet was supervised by *Dorf-Ober* and
Unter-Inspectoren, selected from senior non-commissioned officers. Every officer had to undertake frequent visitations in his
district and render a large number of fixed reports and returns.
In addition, each canton had a number of specialist officers,
including a military judge, styled *Auditor* in the Austrian army,
an engineer, a bookkeeper, and a surgeon. The entire system
was intensely paternalistic and exercised the most minute control over any and all affairs of the Grenzer population.

With this new order the spirit of Austrian cameralism penetrated the military border. Many of the new administrators,
especially in the higher echelons, were convinced physiocrats
and their efforts to improve the agricultural economy of the
Grenzer were well meant and sincere. They were unsuccessful,
however, and in the end the new system proved to be more of
a burden than a boon. From the very outset the canton administration faced the undisguised hostility of most regimental officers, though this aversion might in time have been overcome.
More important, however, was the fact that the basic ideas of
the system were incompatible with each other and, as Lacy
already had pointed out, impossible to achieve. Given Austria's
perennial reluctance to make any large expenditures for the
military border, it was quite impossible to create a prosperous
agricultural economy and maintain a strong military establishment at the same time. Greater encouragement of trade and industry might have improved circumstances somewhat, but, on
the Croatian borders at any rate, the basis for such a development was lacking and the military authorities were openly opposed to this because they feared that it might corrupt the
Grenzer's fighting spirit. Within a very few years the restless
ambition of Joseph II involved Austria in an aggressive war
with the Ottoman Empire that halted all progress. Thereafter,
any further improvement in the economic life of the border was
prevented by the constant wars of the French Revolution.[32]

[33] Explanations given for the failure of the canton system vary with the
political persuasion of the writer. Vaniček, III, 194, blamed the frequent wars
as well as the "mental immaturity" of the officers; on the other hand, the
national-socialist polemicist Rupert v. Schumacher, *Des Reiches Hofzaun*
(3d ed.; Darmstadt, 1942), p. 186, asserted that the system failed because it

Since 1781 the emperor had maintained an alliance with Catherine of Russia, designed in part to bolster the status quo in central Europe, but aimed primarily toward a partition of the Ottoman provinces in the Balkans. As conceived, the agreement looked more profitable to Catherine than to Joseph, but the emperor hoped to utilize it to acquire great parts of Wallachia, Serbia, Bosnia, Herzegovina, and possibly even the Venetian possessions in Istria and Dalmatia. Such great territorial gains not only would wipe out the setback suffered by Austria in the shameful Treaty of Belgrade in 1739, but also would provide additional land for the expansion of the military border settlements. The emperor reconfirmed the alliance during a visit to the Crimea early in 1787, and when in August of that year the much provoked Porte declared war against Russia, he entered the conflict in the spring of 1788 in accordance with his treaty obligations.

Hostile action against Turkey had already been foreshadowed by a forward policy along the frontier. Since the 1740's, standing orders for the frontier guards in the sector facing the troublesome Turkish frontier territories in Bosnia had emphasized caution and restraint. Although incursions were to be repulsed and "violence answered with violence," no reprisal raids were permitted.[33] In 1782, however, Joseph II issued secret instructions authorizing limited reprisal raids,[34] and the following year the Hofkriegsrat began to rearm and to strengthen the permanent fortifications on the Croatian borders which had been allowed to fall into disrepair.[35]

After the Porte declared war on Russia mobilization began in earnest. On September 5, 1787, Vienna informed the Croatian command that "His Majesty has directed the mobilization of His forces along the entire frontier from Transylvania to the Karlstadter Generalcy."[36] Actually, the Croatian regiments

was contrary to the soldierly spirit of the Grenzer. André Blanc, "Les confins militaires Croates au XIX siècle," *Revue d'Études Slaves*, 28 (1951), 115–18, blames the wars, while Rudolf Kiszling, *Die Kroaten* (Graz-Cologne, 1956), p. 47, stressed the rivalry among the regimental and cantonal officers.

[33] Cordon instructions, June 15, 1771, HKR to Banal Gkdo., DAZ Banska gkda. F-1.

[34] Printed in Aleksa Ivić, ed., *Spisi bečkih arhiva o prvom Srpskom ustanku, Zbornik IJK*, X (Belgrade, 1936), 269–74.

[35] HKR to Karlstadt Gkdo., Vienna, Sept. 28, 1783, DAZ Zagr. gkda. F-15.

[36] HKR to all border commands, Vienna, Sept. 5, 1787, DAZ Zagr. gkda. F-17.

were in no condition to sustain major military operations. There was a severe famine in the Karlstadt districts and conditions were but little better in the Banal area.[37] Clearly the regiments were not fit for action and therefore Austrian military planners relied heavily on the enlistment of Balkan Christians to fill the depleted ranks. In October, 1787, the Hofkriegsrat informed the Croatian command that the emperor had decided to spare the Grenzer as much as possible and that the regiments should utilize Christian refugees from Bosnia and Serbia to bring up the battalions to war strength.[38] To encourage recruitment, the emperor enlisted the aid of the Orthodox Church, and a number of clerics were active Austrian agents in Turkish territory even before the official declaration of war.[39]

Thus, once again, the chimera of large-scale Balkan Christian support played a large part in Austrian calculations. In the past, such attempts had usually failed because the Habsburg ties with the Catholic Church had irritated and alienated the Orthodox.[40] But this time it was hoped that the emperor's policy of religious toleration and his alliance with Orthodox Russia would favorably affect Orthodox feelings.[41]

Austria entered the war on February 7, 1788. The two allies had planned to coordinate their operations, but an unexpected Swedish attack in the north prevented Catherine from carrying out her engagement. Therefore, the Austrian forces, some two hundred and fifty thousand strong, faced the major portion of the sultan's army, and during the opening phase of the war things went very badly. The inept Lacy had disposed his forces in six corps drawn up along the extended front from the Adriatic to the Dnjestr. His strategic plan, such as it was, consisted of a general advance all along the whole front.[42] Fortress Belgrade, the Turkish key position, was to be seized by a coup before the declaration of war, but this scheme failed and the

---

[37] Johann A. Demian, *Statistische Beschreibung der Militärgrenze* (2 vols.; Vienna, 1806), I, 67–68.

[38] HKR to Croatian Gkdo., Vienna, Oct. 26, 1787, DAZ Zagr. gkda. F-17. Also instructions from FML de Vins to the regiments on the cordon, Zagreb, Jan. 25, 1788, DAZ Varia Ogulin bgda., F-14, folder 2.

[39] Bishop Joanović of Bać and archpriest Jovan Popović of Kostajnica, were the most active clergymen. Vaniček, III, 365–68.

[40] Gunther E. Rothenberg, *The Austrian Military Border* (Urbana, Ill., 1960), pp. 59–60, 66–67, 92–94, 118–19.

[41] The Toleration Patent of 1781 also applied to the Military Border.

[42] Kotasek, pp. 173–76.

Austrian general advance bogged down almost at once. As for the expected Christian revolts, the emperor and his advisers had badly miscalculated. Although here and there small groups of Serbs joined the imperial colors, hopes for a great Christian uprising against Ottoman rule did not materialize. Instead, Christians as well as Moslems drew together against the invaders and put up stiff resistance in the frontier fortresses.[43] The Austrians made a few minor penetrations, but then rapidly lost momentum as their supply system broke down. By early summer the troops were stricken with typhus and all offensive plans had to be abandoned. Indeed, on the central front, the Turks, recovering some of their old martial spirit, counterattacked and broke through into the Banat, where they caused much damage. Late that summer, Joseph II foolishly assumed personal command of his armies and proved totally incompetent as a field commander. Only the onset of winter saved the imperial forces from complete rout in 1788.

The extreme western sector of the Austrian front was formed by the regiments of the Croatian Military Border, operating for the first time as a separate army corps under Feldmarschall Leutnant De Vins. But the corps designation was purely administrative. There was no staff, insufficient artillery and engineers, and the troops were not concentrated for offensive operations. Instead, in compliance with Lacy's instructions, they were deployed in a rather thin line all along the boundary.[44] Only one brigade, composed of six field battalions from the two Warasdin regiments and from the 2d Banal, were ready to begin offensive operations.[45] These were limited to a number of minor raids conducted with indifferent success. The only major enterprise was the capture of the Turkish fort at Drežnik.[46] In April, 1788, Prince Liechtenstein, a mediocre general at best, assumed command of the Croatian corps and concentrated some ten thousand men to storm Dubica in Bosnia. The assault, however, was repulsed with heavy losses. Only after Field Marshal Laudon, who already had gained renown in leading Grenzer during the Seven Years' War and who was possibly the

---

[43] *Ibid.*, p. 175.

[44] FML De Vins orders of Feb. 10, 1788, DAZ Varia Ogulin bgda. F-14, folder 2.

[45] Order of battle, Vaniček, III, 376–77.

[46] *Ibid.*, pp. 385–88. For the small war, see the reports in DAZ Varia Ogulin bgda. F-14, folders 2 and 3.

ablest Austrian general of his time, assumed command in August, 1788, were offensive operations resumed. Reinforced by several line battalions, the Grenzer corps finally took Dubica at the end of August, and Novi, another Turkish barrier fortress, fell in October. These successes induced a small number of Bosnians to volunteer for the Austrian forces.[47]

Also in 1788 the military border, and in particular the Lika Regiment, was used in an attempt to launch a diversionary attack against the Turkish rear by fomenting an insurrection in Montenegro. Although in the end this enterprise fizzled, it revealed in sharp relief the unstable nature of the Austro-Russian alliance and their sharp rivalry on the Balkans.

Montenegro had never been completely subjugated by the Turks and since 1688 had been in an intermittent state of war against them. A primitive country, almost entirely lacking in resources, its political picture was still dominated by the tribal organization, although since 1697 the Njegoš line of prince bishops had assumed secular as well as ecclesiastic authority. Vienna, as well as St. Petersburg, established contact with the chieftains of the Black Mountain tribes at the beginning of the eighteenth century, but when Austria lost her leading position in the western Balkans after the disastrous Treaty of Belgrade, the Montenegrins turned toward Russia and actually offered to turn the country into a Russian protectorate. When, after worshiping mighty Russia from afar, a Russian mission actually penetrated to Montenegro in 1769, the results were disappointing for both sides.[48] Moreover, Catherine II, anxious to gain Austrian support for her Balkan projects, was increasingly reluctant to continue the Montenegrin involvement. She made no provisions for the Montenegrins in the treaty of Küchük Kainarji (1774), and when in 1777–78 a Montenegrin mission visited St. Petersburg, the empress would not receive the delegates at all. Disappointed, the Montenegrins were now willing to change their alignment and to turn to Austria. In late 1777, a certain knez, Nicolo Marković, claiming to represent the

---

[47] Vaniček, III, 393–472, gives a detailed account of operations. Also assorted documents in F. Berlić, *Die freiwillige Theilnahme der Serben und Kroaten an den vier letzten Österreichisch-Türkischen Kriegen* (Vienna, 1854), pp. 273–340.

[48] Michael B. Petrovich, "Catherine II and a False Peter III in Montenegro," *SR*, XIV (1955), 169–94. See also the literature cited in Branislav Djurdjev *et al.*, *Historija naroda Jugoslavije*, II (Zagreb, 1959), 1284.

pro-Austrian faction in his country, appeared in Vienna and proposed to recruit a Montenegrin free corps for the imperial service.[49]

This proposition greatly appealed to Chancellor Kaunitz, who for years had favored the dismemberment of the Ottoman Empire. In December, 1777, the chancellor sent a memorandum to Maria Theresa and Joseph II in which he pointed out that the dynasty had in the past derived considerable advantages from the recruitment of Balkan peoples and that Marković's scheme presented another opportunity "to utilize the Montenegrins and other subject people of the Porte to augment the military posture of the august house of Austria in a most inexpensive and perfect manner."[50] He continued by pointing out that future operations in the Balkans should be carried out by armies composed largely of "Grenzer, Montenegrins, and other such people, since experience shows that the climate of this region is a veritable graveyard for German troops." The chancellor conceded, however, that too little was known about the actual situation in Montenegro and he urged the dispatch of a reconnaissance mission.[51]

At this point neither Maria Theresa nor Joseph II, involved in the War of the Bavarian Succession, were very enthusiastic. Only after considerable delay, during which some futile negotiations with the main Montenegrin delegation returning from Moscow by way of Vienna were conducted, did the two rulers agree to Kaunitz's suggestion. Colonel Paulić of the 1st Banal was chosen to proceed to Montenegro to make an accurate survey of the country, its political structure, military potential, and possible support requirements.[52] Of course, the mission was to be entirely undercover, and although Paulić was neither able to fool the Turks nor to deceive the Venetians who held the coastal areas, he managed to carry out his task. He penetrated into the interior of the country and despite various Venetian as well as Turkish-inspired attempts on his life returned safely to make a full report. The Montenegrin prince bishop, the *vladika* Sava Petrović, reported the colonel, was sincere in his

[49] Proposal by Count Markovich, KA Mém. XVIII-54.
[50] Memorandum printed in V. Djordjević, ed., *Spisi iz Bečkih Državnih Arhiva. Dokumenti za djelo Crna Gora i Austrija, Zbornik IJK*, IV (Belgrade, 1913), 8–10.
[51] *Ibid.*
[52] Instructions for Col. Paulić, Vienna, Sept. 1781, *ibid.*, pp. 53–57.

intentions toward Austria, but he exercised only a very limited control over the various tribes. Paulić estimated that the country could altogether raise some eight thousand fighting men, but also noted that there existed several factions bitterly hostile to each other. Above all, Paulić noted that since the Venetians held the coast and the Turks controlled all inland routes, shipment of military supplies would present great difficulties.[53] After considering this report, the emperor decided that the "Montenegrin affair was not worthy of any further consideration." [54]

Nonetheless, this was not the end of Austrian relations with Montenegro. When the old vladika Sava died in 1782, his nephew Peter Petrović succeeded him and, as had become customary, departed for Russia to be consecrated by the Patriarch of St. Petersburg. On instructions, however, from Catherine II, eager to retain good relations with Austria, the Russian ambassador in Vienna refused him a passport to continue into Russia. Joseph II seized the opportunity, and with his endorsement Peter went to Karlovci to be consecrated by Patriarch Putnik.[55] After this he returned to Vienna in November, 1782, and requested military stores, mainly powder and lead, in order to defend his country against the designs of Kara Mahmud, the ambitious pasha of Scutari. The Austrian government, however, refused to furnish him with the materials requested, although it did authorize him to purchase them from private sources. But Peter did not have the means to do this and was most dissatisfied. For the next two years he remained in Vienna, constantly trying to make contacts with Russian as well as Prussian agents.[56] Meanwhile, Marković appeared again and renewed his offer to raise a free corps for Austria. But the Hofkriegsrat remained cool and merely advised the authorities on the Croatian Military Border to enlist those Montenegrins who actually presented themselves for service at the Austrian ports of entry.[57]

---

[53] Report of Col. Paulić, Vienna, Aug. 10, 1782, with enclosure describing the country, resources, factions, etc., *ibid.*, pp. 59–111.

[54] Imperial resolution, Vienna, Sept. 4, 1782, *ibid.*, pp. 131–32.

[55] P. Coquelle, *Histoire du Monténégro et de la Bosnie* (Paris, 1895), pp. 237–39, and Djurdjev, II, 1275–76.

[56] *Ibid.*

[57] Instructions from FM Hadik, Pres. HKR to Karlstadt Gkdo., Vienna, March 6, 1784, DAZ Zagr. gkda. F-16.

While Peter and Marković were negotiating without much success, Kara Mahmud, an energetic and ambitious descendant of the great Skanderbeg, who had created himself a nearly independent *pashalik*, was continuing his preparations against Montenegro, from which place the most urgent appeals for aid reached Vienna.[58] Other appeals were directed toward Russia and this time they were heeded. By 1785 Catherine's policy toward the western Balkans had changed again, and from Venice, where Russia had established a center for operations, agents and money poured into Montenegro. And although the Venetians had tried to block the Paulić mission, they did nothing to hamper Russian activities, hoping undoubtedly to play the Russians off against the Austrians.[59] But unless Montenegro was to slip completely into the Russian orbit, Austria had to act. Therefore, early in 1788, Captain Philip Vukassović of the Lika Regiment, who had accompanied Paulić on the previous enterprise, was chosen to take a large Austrian mission, supported by two hundred Likaner with two small guns, into Montenegro. He was given a difficult objective. On the one hand, he was to encourage the Montenegrins to attack neighboring Turkish territories, while on the other, he was to open negotiations with Kara Mahmud, who had hinted that he might turn against the sultan if circumstances were right.[60]

On the whole, Vukassović acquitted himself well. Despite Venetian efforts to prevent him from landing his warlike stores, the resourceful captain was able to smuggle the greater part of his supplies ashore and to make his way inland to Cetinje. Here, however, he found a Russian mission already established and for the next five months, allies or not, the two groups generally were working at cross purposes, supporting various local factions against each other.[61] Moreover, as had always been the experience of missions operating behind the enemy's line, whenever things went badly on the main front, the mission would find the helping hand displaced by the cold shoulder, or even the

---

[58] Djordjević, IV, 138–41.

[59] Adolf Beer, *Die orientalische Politik Österreichs seit 1774* (Prague, 1883), pp. 117–18.

[60] An extensive account of the Vukassović mission in "Die Sendung des österreichischen Hauptmanns Vukassovich nach Montenegro im Jahre 1788," *ÖMZ* (1828), Nos. 5, 6, pp. 170–93, 263–80.

[61] Report, Vukassović to Joseph II, Cetinje, April 9, 1788, Djordjev, IV, 144–45.

dagger in the back. Such was the fate of the Austrian agent Brognard who in July, 1788, set out to contact Kara Mahmud. The pasha, having received information about the misfortunes of the Austrian main army in the Banat, had Brognard assassinated and his head displayed on the walls of Scutari.[62] Meanwhile, Vukassović, despite his difficulties with the Russians, was able to instigate several Montenegrin attacks against Turkish territory. But when Austria's defeats became known and Turkish reprisals threatened, the population turned against him.[63] Vukassović was able to extricate his mission and its guard with great tactical skill and gained the coast where his detachment was evacuated by two small Austrian warships. By September 28, 1788, he arrived back at Senj.[64]

The mission had failed. It was to be the last time that Austria would place reliance on the ephemeral hope of a Balkan rising. Vukassović received a lieutenant-colonelcy, was raised to the hereditary nobility, and was awarded the Maria Theresa order.[65] During the winter of 1788–89 he was employed to raise a free corps to serve against the Turks, but this unit did not play a prominent role when fighting was resumed in the spring.[66]

That year, the Austrian armies, now operating under the overall command of Laudon, finally hit their stride and, renewing their offensive, overran most of Bosnia and Serbia. Belgrade fell on October 8, and Russian troops under Suvorov, assisted by an Austrian corps, entered Bucharest. De Vins resumed command of the Croatian Grenzer and, maneuvering with some skill, took Cetin in Bosnia. After that, operations reverted again to the small war pattern familiar to the Grenzer.[67]

The partition of the Ottoman Empire seemed inevitable, but it was saved by the international situation combined with revolts within the Habsburg realm. The Austro-Russian victories aroused Prussian apprehension, and at the same time Joseph's centralizing reforms aroused opposition which led to armed insurrection in the Austrian Netherlands and threatened rebellion in Hungary. The Hungarian malcontents opened negotia-

[62] Report of Chaplain Kermpotić, accompanying the mission (n.d.), *ibid.*, pp. 158–60.
[63] *Ibid.*, pp. 162–75.
[64] Berlić, pp. 274–75.
[65] Promotion order, Vienna, Dec. 27, 1788 (copy), DAZ Zagr. gkda. F-17.
[66] Vaniček, III, 430–31.
[67] *Ibid.*, pp. 435–71.

tions with Prussia and were arming for open resistance. In addition, on January 30, 1790, Prussia concluded a formal treaty of alliance with the Porte and war appeared imminent.[68]

Such was the situation when Joseph II died in February, 1790, of a disease contracted in the field. He had failed in most of his undertakings. Even on the military borders his well-meant canton system was not working out well and, like most of his other reforms, had to be shelved by his brother and successor, Leopold II.

[68] Robert Gragge, *Preussen, Weimar, und die ungarische Königskrone* (Berlin, 1923), pp. 37–54, 67–68.

5

_—.—.—.—.—_

CRISIS AND REFORM ON THE BORDER: 1790–1809

Following the death of Joseph II the military border underwent a severe and prolonged crisis. The Hungarian and Croatian diets, which under Maria Theresa had been reduced to relatively mild protests against the border institution, became more radical and again demanded its complete dissolution. At the same time, the series of French wars coming hard upon the heels of the Turkish war, strained the population resources of the regiments to the utmost. The canton system failed under stress and had to be abolished. For a time it appeared as if the entire military border establishment would have to be scrapped, but its value to the state was too great and in the end, as part of the reforms introduced by Archduke Charles, it was given a new basic law under which it continued for over four decades.

When Leopold II succeeded to the throne, he found Austria still at war with the Porte, the Belgian Netherlands in open revolt, Hungary on the verge of insurrection, and Prussia arming to support the enemies of the Habsburg. Skillfully mingling force and concessions, the new monarch regained the political initiative. He immediately opened negotiations with Prussia and in the Convention of Reichenbach (July 27, 1790), agreed to accept peace with the Ottoman Empire based on the prewar status quo. Therefore, when the treaty with the Porte actually was signed on August 4, 1791, at Sistova, Austria received only small frontier rectifications. In Croatia, the Turks ceded a strip of land adjoining the Ottoschatz and Lika Regiments, including the forts at Kordun, Drežnik, and Cetin. Actual implementation of the settlement, however, was delayed until 1795, and except for Belgrade, which the Austrians evacuated at once, troops remained in the positions occupied during the final stages of hostilities.[1]

The détente with Prussia deprived the malcontents in the Habsburg dominions of their most important potential ally. Therefore, Leopold was able to bring the Netherlands and Hungary back to their obedience. Troops had to be used to put down the Belgians, but in Hungary a judicious mixture of concessions and threats sufficed to break Magyar defiance. On March 16, 1790, the emperor promised the complete restoration of the Hungarian constitution and not quite two weeks later, on March 29, he issued formal invitations for a meeting of the diet in Buda.[2] But despite these conciliatory moves, the diet, formally opened on June 10, displayed a most uncompromising temper. Going far beyond the customary assertions of the country's constitutional privileges and the perennial demands for additional rights for the nobility, it called for the establishment of a national Hungarian army and the dissolution of the military borders.[3] The latter demands were supported by the Croatian delegation which, though it vigorously protested against the attempted substitution of Hungarian for Latin as the official language of proceedings, allied with the Magyars in opposition to Joseph's centralist reforms. The Croatians pressed for the immediate dissolution of the Warasdin regiments, which once had been conceded by Leopold I in 1704, and the subordination of the Karlstadt and Slavonian regiments to the authority of the Ban. Moreover, they demanded that the functions of the border officers be confined to military matters.[4]

Leopold, however, had no intention of accepting these de-

[1] Treaty cited in Johann C. v. Engel, *Staatskunde und Geschichte von Dalmatien Croatien, und Slawonien* (Halle, 1798), p. 320; Memorandum "Grenzberichtigungen mit der Türkei 1791," KA Mém. XXII-128.

[2] Denis Silagi, *Ungarn und der geheime Mitarbeiterkreis Kaiser Leopolds II* ("Südosteuropäische Arbeiten"), LVII (Munich, 1961), 29–30.

[3] Julius (Gyula) Miskolczy, *Ungarn in der Habsburger Monarchie* ("Wiener Historische Studien"), V (Vienna, 1959), 39–41.

[4] "Gravamina et postulata," of the Dalmatian-Croatian-Slavonian kingdom, and comments from the Hungarian Court Chancery, Gyula Miskolczy, ed., *A horvát kérdés története és iromanyai a rendi állam korában* (2 vols.; Budapest, 1927–28), I, 436–39.

mands, accompanied as they were by threats of armed resistance and continued attempts to reopen Hungarian negotiations with Prussia.[5] Well informed by his agents about the nature and extent of the opposition, he realized that the nobility formed the backbone of resistance. He, therefore, embarked on a determined campaign to drive a wedge between the nobles and the rest of the country.[6] Among his most effective devices was the convocation of the "Greek diet," the Serbian national ecumenical congress, representing the Orthodox clergy and population in southern Hungary and in Croatia, including, of course, the Orthodox Grenzer.[7] This move was decided on late in June, 1790, and on July 12 the Hofkriegsrat issued instructions for the selection of twenty-five military delegates from the various Orthodox dioceses: six from the Karlstadt, three from the Warasdin, four from the Banal, and the balance from the Slavonian-Syrmian regiments.[8] The royal commissioner to the congress, Feldmarschall Leutnant Baron Schmidfeld was instructed to encourage demands for an autonomous Serb region and to support Grenzer requests for the preservation of their special status.[9] The emperor's expectations were met. The congress opened September 1 in Temesvar and on October 24 duly petitioned for an extension of the Leopoldine privileges and the continued imperial administration of the military borders.[10] Leopold replied to these requests in a most favorable manner,[11] and to further underline his determination to counter Hungarian intransigence with concessions to the Serbs, he reconstituted on March 5, 1791, the Transylvanian-Illyrian Court Chancery, which had been dissolved in 1771.[12]

As it was, the last move was no longer necessary. By October, 1790, the Hungarians realized that they were isolated and reluctantly admitted Leopold II as their legal king and elected

[5] Robert Gragge, *Preussen, Weimar, und die ungarische Königskrone* (Berlin, 1923), pp. 72–73.

[6] Silagi, pp. 61–75.

[7] *Ibid.*, p. 34.

[8] Instructions, Vienna, July 12, 1790, DAZ Zagr. gkda. F-17.

[9] Miskolczy, *Ungarn*, pp. 44–45.

[10] Copy of Serb petition, KA Schriftgut F 31/5.

[11] Silagi, p. 35; Henrik Marczali, *Az 1790/1-diki országgyülés* (2 vols. Budapest, 1907), II, 172–80. Cf. Johann v. Csaplovics, *Slavonien und zum Theil Croatien* (2 vols.; Pest, 1819), II, 54–55.

[12] Friedrich Walter, ed., *Die Österreichische Zentralverwaltung, Veröff. Kom. Neu. Gesch. Öst.*, XXXV (Vienna, 1950), 82–87.

his son, the Archduke Alexander Leopold, as their palatine. In addition, the diet repealed all discriminatory legislation against the Orthodox. For his part, Leopold had accomplished his main object and, disturbed by the news from France, was unwilling to push his advantage. In the end, therefore, the resolutions passed by the diet and signed into law by the king were compromises.[13] The Hungarians acknowledged the Habsburg succession in Hungary and its associated kingdoms, while Leopold confirmed the traditional privileges of the Magyar and Croatian nobility. In addition, once the accord had taken effect, Leopold tacitly dropped his support for Serb autonomy. He firmly denied, however, all demands for the abolition of the military borders, declaring them essential for "the welfare of the realm and the maintenance of public security."[14] But as a concession to the Croatian estates, the Banal Border was once again constituted as a separate command under Feldmarschall Leutnant Johann Count Erdödy, the Ban. The Karlstadt and Warasdin regiments remained united under the control of Feldmarschall Leutnant De Vins.[15] Finally, as part of this general reorganization, the Banat regiments were separated from the Slavonian-Syrmian Border.[16]

At the same time, Leopold addressed himself to the problems of the military border administration where the canton system was not functioning well at all. Lacy's misgivings had indeed come true; there was a tremendous difference between the intentions of the government in Vienna and the actual conditions prevailing in the field. Directives, no matter how well intended, could not change the basic incompatibility between the maintenance of large military bodies at little or no expense to the state and the creation of a prosperous farming community. Moreover, the dislocations of the frequent mobilizations and the last Turkish war had hampered the canton officers, whereas the dichotomy between the administrative-economic and the purely military affairs was much resented by the regi-

[13] Miskolczy, *Ungarn*, pp. 46–47; H. Marczali, *Ungarische Verfassungsgeschichte* (Tübingen, 1910), pp. 117–22; and Marczali, *Az 1790/1*, II, 19–24.

[14] Annotation by Leopold, Jan. 2, 1791, Miskolczy, *Horvat kérdés*, I, 445–46.

[15] HKR instructions, Sept. 23, 1790, DAZ Zagr. gkda. F-17; KA HKR 1790-3-1475.

[16] Instructions, Feb. 15, 1791, KA HKR 1791-2-2695.

mental officers. The latter alleged that the division of authority was harmful to discipline and lessened the combat value of the Grenzer. In response to an inquiry made by the Hofkriegsrat in 1791, the great majority of regimental officers stated their belief that the power of the canton officers ought to be drastically curtailed.[17] Nonetheless, with the Austrian state treasury almost depleted, the emperor decided to continue with the canton system and appointed Baron De Vins as Inspector General of the Military Border.[18]

In the last week of 1791 the entire situation of the border was studied by a high-level conference in Vienna. During the deliberations conducted under the chairmanship of Field Marshal Count Wallis, President of the Hofkriegsrat, and attended by military officials as well as representatives of the treasury, the new inspector general vigorously defended the canton system against allegations of waste and inefficiency. He pointed out that the system had never received a fair trial and that it was not uniformly established in all regiments. The welfare of the border as well as the needs of the state, he declared, demanded the application of the principle of uniformity and absolute compliance with all regulations in all districts.[19] In a separate memorandum to the emperor, De Vins blamed the recent war for the difficulties of the canton system and reiterated his convictions that it could make a substantial contribution to the military budget of the monarchy provided that uniformity and good management were enforced. He also asserted that the prevailing taxes, especially the head tax, were most inequitable and suggested that a graduated land tax would encourage better use of the Grenzer lands and provide all the revenue necessary to maintain the regiments.[20]

No change was made in the tax system at this time, but the

[17] Replies filed in KA HKR 1791-23-19/31. Cf. Franz Vaniček, *Specialgeschichte der Militärgrenze* (4 vols.; Vienna, 1875), III, 71–74. Similar problems arose in Prussia where there were many complaints about the impoverishment of the peasants through the canton system. See Otto Busch, *Militärsystem und Sozialleben im Alten Preussen* ("Veröffentlichungen der Berliner Historischen Kommission"), VII (Berlin, 1962), 21–48. One contemporary writer on military affairs described the Prussian Cantonist as "an unhappy compromise between peasant and soldier." Georg Heinrich v. Behrenhorst, *Betrachtungen über die Kriegskunst* (2nd ed., 2 vols.; Leipzig, 1798), II, 210.

[18] Appointment, Vienna, Dec. 21, 1791, KA HKR 1791-3-2324.

[19] Conference protocol, Vienna, Dec. 27, 1791, *ibid.*, 1792-25-336.

[20] Report of De Vins, Vienna, Dec. 28, 1792, *ibid.*

emperor authorized De Vins to proceed with his plans for better organization. For the next seven years the inspector general endeavored to effect a badly needed overhaul of the border administration. He attempted to enforce the many directives and regulations and to improve the economy of the regiments. In Croatia, he continued the consolidation of settlement, already started under Beck, and combined a number of Grenzer households into more compact villages.[21] This was complicated, however, by the problem of the recent immigrants. Shortly before, as well as during, the last Turkish war, a considerable number of Serb and Croat families from Bosnia and Turkish Dalmatia had come over to the Austrians. The majority had been sent on to the Slavonian regiments, but the Karlstadt and the Banal Borders also picked up some four thousand men, women, and children.[22] To accommodate these newcomers, and also as a precaution against the continuing Turkish incursions, De Vins established twelve new villages in the area around Cetin and Drežnik.[23] But there was not enough land for all and many families had to be kept in relocation camps, pending the final, and it was hoped more favorable, demarcation of the Austro-Turkish boundary. When in 1795 the Convention of Dubica finally established the permanent frontier, no more land became available and there was much unrest among the immigrants.[24]

In any case, the outbreak of war with France in the spring of 1792 imposed fresh demands on the border and largely nullified De Vins's efforts. As it was, the regiments were so weakened by the losses of the Turkish war that they could at first furnish only a very small number of troops. Moreover, in the absence of a definite settlement with the Porte, the Karlstadt, Banal, and Transylvanian regiments had to remain alert against hostile moves. This was especially true along the Bosnian frontier where major Turkish troop concentrations remained a source of anx-

[21] Vaniček, III, 75–77; André Blanc, *La Croatie Occidentale* (Paris, 1957), p. 152; relevant documents in DAZ Zagr. gkda. F-14.

[22] Vaniček, III, 64–68; IV, 1–3.

[23] Special privileges, including relief from taxes and robot, granted to the "new Grenzer settled in the territories won from the Turks," Vienna, Dec. 27, 1794, KA HKR 1794-15-3005.

[24] Report from the Ogulin Regiment, March 22, 1796, to Gen. Paulić, Karlstadt, noting that "the regiment was overcrowded and could not receive any more immigrants." Also a letter from Ban Erdödy to the Karlstadt-Warasdin Gkdo., Zagreb, March 26, 1796, complaining about the activities of the recent immigrants. DAZ Zagr. gkda. F-20.

iety for the Austrian command. Therefore, the initial mobilization of the Croation and Slavonian border contingents was not by regiments or battalions, but by individuals, detachments, or at best, companies.[25]

In this fashion two composite battalions — the Warasdin-Karlstadt and the Slavonian — were scraped together. In addition, Croatian and Slavonian Grenzer provided the cadres for the free corps raised by Colonel Mihajlević of the Peterwardein and by Lieutenant Colonel Gyulay of the 2d Banal Regiment. The following year, the Croatian-Slavonian regiments jointly raised a sharpshooter corps commanded by Colonel Franz von Jellačić of the Szluin Regiment. Finally, in 1794–95 the pace of mobilization was stepped up. The Warasdin regiments furnished two composite battalions, while the Slavonian, Syrmian, Banat, and Transylvanian Grenzer provided one battalion each as well as artillery and pontooneer detachments. Also in 1794, encouraged by reports about the performance of the free corps, the Hofkriegsrat decided to raise an additional volunteer unit. This unit, the Wurmser (Styrian) Free Corps, paid for by the contributions of the patriotic citizens of Graz, was composed of cavalry raised among the Croatian and Slavonian Grenzer, while the infantry was recruited from the recent immigrants. In all, over thirteen thousand Grenzer served with the Austrian field armies.[26]

During the campaigns, the regular Grenzer fought with distinction and suffered heavy losses. Indeed, it became difficult to maintain the units at war strength. Officer casualties had to be made good by drafting administrative personnel, and when the heavy losses sustained by the enlisted Grenzer, especially at Arcola and Rivoli, made reinforcements imperative, the Hofkriegsrat suggested that the gaps in the ranks be filled by drafts from civil Croatia and Hungary.[27] This proposal, which would have diluted the unique character of the Grenzer, was not acted upon at this time. In April, 1797, Austria accepted the Armistice of Leoben, and on October 17 the Treaty of Campo Formio temporarily ended hostilities.

[25] Vaniček, IV, 4–71.
[26] Data compiled from Alphons v. Wrede, *Geschichte der K. und K. Wehrmacht*, Supplementary volumes to *MKA* (5 vols.; Vienna, 1893–1903), V, 5, 237–340; III, 923; Johann H. Schwicker, *Geschichte der österreichischen Militärgrenze* (Vienna-Teschen, 1883), pp. 279–88.
[27] Letter of May 14, 1797, KA HKR 1797-9-897.

Throughout the war the regular Grenzer displayed a high degree of discipline and were valued by the Austrian command for their reliability. In the period following the armistice, when the army was plagued by desertions, Grenzer were deployed as a police cordon.[28] Only the Wurmser Free Corps proved troublesome. These recent immigrants lacked discipline and early in 1795 the Grenzer cavalry component had to be detached, lest it become infected by the temper of the infantry. The four hussar squadrons were formed into a provisional *Banatisch-Slavonisch-Croatisch Gränz Husaren Corps.* [29] The Wurmser Free Corps, now all infantry, remained a constant source of difficulties, but realizing that the men had enlisted in the hope of obtaining land for their families and that after the Convention of Dubica there was no longer any hope for this, the Hofkriegsrat decided to keep the unit on active service.[30]

The war caused further deterioration in the economy of the Croatian Border, already suffering from a series of poor harvests. By 1792 there was much unrest in the Karlstadt regiments, and in January, 1793, a petition from the "sharpshooters of the Karlstadt Generalcy" asked the emperor for immediate relief, especially the abolition of the Hauskommunionen. Emperor Francis II, who had succeeded his father Leopold in March, 1792, readily granted tax reductions, remission of robot obligation, and also allocated some nine hundred mustered out army horses for farm use.[31] But this proved of little tangible benefit. The following year the harvest failed again and by 1794 there was acute famine on the Croatian Border.[32] More substantial aid was needed, but the war prevented effective action. "In view of the military situation," the Hofkriegsrat decided in April, 1797, "economic and agricultural matters will have to wait." [33]

To be sure, April, 1797, when the Hofkriegsrat was preparing to evacuate the capital in the face of the advancing French,

[28] Vaniček, III, 89–90.
[29] Circular, Generalkommando Agram, to the 1st and 2d Banal Regiments and the 1st and 2d Banal Cantons, Jan. 30, 1795, in DAZ Banska gkda. 1790-97. Also KA HKR 1793-23-12.
[30] HKR to Haupt-Reichsarmee, April 9, 1796 (copy), DAZ Zagr. gkda. F-20.
[31] Petition and Imperial Resolution, Jan. 29, 1793, KA HKR 1793-23-12.
[32] Engel, p. 265.
[33] HKR to Karlstadt-Warasdin Generalkommando, Vienna, Apr. 13, 1797, DAZ Zagr. gkda. F-20.

was not a good moment for economic considerations, but little was done even after the Peace of Campo Formio. There were, however, certain administrative changes. The seventeen infantry regiments were renumbered consecutively one through seventeen and designated as *National-Gränz-Infantrie Regimenter*, although in practice the territorial appellations remained in use.[34] But new designations helped the Grenzer very little, and when De Vins inspected the regiments in the summer of 1798, he was appalled by the evidence of dire want, poverty, and neglect. He realized then that the canton system had failed, but was taken ill and died in August, 1798, in the Szluin Regiment before he could submit his report. Eventually completed by Feldzeugmeister Alvintzy, the report exposed the defects of the canton system and recommended basic changes.[35] It described the poverty of the Grenzer and proposed that robot obligations and taxes be abolished or at least drastically reduced. De Vins charged that certain officers abused their powers and exploited their men and advised strong action against the offenders. Above all, the report urged an immediate end to the system of divided command, the very heart of the canton organization.

Clearly it was time for a complete change, but the Hofkriegsrat, reluctant to admit the unwelcome truth, attempted to maintain the canton system, albeit in slightly modified form. Feldmarschall Leutnant Wenzel Count Colloredo was appointed the next inspector general and, on his suggestion, the Hofkriegsrat returned administrative officers to the general supervision of the regimental commanders.[36] During his tour in office, Colloredo attempted to raise the level of education on the border, especially among the Orthodox clergy, and tried to prevent abuse of the Grenzer.[37] But when he actually inspected

[34] General orders, HKR, July 1, 1798, KA Mém. XXIII-90. The Croatian-Slavonian-Banat hussars, briefly designated as the 12th Hussars, were disbanded in 1801.

[35] Report of FZM Alvintzy, Oct. 15, 1798, KA Mém. XXIII-90.

[36] Colloredo's suggestions for reform, KA HKR 1798-25-3092; HKR instructions of Jan. 21, 1799, *ibid.*, 1799-47-39.

[37] The education of the Orthodox clergy was extremely primitive; often the priests could neither read nor write. In contrast with the government supported Roman Catholic "German" schools, the Orthodox, or "national" schools received no aid and were supported entirely by their own, often poverty-stricken, communities. Vaniček, II, 580–82; Johann A. Demian, *Statistische Beschreibung der Militärgrenze* (2 vols.; Vienna, 1806), II, 184, 382; H. Marczali, *Hungary in the Eighteenth Century*, (Cambridge, 1910),

the regiments late in 1799, he saw that nothing could save the canton system. His voluminous report recommended its immediate abolition and this time Vienna agreed. On November 1, 1800, an imperial edict ended the experiment.[38] The commanding officers became again the final authority in each regiment. For administrative purposes one senior officer, normally a major, was added to the regimental staff, while subalterns were appointed administrative officers for each company. A number of senior sergeants and corporals completed the personnel of the administrative section. Designated "economic officers" (*Oekonomie-Offiziere*), the administrative specialists were supernumerary to the normal establishment of the regiments and, to ensure continuity in administration, were to remain behind in case of mobilization. Only when the last levy, every man and boy capable of carrying a musket, was called out to defend their homes did the economic officers assume actual command of troops.[39]

In the meantime war with France had broken out again. In March, 1799, France declared war against Austria, which on this occasion was supported by England, Russia, Portugal, and the Ottoman Empire. The alliance with the Porte allowed the reduction of troops on cordon duty along the Turkish frontier, but even so the military border was hard put to muster contingents for active service. Nonetheless, some thirty-six battalions were raised. The Croatian Border regiments, including the Banal, mobilized sixteen battalions; the Slavonian ten, while the Banat and Transylvanian Borders furnished five battalions each. The Croatian and Slavonian battalions were mobilized by regiments, and the other contingents formed composite battalions. In addition, there were the Croatian-Slavonian sharpshooters, two battalions strong, the hussar regiment, and the veteran units of the Wurmser and Gyulay Free Corps. In all, the number of men totalled nearly thirty thousand.[40] During the campaigns of 1799–1800, twenty-four Grenzer battalions

pp. 287–88. Also HKR instructions of Feb. 5, 1799, warning officers not to abuse their Grenzer. KA Mém. XXIII-90.

[38] Colloredo's report, including over 1,000 enclosures (!), KA HKR 1800-23-12. Includes the report of a conference favoring the abolition of the canton system, May, 1800. Copy of the imperial order abolishing the system, DAZ Zagr. gkda. F-21.

[39] The provisional organizational scheme, Sept., 1800, in KA HKR 1800-23-12. Cf. Wrede, V, 134–35.

[40] Figures compiled from *ibid.*, pp. 158–340, passim.

fought in Italy and Switzerland, and twelve battalions, as well as the sharpshooters, the hussars, and the free corps served in Germany. This time, however, the replacement problem proved insurmountable; there were no more reserves in the home districts, and by early 1800 reinforcements had to be found in provincial Hungary, Croatia, and even Moravia.[41]

For Austria the war, once again, proved a disappointment. Although joint Russo-Austrian operations during 1799 in Italy and Switzerland were quite successful, allied cooperation was strained and after Napoleon returned from Egypt and took command the French rapidly recovered the initiative. In June, 1800, Napoleon defeated the Austrians at Marengo, forcing them to accept an armistice, and when operations resumed, Moreau scattered the Austrian army in Germany at Hohenlinden. When, despite the late season, the French pushed into Austria, threatening Vienna, the emperor hastily concluded the Treaty of Lunéville. The unhappy outcome of the war brought a shake-up in the Austrian high command. In January, 1801, Emperor Francis appointed his brother Archduke Charles, the ablest of the Austrian generals and champion of drastic army reforms, as president of the Hofkriegsrat and minister of war. Charles did his best to renovate the cumbersome and antiquated military establishment. Prominent among his plans were the formation of divisions and corps, the training and use of cavalry in large formations, national conscription and careers open to talent. Such ideas aroused opposition of the entrenched interests, while the emperor, who never lost his dread of radical upheavals, half heartedly agreed to his brother's program. As a result, most of the reforms were still in the planning stage when the archduke resigned in November, 1804, in protest against Austria's premature adherence to the Third Coalition against Napoleon.[42]

Also left uncompleted was the reorganization of the military borders. In late 1802, Charles appointed Archduke Ludwig as Director General of the Border (*General-Gränz-Direkteur*) and charged a *Gränz-Organisierungs-Commission*, headed by Major General Klein of the Military Border Department in the

[41] Vaniček, IV, 93. The Gyulay Free Corps had by this time become exclusively Hungarian in character.

[42] Eduard v. Wertheimer, "Erzherzog Carl als President des Hofkriegsrathes 1801-1805," *AÖG*, 66 (1884), 277–314.

Hofkriegsrat, to submit a comprehensive report on the administration of the Grenzer regiments.[43] Circulars were sent to all
officers, and in an unprecedented step, the opinion of the clergy,
Orthodox as well as Catholic, was solicited.[44] All concerned
were asked to submit their replies by the "most direct and the
fastest means" to Vienna.[45]

The various papers and proposals submitted to the commission provided an accurate, although not very encouraging,
picture.[46] Since the early eighteenth century no less than thirty
different schemes, systems, and reorganizations had been tried
out on the border.[47] Each time the primary purpose of these
reforms was to raise the fighting strength of the border; also,
there had been occasional attempts to ameliorate the material
conditions of the Grenzer. Conditions in the different commands
varied in detail, but they were definitely the worst in the four
Karlstadt regiments where the population scraped the barest
living from the hard hills. Here the land was very poor, agricultural methods antiquated, and repeated crop failures had caused
widespread slaughter of domestic animals so that there was an
almost complete lack of fertilizers.[48] In 1802 the Hofkriegsrat
decided that "hard-working and well-reputed Grenzer families
who have lost all their cattle shall be given a few heads to start
anew,"[49] and the following year, with famine threatening again,
the authorities decreed the erection of public magazines and

[43] Vaniček, III, 116–20. Besides Klein, the commission included Maj. Gen.
Martini, Hofrat Grenzreferent Beeg, Col. Devčić, Hofkriegs-Sekretär Pidoll
v. Quintenbach, Hofkriegs-Sekretär Johann v. Engel, Feldkriegs-Kommissar
Stadelmayer, Capt. Schwind, and Feldkriegs-Konzipist Ritter. Wrede, V, 231,
maintains that Ludwig was appointed in 1805. Many of the documents before
this date, however, refer to him as Director General.

[44] Circular to all border commands, Vienna, June 22, 1802, DAZ Zagr.
gkda. F-22.

[45] FML Chernell to all Croatian regiments directing submission of data
to Vienna, Zagreb, Jan. 29, 1803; letter from Archduke Charles, Vienna,
May 24, 1803, thanking all for their cooperation. *Ibid.*

[46] The collected papers of the commission include fascicles 27, 29, and 30
of KA Schriftgut as well as KA Mém. XXIII-90, 91, 92, and 93.

[47] Ognieslav M. Utiešenović, *Die Militärgrenze und die Verfassung. Eine
Studie über den Ursprung und das Wesen der Militärgrenzinstitution und
die Stellung derselben zur Landesverfassung* (Vienna, 1861), p. 32.

[48] Demian, I, 80–82, 112–17; Dominik Teleki v. Szék, *Reisen durch Ungarn und einige angränzende Länder* (Pest, 1805), pp. 266–67; Carl B. v.
Hietzinger, *Statistik der Militärgrenze des österreichischen Kaiserthums* (3
vols.; Vienna, 1817–23), I, 102–6.

[49] HKR to Karlstadt-Warasdin Gkdo., Vienna, Jan. 23, 1802, DAZ Zagr.
gkda. F-21.

provided credits of over two million gulden for agricultural supplies, seed corn, and breeder cattle.[50] Results, however, were minimal, chiefly because of the lack of local skill and resources. The practice of animal husbandry, for instance, was so primitive that the animals usually received very little care and often had no shelter during the harsh winter months.[51] The human population fared but little better. "The habitations of the Karlstadter Grenzer," noted one observer, "are poor, miserable huts, like the dwellings of savages."[52] They commonly possessed no floors, windows, or chimneys. Most of the dwellings were isolated, for despite the efforts of Beck and De Vins, the consolidation of settlement had made little progress. In 1802, out of a total of 16,546 dwellings in the Karlstadt regiments, 4,629 were completely isolated, while about 5,000 were located in hamlets of less than twelve families.[53] Efforts to establish a more compact pattern of settlement were prevented by "the poverty and the decline in population of the Karlstadt Border."[54]

Affairs were somewhat better in the Banal and Warasdin regiments, where the land was more fertile and the climate more favorable for agriculture.[55] In the Banal Border, Petrinja had 664 houses, Kostajnica 594, and Glina 213, although the other villages were mere hamlets and many families remained completely isolated. Houses were better than in the Karlstadt regiments, but they too often lacked chimneys and windows.[56] In the Warasdin district, finally, the villages were more compact, houses more comfortable, and some of the larger places, especially Bjelovar, a privileged military township serving as headquarters for the two regiments, were considered desirable duty stations by many Grenzer officers.[57] In fact, the Warasdin regiments approached a modest well being, perhaps because there was no common frontier with Turkish territory so that the Warasdiner did not have to mount cordon watch. And this was important. Even in normal times the Karlstadters had to

[50] Schwicker, p. 224; Vaniček, III, 133–35.
[51] Demian, I, 112–17.
[52] *Ibid.*, pp. 62–63.
[53] *Ibid.*, pp. 46–47.
[54] HKR to Karlstadt-Warasdin Gkdo., Vienna, May 1, 1802, DAZ Zagr. gkda. F-21.
[55] Hietzinger, I, 102–3, 112–15.
[56] Demian, I, 202–5.
[57] Hugo Kerchnawe, *Die alte k.k. Militärgrenze* (Vienna, 1939), p. 44.

provide 915 men, and the Banal units 315 men weekly to man the cordon line.[58]

Despite the support given by Joseph II, neither trade nor industry had prospered on the military border in Croatia. The Militär Communitäten had stagnated. The military authorities were never too enthusiastic about these townships because they feared that their prosperity would disrupt the rural and patriarchal society of the Hauskommunionen which formed the social basis of the border.[59] Indeed, by 1787, there had been considerable military pressure to dissolve all Militär Communitäten and to return them to regimental jurisdiction. But Joseph II refused to permit this. Gospić, Ottoschatz, Ogulin, and Koprivnica were indeed reincorporated into the regimental organization, but Senj, Karlobag, Ivanić, Kostajnica, and Petrinja continued in their special status.[60] New regulations, however, sharply reduced the number of elective town offices and placed all details of communal life under close military control. Everything from the election of magistrates to the distribution of firewood was minutely supervised, prescribed, and regulated.[61] Joseph II had made special efforts to develop Senj and Karlobag and to establish the nucleus of an Adriatic fleet there. During the 1780's a number of merchant ships were built in both ports and, to protect them from the numerous pirates infesting the lower Adriatic, the emperor issued orders to arm the vessels with two hundred guns from the state arsenals and to draft Grenzer as gunners and marines.[62] But the French wars ended all this. At one time Senj also had manufactured some sailcloth and other naval stores, and even processed some silk, but by 1805 all these enterprises had closed down, while the ships rotted in the harbor. Senj still had 479 houses with some 2,500 inhabitants, while Karlobag was reduced to 185 houses and 656 inhabitants. "It appears," concluded one writer, "that neither manufacture nor trade can prosper under military rule."[63]

[58] Demian, I, 11, 187.

[59] Blanc, pp. 246–47.

[60] Schwicker, pp. 217–19.

[61] Copy of the Communitäten-Regulativ of 1787, KA Schriftgut, ms. vol. 34.

[62] Vaniček, II, 309–10, 658–60; III, 79–82.

[63] Demian, I, 134–55. Also the memo. "Von den Militär-Kommunitäten," Grenz-Organisierungs-Commission, Vienna, Aug. 17, 1803, KA Schriftgut, ms. vol. 35.

Inland, in the regiments, there had also been little progress since the early eighteenth century. A few small cottage industries existed precariously. Near Petrinja primitive ironworks produced some crude implements, some wood was turned at Glina, and in the Ogulin Regiment some rough footwear was made.[64] There were too few artisans on the Croatian Military Border. In the Karlstadt regiments there were only 349, in the Warasdin regiments 442, and the Banal Border counted about 500 poorly trained craftsmen.[65] They were hardly able to keep up with the most necessary repairs to meet local needs and there was little surplus for sale. Commerce, on the Croatian Border, had remained almost completely in the barter stage. By 1805, economic conditions had become very bad and the entire population, so a Hungarian traveler reported, "looked to the government for relief." [66]

But, without a doubt, the most important single factor inhibiting any real improvement was the constant heavy demands for military manpower. In 1799 the total border population, from the Adriatic to the Carpathian Mountains, numbered 823,950, including 101,692 men of military age.[67] Another census, taken three years later, showed that the Croatian military borders, the Karlstadt, Warasdin, and Banal, numbered 182,733, 101,902, and 91,545 inhabitants, respectively, about evenly divided between the sexes.[68] In times of peace, the establishment of the military border was comprised of 54,644 Grenzer under arms; but during the wars from 1792 to 1801, all the regiments of the border together furnished over 100,000 men and suffered 38,000 casualties.[69] In addition, with the exception of the Warasdin regiments, all units continued to man the cordon. Of the total number mobilized for foreign service, the Croatian Border regiments furnished about one-half.[70]

Even so, there was by this time serious doubt about the fu-

[64] Hietzinger, II, 260–72; Demian, I, 128–34, 243–47, 352–53.

[65] *Ibid.* Manufacture was equally retarded in civil Croatia. See the excellent monograph by Miroslava Despot, *Pokušaji Manufakture u Gradanskoj Hrvatskoj u 18. stoljeću, Grada za Gospodarsku Povijest Hrvatske*, XII (Zagreb, 1962), passim.

[66] Szék, p. 271.

[67] Hietzinger, II, 330.

[68] Demian, I, 306–7. Hietzinger, I, 166–69.

[69] Memorandum by Maj. Gen. Klein, Vienna, May 6, 1803, in Vaniček, III, 120–22.

[70] Schwicker, pp. 300–301.

ture military role of the Grenzer. Some highly placed officers even asserted that the combat value of the Grenzer had declined and that the military border institution as a whole had become an obsolete liability. There was, indeed, some truth in the assertion, though this was not caused by any failings of the Grenzer, but rather by an erroneous shift in Austrian military doctrine. Since the end of the Seven Years' War, Austrian military thinking had come to regard major battles as the decisive element in war and had downgraded the importance of light troops. "Regular, well drilled, and steady infantry," maintained the army instructions of 1796, "cannot be impeded by skirmishers. All the shooting and skirmishing decides nothing."[71] Therefore over the years the organization, training, and tactics of the Grenzer had been made to conform more and more with the line regiments. But the Grenzer could never equal the best regulars, while drill and regimentation "spoiled their natural aptitudes that once had made them so formidable."[72] At the same time, the traditional light infantry functions of the Grenzer were now contested by the French light units and tactics developed since 1763.[73] The *tirailleurs*, and later the *voltigeurs* and *chausseurs*, proved most efficient and, together with the revolutionary élan of the individual soldier, allowed the French commanders to operate with relative freedom from the bondage imposed by linear tactics and fixed supply depots. Moreover, Grenzer morale was hard hit by reports about conditions at home and in June, 1800, several squadrons of hussars and two battalions of Peterwardeiner mutinied.[74] After this the view that the Grenzer were "shiftless, false, and totally undisciplined" attained currency among many Austrian officers.[75] Even Gen-

[71] Obervationspunkte für die Generale bei der Armee in Deutschland," in Eugen v. Frauenholz, ed., *Das Heerwesen in der Zeit des Absolutismus* (Munich, 1940), pp. 82–83.

[72] Charles E. P. de Roche-Aymon, *Des Troupes Légères* (Paris, 1817), p. 57.

[73] After 1792 a great number of light, mounted as well as dismounted, troops were formed. These included the "Legions" of the Rhine, the Ardennes, and the North, as well as the "Legion of the Allobroges" under General Dugoumier. Special volunteer companies were raised by Custine in 1793, and frontier areas also raised free corps, *ibid.*, pp. 61–66; John F. C. Fuller, *British Light Infantry in the Eighteenth Century* (London, 1925), pp. 179–81, 204–7.

[74] Carl Pidoll zu Quintenbach, *Einige Worte über die russischen Militär-Kolonien im Vergleiche mit der k.k. österreichischen Militärgrenze und mit allgemeinen Betrachtungen darüber* (Vienna, 1847), p. 75; Vaniček, III, 104.

[75] Demian, I, p. 66.

eral Klein, a staunch defender of the institution, conceded that "the ancient Croats and Pandours, even as late as the Seven Years' War against Prussia, had constituted a much better light infantry than the present regulated and drilled Grenzer."[76] Nonetheless, Klein opposed the dissolution of the Grenzer regiments and argued for a basic reappraisal of their military role.

Klein maintained that attempts to make the Grenzer conform to the pattern of regular infantry were futile because they were contrary to their national custom and temperament. In any case, continued Klein, since the Grenzer also had to look after their farms in order to live, they had "very little time to learn complicated drill and evolutions." This was especially true of the artillery detachments which always would remain half-trained. He suggested that these detachments be reduced from 343 to 50 men in each regiment and that the number of sharp-shooters be raised. Drill and prolonged training not only ruined the economy of the border, but actually made the Grenzer less valuable soldiers. "It is clear," concluded the memorandum, "that the Grenzer cannot be effectively trained or employed as troops of the line, but that their natural aptitudes make them highly suitable as scouts, vedettes, and skirmishers." Some months later, in May, 1803, Klein answered the financial critics of the border establishment. He conceded the existing economic difficulties, but asserted that the question was not whether the state should contribute to the maintenance of the border regiments, but whether the state derived benefits from this outlay. Klein answered this question in the affirmative, pointing out that the cost of a border regiment was but one-fifth that of a regular unit and that the institution, moreover, provided over one hundred thousand trained soldiers in time of need.[77]

By the summer of 1803 the reorganization commission had collected a great amount of data and prepared a number of suggestions for the improvement of the military border. But, before accepting these, Archduke Charles ordered the commission to undertake an on-the-spot survey.[78] The group left Vienna in August and spent nearly nine months traveling the

[76] "Gedanken über Eigenschaften und Widmung der k.k. Militair Gränzer," Hornung 1803, KA Schriftgut fasc. 30.
[77] Excerpt of the memo. in Vaniček, III, 120–22. Cf. KA Mém. XXIII-42 of Jan. 10, 1803.
[78] Travel orders for the commissioners, Aug. 15, 1807, in Vaniček, III, 127–30. Cf. Franz J. Fras, *Vollständige Topographie der Karlstädter Militär-grenze* (Zagreb, 1835), pp. 10–11.

entire extent of the border, discovering that existing regulations and usages formed an entirely irrational patchwork. Therefore, in terms very similar to those expressed by De Vins, the commission recommended the introduction of an entire new set of basic laws for the border. Archduke Charles agreed and the commission set itself to devise a new code to supersede all previous legislation.[79]

Before the new code could be drawn up, however, Austria once more became involved in war with France. In November, 1804, Austria signed the alliance with Russia that led to the resignation of Archduke Charles and to the suspension of most of his reform schemes. In April, 1805, the Third Coalition was formed by England and Russia, soon joined by Sweden and Austria. This time some forty-eight thousand Grenzer were mobilized; twenty-three battalions from the Croatian borders served with Archduke John's army in northern Italy. Although successful on this front, the defeat and capitulation of the Austrian army in Germany forced a precipitate retreat everywhere. The Grenzer, forming the rear guard in Italy, suffered very heavy losses, especially in prisoners. In November, the main operations shifted to Austria, where Vienna was occupied by Napoleon, and then north into Bohemia. On December 2 Napoleon won the battle of Austerlitz. In the meantime, French troops under General Sarras penetrated through Istria and Carniola into northwestern Croatia, easily brushing aside the hastily mustered Grenzer homeguards. Karlstadt itself was menaced and French advance patrols had appeared on the banks of the Sava when hostilities ended.[80]

The unlucky war hastened the introduction of the new border code. Archduke Charles was restored as generalissimo to continue his army reforms. There were apprehensions about the effects of French propaganda on the Grenzer, especially on the several thousand returned prisoners of war. "It grieves me to report," wrote an Austrian police agent early in 1806 from Zagreb, "that the Military Border is no longer steadfast in its allegiance to the house of Austria. Especially among the men returned from captivity, there are many who have succumbed to French influence and are spreading false doctrines."[81] To

[79] Schwicker, pp. 223–25; code draft, KA Mém. XXIII-86.
[80] Vaniček, IV, 103–4.
[81] Report of Vinko Vlatković, Agram, Aug. 6, 1806, in Tomo Matić,

counteract these developments the code was hurriedly debated by the Hofkriegsrat, approved by Archduke Charles, and signed into law by the emperor on August 7, 1807.[82] Although the preamble of the code, designated "Basic Law for the Karlstadt-Warasdin, Banal, Slavonian, and Banat Borders," declared that it "provided a constitution for Our loyal and brave Grenzer, more in keeping with the times and with their national character," it was hardly more than a well-intentioned elaboration of the central features of the Theresian settlement.[83] Two principal, yet conflicting, motives were behind this document and underlined the cross-purposes always present in the administration of the military border. On the one hand there was a sincere desire to lighten the lot of the Grenzer, and on the other there was the pressing need to call on them for the maximum number of trained soldiers. As always the second objective won out.

The code consisted of 7 major titles and 155 lengthy paragraphs. Title I dealt with the land allotments.[84] Like the law of 1754 it stressed that the homesteads were granted in return for military service, but declared them hereditary military fiefs, which, as long as the family carried out its obligations, could not be confiscated or withdrawn. Only Grenzer had the right to own land within the military borders. As for their homesteads, these varied in size. The code recognized full homesteads, three-quarter, one-half, and even one-quarter allotments. In the Karlstadt and Banal Borders, as well as in the Wallachian Illyrian Regiment in the Banat, a full homestead was defined as eighteen yokes of arable land and six yokes of meadowland. In the Warasdin and Slavonian Borders and in the German Banat Regiment, a full allotment consisted of twenty-four yokes of arable land and ten yokes of meadows.[85] In addition, the Gren-

"Pabirči iz arhiva Austrijske Polizeihofstelle iz godina 1797–1810," JAZU, *Starine*, 46 (1956), 48.

[82] Schwicker, pp. 261–63.

[83] *Grundgesetze für die Carlstädter-Warasdiner, Banal, und Banatische Militär-Gränze* (Vienna, 1807). The best commentary on the code and its frequent modifications is the semiofficial manual by Mathias Stopfer, *Erläuterungen der Grundgesetze für die Carlstädter, Warasdiner, Banal, Slavonische, und Banatische Militär-Gränze* (Vienna, 1831). The code never applied to the Transylvanian regiments where there was no clear division between military and civilian territories.

[84] "Von dem Rechte auf unbewegliche Güter," arts. 1–41, *Grundgesetz*, pp. 9–22.

[85] Arts. 3–7, 13, *ibid.*, pp. 9–11, 15.

zer everywhere enjoyed grazing and woodcutting rights in the
state pastures and forests. As some traffic in land was considered necessary, and this was a concession compared to the
Theresian settlement, all families had a portion of their land
designated as surplus and could dispose of it freely to eligi-
ble persons. Non-transferrable land, *Stammgut*, however, still
amounted to well over two-thirds.[86] Subject to strict controls,
the law also permitted the division of individual *Hauskommunionen*, provided that each of the resulting households held
enough land to support one family and to maintain one Grenzer.[87] Finally, if families were unable to work their land because
their men were absent on military service or incapacitated, the
authorities were to detail neighbors to help out without re-
muneration.[88]

Title II enumerated the "Right of the Grenzer to pursue
Trades, Commerce, and Sciences."[89] In theory the Grenzer
were allowed to follow any occupation as long as it did not interfere with the performance of their military duties; in practice, however, only men not capable of bearing arms were allowed to learn a trade leading to guild membership. Casual
work was permitted to all. The interchange of goods with the
Turkish territories was encouraged, but commerce between
the military border and other parts of the monarchy had to be
licensed. Finally, while there was no limit on the number of
boys permitted to study for the Catholic priesthood, the number of aspirants for the Orthodox clergy was strictly limited.

Following precedents set by previous legislation, Title III,
"Concerning the Hauskommunion," recognized these as the
basic social and economic units. The authorities believed that
communal households permitted the mobilization of larger
numbers, and also supported the Hauskommunionen as the
basic unit of military control. The authority of the housefather,
the *starješina*, who was elected by the members of the household
and confirmed by the military, served to supplement the command structure. The housefather transmitted orders from above

---

[86] These regulations were soon modified. Families willing to accept military
obligations were allowed to buy land and retired officers were also permitted
to own farms. Schwicker, pp. 230–34. Arts. 13–17, *Grundgesetz*, pp. 13–15.

[87] Arts. 13–17, *Grundgesetz*, pp. 13–15.

[88] Art. 19, *ibid.*, p. 15.

[89] "Von dem Rechte der Gränzer sich auf Gewerbe, Handel, und Wissen-
schaften zu verlegen," arts. 42–54, *ibid.*, pp. 23–25.

and was responsible for the actions of the members of his household.[90] Military purposes then remained the preeminent considerations, and the provisions of Title IV were of the greatest importance. "All Grenzer capable of bearing arms are, without exception, obliged to render military service in, as well as outside, the border region."[91] Every household providing at least one soldier received an allowance of twelve florins yearly, the *Dienstkonstitutiv*, which was applied against the land tax, and the surplus, if any, was paid to the family. In peacetime, the Grenzer were issued arms and ammunition, and while on active service they received equipment and clothing, which they were allowed to retain on demobilization. They were responsible for the upkeep of all issue items and in addition had to furnish the undress uniform, worn on frontier watch and regimental duties, out of their own pockets.[92]

The code continued the obligation of the Grenzer to render *corvée* for military and administrative purposes. Since this obligation had been much abused, however, Title V, "Concerning Governmental and Communal Labor on the Border," minutely outlined the duties and rights of each family and individual.[93] The Grenzer were liable for twelve days of paid labor each year and in addition had to provide relays (*Vorspann*) for certain enumerated classes of traffic at fixed rates. Unpaid labor was limited to the "erection and repair of government buildings and churches" and to the "rebuilding of houses which had burned down without negligence on the part of the inhabitants."[94] The last two major sections, Titles VI and VII, regulated taxation. The land tax now became the main tax burden, but it was differentiated according to the quality of the land in the various regiments. It was lowest in the Karlstadt regiments, slightly higher in the Banal, and highest in the relatively well-to-do Warasdin regiments. Title VII regulated the taxes on trade and industry, but these were of very little importance on the Croatian Border.[95]

[90] "Von den Haus Communionen," arts. 55–90, *ibid.*, pp. 26–34.

[91] Art. 91 of "Von der militärischen Widmung der Gränzer," *ibid.*, p. 35.

[92] Arts. 92–104, *ibid.*, pp. 35–38.

[93] "Von der Gränz-Aerarial-und Gemeinde Arbeit," arts. 105–39, *ibid.*, pp. 39–50.

[94] Art. 105, *ibid.*, p. 49.

[95] Arts. 140–55, "Von der Grundsteuer," and "Von der Industrie-und Schutzsteuer," *ibid.*, pp. 51–57.

The provisions of the code went into effect on May 1, 1808, supplemented by regulations issued by the Director General of the Border, Archduke Ludwig.[96] These regulations clarified the position of the economic-administrative personnel and the regimental officers. In each regiment, with the exception of the Transylvanian Border, the commanding officers, normally colonels, were to be in complete control of all military, economic, and judicial affairs. But in matters normally handled by civilian authorities, they were to be assisted by administrative officers permanently assigned to each unit. These specialist officers, though subject to the overall authority of the colonels, formed a separate branch with its own promotion and seniority roster. In 1807 a special school, the *Gränz-Verwaltungs Institut*, with a two-, and later a three-, year curriculum was established in Graz. The regulations standardized the normal strength of each regiment at 2,570 officers and men, including an administrative section of 228.[97]

Simultaneously, steps were taken to improve the performance of the Grenzer in the field and to return them to their original duties as light infantry. The field and the undress uniform were merged into a general service dress consisting of a brown button-up jacket with short skirt, and light blue Hungarian trousers. Crossbelts, pouches, and other leather equipment were black, as was the newly introduced leather shako. Regimental differences were retained in the colored facings on the jackets, while the Czaikisten battalion retained its dark blue uniform with an anchor insignia on the shako.[98] At the same time, prodded by Archduke Charles, the Hofkriegsrat issued new field and training regulations for the Grenzer, which simplified drill and evolutions and stressed marksmanship and skirmishing.[99]

Withal it was hard to break the grip of the old military bureaucracy. While Archduke Charles attempted to get the Austrian forces ready for another contest with Napoleon, the Hofkriegsrat continued to worry about paperwork. In October,

[96] Stopfer, pp. 256–70; Ignaz F. Bergmayr, *Verfassung der k.k. Militär-Gränze und Oesterreichischen Kriegsmarine* (Vienna, 1845), pp. 95–118.
[97] Vaniček, III, 289–90.
[98] Clothing and equipment regulations (printed), Vienna, Aug. 24, 1808, in KA Schriftgut F-42.
[99] *Exercier Reglement für die kaiserlich-königliche Gränz-Infantrie* (Vienna, 1808).

1807, Count Colloredo, now president of that august body, complained that strength returns and other periodic reports from the border had been rendered late and threatened stern action against offenders.[100] Also, there were objections and footdragging in the lower echelons of the border administration against the introduction of the new code, and many of the old abuses, especially the misuse of the *corvée*, continued.[101]

In any case, the new basic law did not solve the troubles of the military border in Croatia. It was essentially the last of the eighteenth-century reform schemes and it did not envisage, and it was not designed to deal with, the problems of the nineteenth century that were drawing ever closer to the border. Across the frontier in Serbia and Bosnia, there was a national revolt against Turkish misrule, which could not fail to engage the hearts and the active support of the Grenzer, and the ideas of the French Revolution would soon be carried into Croatia. And within two years, the Karlstadt and Banal regiments would actually come under French rule.

[100] Pres. HKR to Banal Gkdo., Vienna, Oct. 29, 1808, DAZ Zagr. gkda. F/25-26.

[101] Pres. HKR to Karlstadt-Warasdiner Gkdo., Vienna, March 6, 1808, warning against abuse of corvée and *Vorspann. Ibid.*

6

—·—·—·—·—

THE MILITARY BORDER IN THE PERIOD OF THE SERB REVOLT AND THE FRENCH OCCUPATION: 1804–14

Even while Archduke Charles was struggling to introduce a new, and as he hoped better, order on the military border, events occurred in Serbia and Bosnia that seriously prejudiced the traditional loyalties of the Croatian and Slavonian Grenzer regiments. In February, 1804, Serbian patriots led by Djordje Petrović, better known as Karadjordje, rose against the misrule and the intolerable excesses of the Turkish janissaries then controlling the Belgrade pashalik. Taking the enemy by surprise, the insurgents were initially victorious and by April had forced the Turks to hole up in a few strong fortresses. At the outset the revolt was not directed against the rule of the sultan; the Serbs fought against the local authorities that, so they confidently believed, were flouting the sultan's commands. Even so, the insurgents were aware that the Porte might support the janissaries, and they looked for outside support. In the past Austria had usually aided anti-Turkish movements and many of the Serb leaders had gained military experience in the ranks of Austrian *frajkorci* during the last Austro-Turkish war.[1] It was therefore not surprising that Karadjordje approached Austria and in return for support offered to place himself and the country under Habsburg rule.[2]

The offer was tempting indeed. Austria had gained and lost

[1] Matthias Bernath, "Die Südslawen," in Hans Kohn, ed., *Die Welt der Slawen* (Frankfurt, 1960), pp. 236–37.

[2] Adolf Beer, *Die orientalische Politik Österreichs seit 1774* (Prague, 1883), pp. 183–84, 188.

Serbia three times within the last century and possession of fortress Belgrade was a dream since the days of Prince Eugene. But in 1804 Austria faced the probability of another war with France and therefore Vienna decided to reverse her long standing policy of supporting Balkan Christians against Turkish rule and refused to aid the Serb revolt. On May 25, 1804, the *Staatskanzlei* sent a memorial to Emperor Francis declaring the stability of the Ottoman Empire a necessity and warning that the close relations between the Serbs and their compatriots in Croatia-Slavonia, and especially on the military borders, might well embroil Austria in unwanted hostilities with the Porte. In fact, the diplomats asserted that quite possibly "some Grenzer subaltern misled by ties of family and friendship," had induced the Serbs to make their offer. Therefore, continued the memorial, the Serb offer ought to be rejected and the Grenzer most closely supervised.[3] Archduke Charles, on the other hand, favored limited intervention, especially the occupation of Belgrade, but was overruled. The Staatskanzlei carried the day and the emperor endorsed a policy of strict neutrality.[4]

Although there was at this time still very little awareness of a common South Slav identity, the constant warfare between Austria and the Ottoman Empire had brought the Grenzer into frequent contact with their kinsmen across the frontier. While the rifts between Catholics and Orthodox were deep, the military borders, where Orthodox Serbs and Catholic Croats shared a common fate, constituted a unique link between the various South Slav groups. From the very beginning, the Serb revolt was supported with arms and supplies from the Serb civilian community in southern Hungary and Slavonia and to a lesser degree from Croatia. The Grenzer, of course, were particularly eager to help and the decision to deny aid caused much resentment, especially in the heavily Orthodox Karlstadt, Banal, and Slavonian regiments.[5] The situation became even more tense

[3] Memorandum, Vienna, May 25, 1804, in Aleksa Ivić, ed., *Spisi bečkih arhiva o Prvom srpskom ustanku, Zbornik IJK*, 2d Series, (vols. 8, 10, 12, and 14; Belgrade, 1935–39), VIII, 154–60.

[4] Beer, pp. 188–90, 196. See also the directive from Archduke Ludwig, June 21, 1804, to all Border commands, in Aleksa Ivić, ed., "Dokumenti o ustanku Srba pod Karadjordjem Petrovičem," *VZA*, 21–22 (1920), 55.

[5] The census of 1802 revealed the Banal regiments as two to one Orthodox, the Karlstadt regiments about evenly divided, and the Lika Regiment nearly solid Orthodox. In the Warasdin regiments, on the other hand, the Roman Catholics predominated heavily. There also were strong Catholic majorities

when the Turks regained the initiative in Bosnia and made several incursions, murdering, looting, and burning in the Banal regiments.[6] On June 24, 1804, Feldmarschall Leutnant Baron Chernell, commanding in Croatia and on the military border, placed the Banal regiments on full alert and brought up reinforcements from the Szluin Regiment.[7] When frontier violations continued, the Hofkriegsrat, in accordance with the standing instructions of 1782, authorized the Croatian command to undertake limited reprisal raids against Turkish bases in Bosnia.[8]

In the meantime, denied Austrian assistance, the Serbs turned to Russia and in September, 1804, sent a delegation to St. Petersburg to request aid. Tsar Alexander, however, also faced with the prospect of war with France, took an ambivalent position. He provided the delegates with some funds and promised to send officers and arms, but he would not openly intervene. In fact, the Russians advised the Serbs to seek a negotiated settlement,[9] but attempts to reach such a settlement failed. Sultan Selim decided to treat the Serbs as rebels and proclaimed a holy war against them. In 1805 a large Turkish army entered Serbia, but was defeated. The next year the Serbs took the offensive, capturing Belgrade in December. Even so, the position of the insurgents remained precarious, and they repeatedly appealed for arms and munitions from Austria, only to be turned down each time.[10] The only concession made to the Serbs was permission for disarmed refugees to enter the Austrian lines.[11]

The international situation changed late in 1806 when the sultan decided to throw in his lot with Napoleon. Turkey was immediately attacked by England and Russia and Karadjordje, rejecting a hasty Turkish offer of autonomy, signed an alliance with Russia on July 10, 1807. Russia promised arms, supplies, and military missions, but within six weeks Alexander deserted

in the Brod and Gradiska Regiments, and the Peterwardein Regiment was almost exclusively Orthodox. Johann A. Demian, *Statistische Beschreibung der Militärgrenze* (2 vols.; Vienna, 1806), I, 274–80, 307–8.

[6] Franz Vaniček, *Specialgeschichte der Militärgrenze* (4 vols.; Vienna, 1875), III, 138–39.

[7] Ivić, *Spisi bečkih arhiva*, X, 255–56.

[8] Thus Archduke John, acting for Archduke Charles, informed the Staatskanzlei, Vienna, Aug. 27, 1804, *ibid.*, pp. 265–66.

[9] Aleksije Jelačić, *Russija i Balkan* (Belgrade, 1940), pp. 44–45; Beer, p. 185.

[10] Francis II to Count Stadion, Vienna, April 6, 1806, outlining policy of Austrian neutrality, Ivić, *Spisi bečkih arhiva*, XI, 34–35.

[11] Beer, p. 194.

his new allies and concluded a treaty with the Porte, leaving the Serbs to fight on alone. The changing fortunes of the Serb revolt were followed on the military borders with intense interest, since many favored active participation in the struggle. In April, 1807, Archduke Ludwig informed Feldmarschall Leutnant Ignaz Count Gyulay, commanding the Banal regiments, that "numerous confidential reports indicate a most dangerous disposition among the non-Uniat Greeks."[12] Gyulay was directed to keep a close watch and to halt all pro-Serb agitation. Several months later, on October 14, Ludwig warned Gyulay again about the dangerous connections between certain "k.k. subjects of the Illyrian rite and the Serbs."[13] All such contacts, even when they were masked as harmless trade relations, should be suppressed. Special attention, so the Archduke continued, should be paid to the activities of Russian agents in Belgrade. Ludwig remained suspicious even after Gyulay reported that investigation had not turned up any substantial evidence of subversive activities.[14] In January, 1808, he repeated his instructions concerning close surveillance of the Orthodox Grenzer. This, the archduke emphasized, was "a direct order from the emperor who considered this matter of great importance."[15]

As it was, Archduke Ludwig's fears were not unjustified. There was considerable unrest among the Grenzer and it was not confined to the Banal Border. Everywhere the authorities were plagued by the perennial problem of desertions. Especially in the Karlstadt regiments, the number of deserters either joining the bandits in the hills or crossing the frontier to help the Serbs swelled to alarming proportions.[16] Conditions were also serious in the Slavonian command where in June, 1807, Feldmarschall Leutnant Joseph Baron Simbschen took over from the ninety-six year old Geneyne.[17] Here the privileged military townships, especially Zemun, were centers of the illegal arms traffic with Serbia, while the three Slavonian regiments were

---

[12] Archduke Ludwig to FML Gyulay, Vienna, April 14 and July 14, 1807. DAZ Banska gkda. F-3.

[13] The same, Oct. 14, 1807, *ibid.*

[14] Intelligence summary (copy), Croat. Gkdo. Zagreb, Dec. 14, 1808, *ibid.*

[15] Archduke Ludwig to Gyulay, Vienna, Jan. 21, 1808, *ibid.*

[16] Report from Zagreb, Dec. 18, 1808, in Ivić, *Spisi bečkih arhiva*, XIV, 1037, and instructions from Archduke Ludwig to the Karlstadt-Warasdin Gkdo., Vienna, Feb. 14, 1809, DAZ Zagr. gkda. F-25-26.

[17] Franz v. Krones, "Josef Freiherr von Simbschen und die Stellung Österreichs zur Serbischen Frage, 1807–1810," *AÖG*, 76 (1890), 138.

openly disaffected.[18] Early in 1808 Archduke Charles, alarmed about the state of the border, instructed Simbschen to enter into negotiations with Karadjordje. The main purpose of this move was to block Russian influence and to halt Grenzer disaffection. In a secret addendum to his instructions, Simbschen was told to prepare contingency plans to seize Belgrade by a coup with troops from the 1st Banal Regiment, supported by Grenzer artillery and regular cavalry.[19]

Simbschen and Karadjordje met early in April, 1808. But by then the Serb leader had grown wary, and though he did not reject the Austrian propositions out of hand, he did insist on immediate delivery of supplies and on guarantees that Serbia would never become subject to Hungary but always constitute an integral part of the military border.[20] The Staatskanzlei did not like these military negotiations and convinced the emperor that support for Karadjordje, or the occupation of Belgrade, could only lead to war with the Porte. The most that could be done for the Serbs, argued the ministers, was to provide them with some victuals. These, the Staatskanzlei continued, should not be furnished from army stores, but supplied through private channels.[21] This time, however, the military won their point. Simbschen was permitted to continue his negotiations. He was authorized to give verbal assurances of Grenzer status to the Serbs, but was to make no definite commitments. But if Russian occupation of Belgrade appeared imminent, he was to take all necessary actions up to and including military seizure.[22] Word of these intentions leaked out to the Russians who promptly protested to Vienna. The Austrian government did not want to lose Russia's goodwill and Archduke Charles now instructed Simbschen to cease all military preparations and restrict himself to observation.[23] Even so, there were periodic con-

---

[18] *Ibid.*, pp. 146–47, and Simbschen's reports to Archduke Ludwig, Peterwardein, July 25 and Dec. 28, 1807, in Aleksa Ivić, ed., *Arhivska gradja o srpskim i hrvatskim književnim i kulturnim radnicima, Zbornik IJK*, 3 (Belgrade, 1931), 30–31, 380–81.

[19] Instructions to FML Simbschen, Feb. 18, 1808, in Ivić, *Spisi bečkih arhiva*, XIV, 173–78.

[20] Simbschen's report to Archduke Charles, Zemun, April 5, 1808, *ibid.*, pp. 414–19.

[21] Opinion of Count Philip Stadion, April 13, 1808, *ibid.*, pp. 444–46.

[22] Report of Archduke Charles, Vienna, May 1, 1808, *ibid.*, pp. 573–78. HKR instructions to Simbschen, Vienna, May 28, 1808, Krones, pp. 176–78.

[23] Revised instructions to Simbschen, Vienna, June 8, 1808, *ibid.*, pp. 184–85. Report by Archduke Charles concerning the outcome of the Simb-

tacts with Karadjordje throughout the next few years, but nothing definite came out of this.[24]

Austria's indecisive policy was in part due to her desire to remain on good terms with both Russia and the Porte, but it also derived in large part from the mounting fears about the spread of South Slav national feeling and its effect on the loyalty of the Grenzer. Between 1806 and 1809 it appeared as if the Serb revolt might become a Balkan revolution. There were rebellions in the Peloponnesus, in Bosnia, western Bulgaria, Macedonia, and Thessaly. In Vienna the Hofkriegsrat was apprehensive.[25] These apprehensions gained real substance when in June, 1808, there was a mutiny in the Wallach-Illyrian Regiment in the Banat. Although the affair involved but one Orthodox priest, several subalterns, and a handful of enlisted men, Vienna was alarmed.[26] Suspicions that Serbian intrigues were at the bottom of this incident appeared confirmed by a report from Simbschen that the Serbs were encouraging Grenzer desertions.[27] All this tended to reinforce Austria's policy of neutrality. But at the same time, this very policy alienated the Grenzer and made them more receptive to foreign propaganda. Indeed, Austria's refusal to aid the Serb revolt, combined with the continuing economic hardships and the heavy military obligations, explain why the Grenzer readily accepted the French occupation, hoping both for relief from their military duties and for help in the achievement of the Serb national aspirations.

French influence in Serbia and the military border had steadily increased since 1806 when in the Treaty of Pressburg Napoleon acquired Venetia, Istria, and Dalmatia, including the Ragusan republic, and also was accorded the right to maintain

schen negotiations, Vienna, June 27, 1808, Ivić, *Spisi bečkih arhiva*, XIV, 816–20.

[24] Beer, pp. 235–40. During negotiations in 1810 Simbschen apparently was led to believe that he did have authority to make definite arrangements for the occupation of Belgrade. By this time, however, Austria was allied with France and he was disavowed by Vienna and recalled. Russian troops occupied Belgrade in February, 1811.

[25] Traian Stoianovich, "The Social Foundations of Balkan Politics, 1750–1941," in Charles and Barbara Jelavich, eds., *The Balkans in Transition* (Berkeley, 1964), pp. 309–10; Reports about Serb propaganda among the Grenzer, Ivić, *Arhivska gradja*, 3, 64–68; *Spisi bečkih arhiva*, XIV, 193–94; Krones, p. 175, and the reports for January through April, 1808, in DAZ Banska gkda., F-3.

[26] Vaniček, *Specialgeschichte*, III, 296–98.

[27] Simbschen to Archduke Ludwig, Peterwardein, Dec. 1, 1808, Ivić, *Dokumenti o ustanku Srba*, pp. 306–7.

a military road through civil and military Croatia from Venetia to Dalmatia. The frequent passage of French detachments through the Karlstadt regiments was a great irritant to the Austrian administration. To be sure, the soldiers marching along the road from Karlstadt through Ogulin, Ottoschatz, and Gospić to Dalmatia found little of interest to detain them en route. They had to take precautions against the bandits infesting the hills, and they were appalled by the extreme poverty and economic backwardness of the region. There is little evidence that the French carried on any deliberate propaganda, but, finding a ready means of communication in the crude soldier-German spoken by both sides, they brought news of the outside world and stories of the great changes taking place in the territories under French rule.[28] And often these tales were confirmed by Grenzer returning from French prisoner of war camps.[29]

In March, 1809, Austria mobilized once more and war against France was declared in April. This time the military border put forth a maximum effort. In all, including all reserves and the levies of the armed population, the regiments put over one hundred thousand men into the field. The bulk of the field battalions marched off to join the Austrian main armies in Germany and Italy, and a special Grenzer corps, well over ten thousand strong, concentrated in the Lika for an invasion of French Dalmatia.[30] Although the French forces were outnumbered, neither the Austrian commander Major General Stojčević nor his troops, consisting mainly of reserve battalions and levies, were a match for the seasoned veterans under Marshal Marmont. Marmont's task was to contain the greatest possible number of the enemy and to join the French army operating in northern Italy under Eugène Beauharnais when the favorable moment came. Therefore, Marmont conducted an active defense, garrisoned half a dozen major strong points and abandoned all others, and by requisitioning two thousand pack mules managed to make his forces mobile.[31] During the fight-

---

[28] See the account in Charles Desboeufs, ed., *Souvenirs du Capitaine Desboeufs* (Paris, 1910), pp. 63–66.

[29] Report by Capt. Holevać, Lika Regt., Feb., 1808, in Ivić, *Spisi bečkih arhiva*, XIV, 191.

[30] Vaniček, IV, 114–19.

[31] *Mémoires du Maréchal Marmont, Duc de Raguse, de 1792 à 1841* (9 vols., 3d ed.; Paris, 1857), III, 131–35; Emil v. Woinovich, *Die Kämpfe in der Lika, Croatien, und Dalmatien 1809* (Vienna, 1906), passim. Also the ms. "Feldzug in Dalmatien 1809," KA Mém. III-135.

ing, Stojčević made a small advance, but within days his offensive stalled before the expert French musketry and grape, and in early May, 1809, Marmont counterattacked and drove into the Lika. When the Bosnians instigated by Marmont, raided in force across the almost totally undefended Banal frontier, burning a number of villages and destroying several homeguard detachments, the Grenzer corps virtually dissolved as men deserted to protect their homes against this new danger.[32] The Croatian Border appeared lost, and from Pest, where the Hofkriegsrat had moved to avoid Napoleon's capture of Vienna, cautionary orders were issued for an evacuation of military personnel, records, and stores.[33] In the meantime, however, Napoleon suffered a repulse at Aspern (May 21, 1809) and Marmont was now ordered to bring his corps to reinforce the main army in Austria. The Austrians were unable to block Marmont's fast march along the coastal road to Senj and then across to Karlstadt and into Carniola, but in the interior Feldmarschall Leutnant Vincenz Baron Knežević rallied the Grenzer, expelled the Turks, and penetrated once more into Dalmatia, where he took Zadar (Zara), only weakly held by the French.[34]

The ultimate fate of the Croatian Military Border was decided by the battle of Wagram (July 5–6, 1809). After this defeat the Austrian government sued for peace, and in the Treaty of Schönbrunn, signed October 14, it ceded Croatia on the right bank of the Sava, including the six Karlstadt and Banal regiments, to Napoleon. These territories, together with parts of Carniola, Carinthia, Istria, and Dalmatia were constituted as the Illyrian Provinces with the capital at Ljubljana (Laibach). Prince Eugène Beauharnais, Napoleon's viceroy in Italy, became the titular head of French Illyria; actual administration was confided to Marshal Marmont who received the title of Duke of Ragusa and was named governor general and commander of all military forces.[35]

Officially the French were scheduled to take over the six ceded regiments on December 1, 1809. Until then the Austrian

[32] Vaniček, IV, 126–30.

[33] Instructions from FZM Baillet de Latour, Pest, May 22, 1809, DAZ Banska gkda. F-3.

[34] Marmont, III, 342.

[35] Napoleon's instructions to Eugène, Schönbrunn, Oct. 14, 1809, in *Correspondance de Napoléon Ier publiée par l'ordre de l'Empéreur Napoléon III* (32 vols.; Paris, 1858–70), XIX, no. 15,945.

administration continued, plagued by a recurrence of Turkish incursions from Bosnia. For a while this problem became so bad that the Hofkriegsrat instructed Simbschen to prepare his Slavonian regiments to march to the aid of Croatia.[36] This, however, did not become necessary. At the same time, the Austrian authorities sought to salvage as much military equipment as possible from the ceded areas. Knežević was appointed imperial commissioner to supervise the transfer and to collect all modern weapons from the Grenzer.[37] Every regiment was to retain only four hundred obsolete muskets, dating back to the Seven Years' War, as a defense against raids. The remainder, as well as all regimental artillery and other stores, was to be removed across the Sava to Zagreb. Foreseeing difficulties in the collection of arms, Knežević asked and received authorization to pay a bounty of five gulden for every modern musket handed in by the Grenzer.[38] Knežević also ordered a series of stand-down parades. On November 29, the aged and popular Feldmarschall Leutnant Franz Baron Jellačić held the final parade and in the name of the emperor bade the Karlstadt and Banal Grenzer farewell.[39] His exit was coupled with the arrival of the first French officials and two days later the mounted advance guard of Marmont's corps clattered across the Kupa bridge into Karlstadt.

The often repeated story of the "undying loyalty and devotion" of the Grenzer and of their grief about the passing of Austrian rule must be considered a patriotic legend.[40] In fact, the nobility in civil Croatia, fearing the loss of its feudal privileges, and the Catholic clergy that held strong views against Napoleon, the gaoler of Pope Pius VII and the champion of state control over the church, were hostile. But in the regiments the French were well received. The Grenzer expected economic

[36] HKR to FML Simbschen, Vienna, Aug. 10, 1809, Krones, pp. 191–92.

[37] Instructions and appointment, Francis II to FML Knežević, Pesth, Oct. 21, 1809; also instructions from FZM Colloredo, Pres. HKR to Knežević, Pesth, Nov. 1, 1809, DAZ Zagr. gkda. F 25-26. Also instructions from Knežević to FML Lattermann, commanding in Zagreb, Rijeka, Nov. 4, 1809, *ibid*.

[38] Instructions Knežević to Lattermann, Rijeka, Nov. 6 and 10, 1809, *ibid*.

[39] Report of FML Jellačić, Dec. 3, 1809, DAZ Banska gkda. F-9.

[40] Among others the story was told by Carl B. v. Hietzinger, *Statistik der Militärgränze des österreichischen Kaiserthums* (3 vols.; Vienna, 1817–23), I, 37–38; repeated by Vaniček, 3, 199, embroidered by the national-socialist pseudo-historian Rupert v. Schumacher, *Des Reiches Hofzaun* (3d ed.; Darmstadt, 1942), p. 249, and again repeated by Rudolf Kiszling, *Die Kroaten* (Graz-Cologne, 1956), p. 48.

improvements, relief from their heavy military burdens, and they also had high hopes that France would lend a hand in the liberation of Serbia. This hope was also shared by the Serb insurgents and in August, 1809, Karadjordje asked for help from Napoleon and assured him that Serbs everywhere would rally to the imperial eagles.[41] The enlisted Grenzer followed the example of their officers. While all officers of general rank, the colonels commanding the regiments, and many of the administrative officers left the country, the regimental officers remained at their posts and were taken over en bloc by the new regime. One Austrian agent even blamed the conduct of the Grenzer entirely on those officers who "have seduced the crude and ignorant men from their rightful allegiance." Civilians, the report continued, were generally downcast by the arrival of the French, but the company grade officers rejoiced. "The earth," concluded the agent, "is too good for these monsters. They ought to be killed and their ashes scattered in the four winds."[42]

French rule of the Croatian Military Border lasted four years. During this time roads were built, hospitals established, and harbors improved, but even so the French administration brought few radical innovations. Napoleon regarded the military border above all as a defensive bastion to protect the flanks of his empire and as a potential springboard for an advance into the Balkans.[43] Therefore military considerations came first and the Grenzer passed from Austrian to French rule and back without any real changes in their circumstances. From the first Marmont intended to retain the regimental administration intact. He confirmed the Grenzer officers in their positions and promoted the highest ranking, Major Slivarić of the Ogulin Regiment to Lieutenant Colonel in command of the Lika Regiment. French commanders were appointed for the other five regiments with Grenzer second in commands to assist them.

[41] Karadjordje to Napoleon, Aug. 16, 1809, in P. Boppe, ed., *Documents inédits sur les relations de la Serbie avec Napoléon I, 1809–1814* (Belgrade, 1888), p. 6.

[42] Report from Zagreb, Dec. 10, 1809, in Tomo Matić, "Pabirči iz arhiv Austrijske Polizeihofstelle iz godina 1797–1810," JAZU, *Starine*, 46, 54–55, 59. These reports confirm the account of Gen. Guillemont, Karlstadt, Jan. 9, 1810, AN AF IV-1713. See also Imbro Tkalac, *Uspomene iz Hrvatske* (Zagreb, 1945), pp. 3–34.

[43] Ernst Birke, *Frankreich und Ostmitteleuropa im 19. Jahrhundert* (Cologne-Graz, 1960), p. 21.

Continuation of the regimental structure was officially proclaimed in a special organization decree of June, 1810, which
also divided the Illyrian provinces into two military districts.
The first, with headquarters at Ljubljana, comprised the Ogulin, Szluin, and the two Banal regiments; the second, with
headquarters in Zara, included the Ottoschatz and Lika Regiments as well as forces locally raised in Dalmatia. In addition,
there also were some French and Italian units, mainly of poor
quality, stationed in Croatia, Carniola, and Dalmatia.[44] *La
Croatie Militaire*, as the French officials called it, was supervised by an inspector general at Karlstadt, but beyond that
Marmont contemplated no changes in the internal structure or
the service regulations. He regarded the military border as an
extraordinarily successful military society. "The more I studied
the Austrian system," he wrote to General Clarke, Napoleon's
minister of war, "the more I have become convinced that it
should be preserved in its entirety and no changes whatso-
ever should be made." [45] Marmont's views were supported by the
minister's adjutant, Colonel Leclerc who, after returning from
a visit to Croatia, warmly endorsed continuation of the Austrian organization.[46] But the emperor was not persuaded. Although he provisionally confirmed Marmont's actions, he also
announced that permanent dispositions for military Croatia,
as well as for the Illyrian provinces in general, would have to
await the results of a more thorough investigation and study.[47]

The Turks, meanwhile, constituted Marmont's most urgent
problem. He had encouraged them initially to resume their
raids and the Austrian withdrawal and the partial disarmament
of the regiments provided additional opportunities. And this
time the incursions were not simple expeditions for loot and
plunder. The Turkish frontier governors, hoping to recover the
territory lost at Sistova in 1791, backed the raiders with regular troops and occupied a strip of land in the Ogulin Regiment,
including the fort at Cetin. Throughout the first winter Marmont repeatedly requested weapons to arm the Grenzer, but

[44] Marmont, III, 346–48; P. Boppe, *La Croatie Militaire (1809–1813)*
(Paris, 1900), pp. 17–22. Copy of the organizational decree, June 2, 1810,
enclosure to "Illyrische Grenz Administration," KA Schriftgut F-39.
[45] Letter to Gen. Clarke, Ljubljana, Dec. 11, 1809, Marmont, III, 378–79.
[46] Report by Col. Jean de Montpye Leclerc to Gen. Clarke, "Rapport sur
la marche du gouvernement et l'esprit du peuple en Croatie civile et Croatie
Militaire," Paris, Feb. 27, 1810, AHG Recon. Autriche, 1598.
[47] Boppe, *La Croatie Militaire*, p. 26.

Napoleon, still dubious about their loyalty, refused. "The demand for fifteen thousand muskets," he wrote on January 9, 1810, "is premature and dangerous. At the most one company in each regiment may be armed, but no more."[48] In the early spring, when there were increasing signs that the Turks were preparing for major operations, the emperor changed his mind and decided to rearm the Grenzer. Even so, he instructed Marmont to confine his activities to reconnaissance and defense.[49] But the marshal was resolved that the Turks should fear him and decided on a forward policy. After several peremptory demands had failed to bring the cessation of raids or the evacuation of Cetin, Marmont concentrated a striking force of four Grenzer and two French battalions, supported by French artillery. Izačić, the main Turkish raider base, was attacked and destroyed. This action was followed by a demonstration against Bihać, the Turkish administrative center in northern Bosnia, and resulted in the cessation of raids and the prompt evacuation of Cetin.[50] But Napoleon was furious about the use of French troops. "French blood," he angrily wrote to Clarke, "is too precious to be shed for such trifles."[51] Nonetheless, the vigor and speed of Marmont's operations pacified the Turks for the next three years and gained the French much prestige among the Grenzer.[52]

Even so, the preservation of the military border in the Illyrian Provinces was by no means a foregone conclusion. Napoleon had not made up his mind and there was a considerable body of opinion in Paris which held that the system was a relic of the feudal past which ought to be abolished.[53] All measures taken thus far in Illyria were regarded as provisional only and subject to revision following the comprehensive study ordered by the emperor. This investigation got under way early in 1810. Marmont had been directed to send a special delegation to Paris, drawn from all parts of the Illyrian Provinces, civil as well as military.[54] Also included by special imperial

[43] Napoleon to Clarke, Paris, Jan. 9, 1810, *Correspondance*, XX, No. 16,123.
[49] Boppe, *La Croatie Militaire*, pp. 28–29.
[50] Reports to Clarke, May 3, 9, and 12, 1810, Marmont, III, 398–408; Desboeufs, pp. 134–36.
[51] May 15, 1810, *Correspondance*, XX, No. 16,472.
[52] Boppe, *La Croatie Militaire*, pp. 35–36.
[53] Marmont, III, 345–47.
[54] Instructions from Clarke to Marmont, Paris, Jan. 24, 1810, AN AF IV 1713; list of delegates in Boppe, *La Croatie Militaire*, pp. 194–96.

command was General Antoine François Andréossy, a former artillery officer turned diplomat and lately Napoleon's governor of occupied Vienna, who was considered a specialist on the problems of southeastern Europe.[55] Andréossy was the most outspoken opponent of Marmont's plans to keep the border establishment intact. The general argued that conditions of service in the regiments were degrading and produced a society in which there was neither justice nor equality, but constant fear and want. He wanted to abolish the system and advocated a single, centralized and uniform administration for all of the Illyrian provinces. But Andréossy was unable to persuade the other members of the delegation to his point of view and the investigation remained deadlocked throughout the summer of 1810.[56]

At length Napoleon grew impatient. He sent an aide, General Mouton, to poll the delegates and dispatched another, General Lauriston, to Croatia for a first-hand report.[57] By the end of the year, General Clarke, the war minister whom Marmont had bombarded with a constant stream of memoranda, decided to support continuation of the Austrian system. In November, 1810, he submitted a lengthy report to the emperor. After summarizing the various arguments for and against the preservation of the military border establishment, he concluded with the recommendation that the system be continued. In fact, he practically quoted Marmont's latest communication. "Military Croatia," wrote Clarke, "should not be regarded as just another province but as a vast military encampment; its population was an army that maintained and reinforced itself."[58] Such military potential outweighed reform sentiments, and Napoleon decided to continue the military border system unchanged.

[55] *Ibid.*, pp. 39–40. Despite his Hungarian name, Gen. Andréossy, "a deserving man who had shown his mettle not only on the battle field but also on the Eighteenth Brumaire," came from an old French military family. After the Treaty of Amiens, he briefly served as Napoleon's ambassador to England, later, 1808–9, as ambassador in Vienna, and then as military governor of that city. Alfred Vagts, *Defense and Diplomacy* (New York, 1956), p. 17.

[56] Boppe, *La Croatie Militaire*, pp. 41–53; documents in Melitta Pivec-Stelè, *La vie économique des Provinces Illyriennes* (Paris, 1930), pp. 267–69.

[57] Instructions to Gen. Lauriston, Oct. 10, and to Gen. Mouton, Oct. 18, 1810, *Correspondance*, XXI, Nos. 17,031, and 17,061.

[58] Clarke's report, Paris, Nov. 21, 1810, AN AF 1713, and printed in Boppe, *La Croatie Militaire*, pp. 41–53. Marmont's report from which Clarke cited, Oct. 27, 1810, AHG Recon. Autriche, 1595.

Marmont, however, was not to enjoy his victory for very long. The marshal was dissatisfied with the general arrangements made for the government of the Illyrian provinces. The final organizational decree of April 15, 1811, left very little power in the hands of the governor general and Marmont considered this incompatible with his dignity. He asked for an operational command and Napoleon granted his request. As his successor the emperor appointed General Bertrand, another former aide-de-camp.[59]

Once the decision regarding the future status of the six Grenzer regiments was made, they were assimilated to the light troops of the imperial service. French replaced German as the official language of command and instruction, though German continued to be used even in official correspondence.[60] Translations from French military manuals were made, selected subalterns and sergeants were seconded for instruction to French regiments, and two hundred Grenzer boys were sent to receive a military education in France.[61]

But the French were not left in peace to carry out their new measures. For much of the remainder of their stay they were harassed by a number of British seaborne attacks, for the most part under the command of the remarkable Captain William Hoste. Defense against these raids was provided by Grenzer units, now styled *Chausseurs d'Illyrie*. But Napoleon still did not trust the Grenzer completely; essentially he would always consider them unreliable and expendable.[62] In July, 1811, he warned Bertrand not to entrust the coastal defenses of Ragusa (Dubrovnik) to Grenzer alone, but always to brigade them with French or Italian troops.[63] The following month the emperor advised the governor general not to expose French troops unnecessarily to the unhealthy climate of the Adriatic littoral marshes. Grenzer regiments, held Napoleon, were good enough for such assignments.[64]

Despite the emperor's misgivings, the continuing demands

---

[59] Boppe, *La Croatie Militaire*, pp. 61–62.

[60] Marmont, III, 374–75.

[61] *Ibid.*, 376.

[62] Pivec-Stelè, p. 332, and Napoleon to Clarke, May 15, 1810, *Correspondance*, XX, No. 16,472.

[63] Napoleon to Bertrand, Trianon, July 15, 1811, *ibid.*, XXI, No. 17,923. This contrasts rather sharply with Marmont's account concerning Napoleon's enthusiasm for the Grenzer, "the world's best soldiers." Marmont, III, 348.

[64] Napoleon to Bertrand, St. Cloud, Aug. 23, 1811, *ibid.*, XXII, No. 18,077.

for military manpower forced the employment of the Grenzer in more active roles. When late in 1811 the emperor began to assemble his Grand Army for the invasion of Russia, the Grenzer were included. Three field regiments — designated as the 1st, 2d, and 3d Provisional Croatian Regiments — were organized, equipped, and uniformed on the French light infantry pattern. The 1st Regiment, drawn from the Lika and Ottoschatz regiments, and the 3d Regiment, composed of units from the two Banal regiments, eventually marched with the Grand Army to Moscow. The 2d Regiment, with units from the Ogulin and Szluin regiments, was not activated until the spring of 1813 and saw service in Germany against the Prussians. Other Grenzer units, mainly second- and third-line troops, were deployed for coastal defense and internal security duties. A Croatian hussar regiment was recruited in 1813 but saw no fighting.[65]

Meanwhile, affairs proceeded routinely in the Warasdin regiments that had remained under Austrian control. The command had no common frontier with the Turks and did not suffer any incursions. Implementation of the provisions of the Law of 1807, routine duties, and training continued without interruptions. There were no reports of propaganda and no disturbances.[66] Although the Austrian government was careful not to antagonize the French, some activity, for the moment covertly, was directed toward the day when Austria would recover the lost regiments. Skeleton staffs for the ceded regiments were maintained and the Warasdin Border, a mere two regiments, retained the status of a separate general command. From 1809 to 1812 Baron Knežević was in command, succeeded by Baron Gyulay.[67]

Austrian officials also encouraged a certain amount of surreptitious contact with the lost territories. As early as October, 1809, Grenzer families had been offered asylum in the unoccupied border regions and throughout the next few years there was a steady trickle of refugees from military Croatia, ascribed by French officials to Austrian machinations. In May, 1810, for instance, Marmont reported that Austrian officers, especially

---

[65] Boppe, *La Croatie Militaire*, pp. 93–152, provides a detailed account of the fortunes and misfortunes of the Grenzer on active service with the French armies.

[66] Records of the Warasdiner Gkdo., 1809–1812, DAZ Zagr. gkda. F 27-29.

[67] HKR to Knežević, Vienna, April 1, 1812, *ibid.*, F-29.

Knežević, were deliberately spreading false rumors and that by these means they "induced a number of families from the 2d Banal regiment, which is closest to the Austrian frontier, to cross the Sava."[68] Similar complaints were made by Bertrand the following year.[69] Undoubtedly there was some Austrian propaganda, but there was also growing disappointment among the Grenzer over the failure of the French administration to alleviate the economic hardships and about the French refusal to back the Serb revolt. Even so, the total numbers involved in this emigration were small—about three hundred families in all. The Austrian authorities attempted to resettle the refugees in the Warasdin, Slavonian, and Banat regiments, but this proved difficult because of the shortage of available agricultural land.[70]

Beyond accommodating, and perhaps encouraging, these Grenzer emigrants, Austria carefully observed the terms of its agreement with Napoleon. Two battalions of Warasdiner participated in the auxiliary corps furnished for the Russian campaign. Although this corps, commanded by Prince Schwarzenberg, saw little fighting, the Grenzer suffered heavy casualties.[71]

In early 1813 the French position in Illyria deteriorated rapidly. The Bosnian Turks, encouraged by the withdrawal of troops and by the news of the French debacle in Russia, renewed their incursions. They appeared in force in the Szluin Regiment, rushed a number of positions, and massacred the weak garrisons. After the first surprise, however, resistance stiffened and by late April the situation was stabilized.[72] Meanwhile, the English intensified their operations on the Adriatic sea coast and temporarily occupied Rijeka (Fiume). They were only half-heartedly opposed by the Grenzer detachments stationed on the islands and in the ports of the littoral.[73] French

[68] Marmont to Clarke, Ljubljana, May 15, 1810, Marmont, III, 411.

[69] Bertrand to Clarke, cited in Pivec-Stelè, p. 272.

[70] Warasdiner Gkdo., Zagreb, June 11, 1812, DAZ Zagr. gkda. F-29, and Karl v. Czoernig, *Ethnographie der österreichischen Monarchie* (3 vols.; Vienna, 1857), III, 111–13.

[71] Vaniček, IV, 139, and Anton Springer, *Geschichte Oesterreichs seit dem Wiener Frieden 1809* (2 vols.; Leipzig, 1863–65), I, 207.

[72] Boppe, *La Croatie Militaire*, pp. 68–70. Intelligence report, (n.d. [1813]), Warasdiner Gkdo. to HKR (copy), DAZ Zagr. gkda. F-30.

[73] M. H. Weil, *Le Prince Eugène et Murat, 1813–1814* (5 vols.; Paris, 1901–2), I, 126–27.

prestige declined sharply and an increasing number of Grenzer took to the hills where they constituted large armed bands.[74] On the other hand, a considerable number of officers remained loyal to the French and their influence could still raise new units. In April, 1813, Slivarić, recently promoted to brigadier general, returned to Croatia and issued a successful appeal for a thousand volunteers to fill the depleted ranks of the 1st Provisional Regiment.[75]

Even so, Napoleon realized that the Illyrian provinces could not be defended if Austria entered the war against him. Bertrand had been recalled in 1812 to serve on Napoleon's staff during the Russian campaign. His replacement, General Junot, became incapacitated in the spring of 1813, and on July 17 the emperor appointed Fouché, the wily former police minister, as governor general, with General Fresia to command the troops.[76] Neither the emperor nor Fouché had any illusions that Illyria could be defended. There were but a few French and Italian units left in the provinces and the local forces, consisting of six battalions of Grenzer and conscripts and national guards from civil Croatia and Slovenia, were largely unreliable. There were fewer than twelve thousand men.[77] The overall plan was for Eugène Beauharnais to assemble a strong corps along the Isonzo and to advance into Inner Austria to cover the right wing of Napoleon's main army in central Germany.[78] Illyria was considered expendable, and the main task for the new governor general was to conduct a rear-guard action, saving all that could be saved of French officials, troops, treasure, and stores.[79]

Austria, however, still moved cautiously. Although during the early spring of 1813 a number of schemes for raising Croatia and Dalmatia against the French were urged in Vienna, Metternich was determined to avoid any disturbances before the outbreak of general hostilities. He opposed a national rising and

[74] Appeal for volunteers in Paul Kussan, *Kurzgefasste Geschichte des Oguliner dritten National-Grenz-Infantrie Regiments* (Vienna, 1852), pp. 40–41.

[75] Desboeufs, p. 135.

[76] Napoleon to Fouché, Dresden, July 17, 1813, *Correspondance*, XXV, No. 20,284.

[77] Fouché to Napoleon, Ljubljana, Aug. 3, 1813, Beauharnais Archive.

[78] Weil, I, 81–83, 94–95, 107–8.

[79] Louis Madelin, *Fouché* (2 vols., 4th ed.; Paris, 1913), II, 242–43, and the excellent article by Cyril Black, "Fouché in Illyria," *JCEA*, 2 (1943), 386–95.

so instructed the Austrian commanders.[80] But, when Austria was moving ever closer to conflict with Napoleon, he countenanced plans to recover the southeastern territories lost in 1809. By June preparations were in full swing. An army of observation was assembled in Bohemia and another, fifty thousand men strong, was concentrated in Inner Austria under the command of Feldzeugmeister Johann Friedrich von Hiller. The main objective of this force was to contain Beauharnais and to push on into Italy, while a detached corps under Feldmarschall Leutnant Paul von Radivojević, some ten thousand strong, was to occupy Croatia and the other parts of the Illyrian provinces.[81] on August 11, the day Austria actually declared war, orders from Vienna further clarified Radivojević's mission. His corps, consisting of one battalion each of Kreutzer, St. Georger, Broder, and Gradiskaner Grenzer, two battalions of line infantry, six squadrons of the 5th Hussars, and some support units, was to reoccupy the six ceded regiments, reestablish Austrian control, and arm the population. For this purpose the Hofkriegsrat provided twelve thousand muskets and also prepared lists of reliable Grenzer officers to be reappointed to command. When the military border had been recovered and rearmed, Radivojević was instructed to turn one part of his forces toward Istria and Trieste, whereas another part was to press down the Dalmatian coast towards Ragusa.[82] Operations in the military border proper were entrusted to Major General Laval Nugent. Nugent had on previous occasions suggested that Croatia could be recovered by an insurrection against French rule, and he now asked and received permission to advance rapidly in the direction of Karlstadt. Relying on reinforcements from the Grenzer, Nugent took less than two thousand men with him.[83]

The Austrian offensive into Illyria finally got under way on August 16. Two days later, Nugent reached Karlstadt where

[80] Staatskanzlei to FZM Hiller, Slavon. Gkdo., Vienna, Jan. 12, 1813, cited in Arthur G. Haas, *Metternich, Reorganization and Nationality, 1813–1818* (Wiesbaden, 1963), p. 18. Also intelligence estimate, Zagreb, Aug. 1, 1813, KA FA 1813, Hiller, VIII-1.

[81] Instructions from FM Count Bellegarde, Pres. HKR to Hiller, Vienna, Aug. 3, 1813, KA FA 1813, Hiller, VII-38a.

[82] Instructions from Bellegarde to Hiller and FML Radivojević, *ibid.*, VII-45, 45a.

[83] On Nugent, an Irishman in the Austrian service, see Haas, p. 189. For his operations consult KA FA 1813, "Journal des detachierten Corps des Generals Grafen Nugent".

the French commander, General Jean Baptiste de Jeanin, attempted to make a stand along the bank of the Kupa. His attempt to demolish the strategic Kupa bridge was prevented, however, by a rising of the local citizenry.[84] And when two companies of the Szluin Regiment mutinied, Jeanin was forced to make a hasty withdrawal.[85] The Szluiner immediately returned to their old allegiance and in similar fashion Grenzer of all six regiments rallied to the Austrian colors during the next few weeks.[86] Istria was occupied without fighting by Captain Lazarić and some fifty Grenzer,[87] and only in the forts along the coast, where Grenzer officers remained stubbornly loyal to the French, was there any resistance. Fighting was of short duration, and by mid-September the Austrians were again in complete control of the Karlstadt and Banal Borders as well as of civil Croatia.[88]

Radivojević and Nugent were now ordered to rejoin Hiller's main army fighting its way into Italy. Feldzeugmeister Christoph Baron Lattermann was appointed provisional military governor in Illyria, while a hastily raised Grenzer force under Feldmarschall Leutnant Franz Baron Tomassić, supported by a British squadron under Hoste, continued operations against the French in southern Dalmatia.[89] In Zadar, held by a weak garrison, a battalion of the Lika Regiment still in the French service mutinied, and although only about half of the officers supported this move, the Grenzer were able to force their way out of the fortress and join the Austrian forces.[90] Zara then capitulated on December 5, 1813. But farther south Kotor (Cattaro) and Ragusa held out until January. Here the situation was complicated by the Montenegrins. Eager to gain an outlet to the sea, the vladika, aided and abetted by British agents, had since 1811 been trying

[84] Velimir Deželić, ed., "Kako su Francuzi g. 1813 otišli iz Karlovca," *VZA*, 15 (1913), 198–202.

[85] Jeanin's report from Venice, Dec. 14, 1813, AN AF IV 1713, and Fouché's report, Ljubljana, Aug. 18, 1813, Beauharnais Archive.

[86] Hiller to Emperor Francis, Aug. 25, 1813, KA FA 1813, Hiller, VIII-211.

[87] Weil, I, 347–56.

[88] Radivojević to Hiller, Karlstadt, Sept. 17, 1813, KA FA 1813, Hiller, VIII-207; Boppe, *La Croatie Militaire*, pp. 78–81.

[89] KA FA 1813–14, Krieg mit Frankreich in Croatien und Illyrien-Tommassić, XI-1.

[90] A report by the commandant of Zadar, Gen. Claude de Roize, printed in Boppe, *La Croatie Militaire*, pp. 86–90. Proclamation announcing awards for those who had risen against the French and demoting officers who had remained loyal to them, Karlstadt, Feb. 8, 1814, DAZ Zagr. gkda. F 30–31.

to foment an insurrection in the Gulf of Kotor region. Neither Marmont nor Bertrand had been able to assemble enough reliable troops for an expedition against Cetinje.[91] In October, 1813, the Montenegrins came down in force from their mountain fastnesses, and reinforced by local volunteers and aided by the British, drove the French out.[92] Ragusa still remained in French hands, but was besieged by a mixed force of Montenegrins and local volunteers.

When the Austrians arrived to find the Montenegrins in territory they regarded as their own the situation grew very tense. After some hasty diplomatic moves, Alexander of Russia declared his support of the Austrian position and in the meanwhile, too, Austrian troops had managed to enter Ragusa ahead of their embarrassing allies.[93] But incidents between the troops, mainly Grenzer from the Lika, Ogulin, and Szluin Regiments, and the Montenegrins soon led to open fighting, and it was not until the summer of 1814 that the Gulf of Kotor region was secured for Austria.[94]

Meanwhile, the Grenzer formations serving with the French field armies had ceased to exist as fighting units. On November 25, 1813, Napoleon ordered the disarmament of all foreign corps and their conversion into labor units. By then the order affected only a few remnants of the 1st and 3d Provisional Croat Regiments, the hussars, and some scattered detachments. The order could not be carried out in the 2d Provisional Regiment forming part of the Magdeburg garrison invested by the Prussians.[95] After the emperor's abdication all Croatian units made their way home and by May, 1814, the last stragglers had returned. Thus the French interlude on the military border came to an end.

[91] Boppe, *La Croatie Militaire*, pp. 71–72, and Spiridion Gopčević, *Beiträge zur neueren Kriegsgeschichte der Balkan Halbinsel* (Leipzig, 1887), pp. 23–76.

[92] Haas, pp. 17–19.

[93] Johann Sporschil, *Feldzug der Oesterreicher in Illyrien und Italien in den Jahren 1813 und 1814* (Braunschweig, 1844), pp. 75–77.

[94] Vaniček, IV, 171–76.

[95] Order to Clarke, Nov. 25, 1813, *Correspondance*, XXVI, No. 20,940; Boppe, *La Croatie Militaire*, pp. 155–59; Kussan, pp. 41–42.

7

THE MILITARY BORDER IN THE
ERA OF METTERNICH: 1815–47

In the years between the fall of Napoleon and the Revolution of 1848, Austrian military policy was primarily directed toward maintaining the status established by the treaties of 1815 and safeguarding internal security. Perennially short of funds, the army was drastically reduced in size and rigidly limited in its training and equipment expenditures. Under these circumstances the ever-ready and cheaply maintained Grenzer assumed increased importance within the Austrian military establishment. Together with the army of Italy they constituted the only combat-ready units.[1] They maintained their guard along the Turkish frontier, and though with the patent decline in Ottoman power emphasis had changed to the control of the plague and the prevention of smuggling, there still were frequent incursions from Bosnia, which on occasion flared up into full-scale battles. At the same time, the Grenzer were repeatedly mobilized to bolster the imperial forces in Italy and to maintain civil order in Hungary. There was, however, continued economic hardships and increasing discontent with the military bureaucracy, as well as indications that the quality of officers was declining. And despite efforts to keep the Grenzer "uncontaminated," new ideas, especially the spirit of nationalism, were slowly filtering through civil Croatia into the military border.

At the close of the Napoleonic wars the Croatian Military

[1] Rudolf Kiszling, "Das Nationalitätenproblem in Habsburgs Wehrmacht, 1848–1918," *DR*, 4 (1959), 82–83.

Border was not a happy place. Almost every household had lost at least one member; one-ninth of the male population of the eight Croatian regiments never came back from the wars.[2] Then, too, the burden of taxation lay heavily on the poverty stricken land. The harvest was extremely poor in 1814, and crops failed in 1815 and again the following year. By May, 1815, a report from Warasdin spoke about the "general misery and discontent" and blamed inflation and high taxes on essential commodities, especially on salt, for the prevailing unrest.[3] Other reports of the same year alleged continued pro-French sentiments in the Ogulin Regiment and hinted darkly at Bonapartist machinations.[4]

The problem of residual French influence engaged the attention of the authorities, especially the question of what should be done with the Grenzer officers who had served the French. Although there was some sentiment in favor of punishment, it was remembered that the regiments and their personnel had been ceded to the French. An imperial order, dated October 3, 1813, directed that all former officers should be received back in their current rank, even if that rank was the result of a French promotion. Individuals who had revealed strong sentiments against the dynasty, however, were to be suspended pending investigation.[5] The same disposition was applied to those who had stayed with the French to the bitter end, although most were given an opportunity to redeem themselves in the campaigns against the Montenegrins. In the end, only about two dozen officers, including General Slivarić, either lost their commissions or were retired; some others were reduced in rank, and still others were posted away from the border.[6]

There were also problems with the rank and file. There were no reprisals against Grenzer having served the French, but enlisted men who had distinguished themselves in that service were not allowed to wear their decorations and also gained

[2] "Über die Population der Gränze im Jahre 1813," (draft), KA Schriftgut F-29, fold. 3.

[3] FML Gramont to HKR, Karlstadt, May 10, 1815, KA HKR 1815-5-16.

[4] Maj. Gen. Leutner to HKR, Karlstadt, *ibid.*, 1815-4-23, 27.

[5] Imperial cabinet order, Teplitz, Oct. 3, 1813 (copy), DAZ Zagr. gkda. F 30-31. Also instructions from FM Bellegarde to the Karlstadt-Banal prov. Gkdo., Vienna, Oct. 6, 1813, ibid., 1815-29-30.

[6] Correspondence regarding the disposition of Grenzer officers, March to September, 1814, KA HKR 1815-5-7, *ibid.*, 1815-30-31.

slower promotions.[7] Reabsorption of families that had emigrated during the French occupation also proved quite difficult. In general their properties were restored, but other families had to be resettled.[8] This, as well as the arrogance and harsh behavior of some of the returned officers, caused considerable resentment, and in August, 1814, the Hofkriegsrat had to issue a stern warning against abuse of the enlisted men.[9]

The Hofkriegsrat was determined to make the greatest possible use of Grenzer manpower, and to this end instructions were issued in 1814 for a detailed census, a conscription, to be taken every five years and revised annually.[10] Heads of all zadruge were to appear before special commissions to give an account of their land holdings, the number of persons in the household, and other such details. The entire male population was enumerated and classified into three major categories: active duty (*dienend*), liable for duty (*dienstbar*), and exempt or unfit for duty (*undienstbar*). The first category included Grenzer actually serving under arms, regimental cadres and staff, custom agents, quarantine station employees, forest guards, and Seressaner. The second group included all able-bodied Grenzer between the ages of eighteen and sixty. Here there were a number of subcategories. Men over fifty, or those in poor health, were considered fit for limited service (*hausdienstbar*) only. A special roster was maintained showing which men could best be spared by their households. Finally, the third category, the unfit and exempt, included besides invalids and cripples, men over sixty and under eighteen, priests, members of religious orders, public officials, and the families of line officers. Of course, the citizens of the Militär Communitäten were exempt by statute.

The census of 1815 revealed that the population of the Karlstadt regiments was 193,607; the Banal regiments, 96,281; and the Warasdin regiments, 107,589.[11] Of these totals slightly

---

[7] Imbro Tkalac, *Uspomene iz Hrvatske* (Zagreb, 1945), pp. 49–50.

[8] Directive HKR to commanding general, Karlstadt, Vienna, Feb. 25, 1815, KA HKR 1815, B-2-8/1-3.

[9] HKR to Karlstadt-Banal mil. govt., Vienna, Aug. 10, 1814, DAZ Zagr. gkda. F 30-31.

[10] "Conscriptions Normal," of Nov. 3, 1814, modified Aug. 12, 1821, in Mathias Stopfer, *Erläuterungen über die Militär-Gränz Verwaltung des österreichischen Kaiserthums* (Vienna, 1838), pp. 204–48.

[11] Conscription summary for 1815, KA HKR 1815, B-2-44. Other statistics in KA Schriftum F-32, fold. 6.

more than one-half were men, and of these about one-quarter were fit for field service, and about one-half were classified fit for limited service. The census also revealed that the religious composition of the regiments had remained substantially unchanged. The Orthodox prevailed in the Banal regiments, while the Catholics formed a two to one majority in the Warasdin units. In the Karlstadt regiments the Ottoschatz and Ogulin units had the most Catholics; the Lika Regiment was almost solidly Orthodox. Uniats, numbering about four thousand were concentrated almost exclusively in the Szluin Regiment. A handful of Protestants existed in the Militär Communitäten, but in military Croatia Jews were still completely excluded.[12]

Except for the natural increase, the population was stabilized. There no longer were any immigration waves. To be sure, approximately one hundred thousand Serbs fled into the border territories after the collapse of the Serb revolt in 1813, but most of these returned to their homes after 1815 and the rest settled mainly in southern Hungary. Austria now actively discouraged immigration from Turkish controlled areas. In 1814 and again in 1815 the Hofkriegsrat directed the border commands to discourage immigrants from Bosnia and Serbia, and in 1822 orders were issued not to admit any refugees without means.[13] In 1826 a small number of Czech families were settled in the Warasdin regiments, but they were rapidly assimilated.[14] The natural increase, however, was considerable. By 1830 the census showed 240,814 persons in the Karlstadt regiments, 121,032 in the Warasdin, and 111,268 in the Banal units.[15] By 1843 the eight regiments of the Croatian Military Border had a total population of 572,752 of whom 246,687 were considered Serbs. The same year the Slavonian regiments numbered 162,898 with 92,986 Serbs.[16]

There was also some administrative reorganization. Soon

[12] Carl B. v. Hietzinger, *Statistik der Militärgränze des österreichischen Kaiserthums* (3 vols.; Vienna, 1817–23), III, 492.

[13] The Karlstadt-Warasdiner Gkdo. transmits the HKR directives of Nov. 23, 1814, and March 18, 1815, to all regiments, DAZ Zagr. gkda. F 32-33. Also Johann H. Schwicker, *Geschichte der österreichischen Militärgrenze*, (Vienna-Teschen, 1883) p. 187, and Franz Vaniček, *Specialgeschichte der Militärgrenze* (4 vols.; Vienna, 1875), III, 336–37.

[14] Karl v. Czoernig, *Ethnographie der österreichischen Monarchie* (3 vols.; Vienna, 1857), III, 107–9.

[15] Conscription summary for 1830, KA Schriftgut F-32, fold. 6.

[16] Alexius v. Fenyes, *Statistik des Königreiches Ungarn* (2 vols.; Pest, 1843–44), II, 205–12.

after the area was recovered from the French, the Hofkriegsrat recombined the Karlstadt and Warasdin regiments into one command. The Banal Border for the time being remained separate, but with the shortlived Illyrian Kingdom Metternich's concession to the South Slavs came to an end in 1822, the three Croatian borders were merged into a single command, the Banal-Warasdiner-Karlstadter Generalkommando, with headquarters in Zagreb.[17] In addition, brigades of two regiments each were formed. The Gospić Brigade comprised the Lika and Ottoschatz Regiments; the Karlstadt Brigade was formed from the Ogulin and Szluin units. The Banal regiments were assigned to the Petrinja Brigade, and the Warasdin regiments, with headquarters at Bjelovar, formed the fourth brigade. Regimental organization remained much the same. Normally each regiment raised four battalions, grouped into three levies according to age. The first two battalions were considered on active service and in rotation, every man serving about five months each year, furnished frontier guards and troops for other duties. Fully mobilized, the first and second battalions combined mustered twelve companies, 2,570 men, including a regimental staff of 48 and an artillery detachment of 50. When necessary, the third and fourth battalions, trained but only partially equipped, could be called out, and in an emergency every man, regardless of age who could carry a musket, formed the fifth battalion, the *populace* or *Landesaufgebot*.[18] In addition, there were the Seressaner of the Banal and Karlstadt regiments, who received a more detailed regulation in 1835.[19]

Within each regiment the commanding officer exercised complete control in civil as well as military affairs. There continued, nonetheless, the special administrative branch, the *Verwaltungsabteilung*, some 170 officers and men in each regiment.

[17] Ignaz F. Bergmayr, *Verfassung der k.k. Militär-Gränze und Oesterreichischer Kriegs-Marine* (Vienna, 1845), pp. 198–200. Other major commands during this period were the Slavonian-Syrmian at Peterwardein, the Banater at Temesvar, and the Transylvanian at Hermannstadt.

[18] Complete tables of organization in Mathias Stopfer, *Erläuterungen über die Militär-Gränz Verwaltung des osterreichischen Kaiserthums* (Vienna, 1838), pp. 273–92. Also Carl v. Bundschuh, *Handbuch aller seit dem Militärjahre 1767, als dem Anfange des in der k.k. österreichischen Armee itz bestehenden Militär-Oekonomie-Systems bis zum Schlusse des bürgerlichen Jahres 1827 erflossenen und noch als Gesetz bestehenden Normal-Vorschriften* (3 vols.; Prague, 1832), I, 8–10.

[19] Vaniček, III, 338–47.

Administrative service constituted a separate career for officers, and after 1822 entrance into this branch was by competitive examination.[20]

In times of peace cordon guard was the most burdensome obligation of the Grenzer. Duty here was usually for a week at a time, every six or seven weeks.[21] Except in the major frontier crossing stations, the Grenzer on cordon duty wore an undress uniform. "Over the usual peasant frocks," one account related, "they wore knapsacks fastened to a leather strap. Their legs were wrapped in linen or woolen cloth, and their feet covered with those sandals, fastened with red bindings. . . . They wore peasant caps and most of them had a knife sticking in their girdle."[22] In times of suspected plague, the cordon line was reinforced and regulations rigorously enforced. "If you dare to break the laws of the quarantine," reported an English traveler, "you will be tried with military haste; the court will scream out sentence to you from a tribunal some fifty yards off; . . . [and] you will find yourself carefully shot and carelessly buried."[23] Another contemporary observer, however, described the cordon as much less rigorous and claimed that the poor Grenzer could always be bribed to let smugglers and others anxious to avoid the quarantine pass.[24] In any case, cordon duty was a major and unpopular burden, especially when additional troops were required and the third battalion was pressed into service.[25]

During this period Grenzer troops were also employed for a variety of other duties. In 1820 the Ogulin Regiment furnished three companies to guard the Congress of Ljubljana, and in 1820, 1821, and again in 1831, one battalion from each regiment went to reinforce the Austrian army in Italy.[26] These

[20] Bergmayr, pp. 100–102.

[21] Hietzinger, II, 362–64. By 1841 Stopfer's *Lehrbuch der Militär-Gränz-Verwaltung* (Graz, 1841), pp. 82–83, considered the cordon the primary task of the border.

[22] Johann G. Kohl, *Austria, Vienna, Prague, Hungary, Bohemia, the Danube, Galicia, Styria, Moravia, Bukovina and the Military Frontier* (London, 1843), p. 267. Another contemporary description, anonymous, *Caragoli: Ungarn, Militairgrenze, Slavonien, Croatien* (Berlin, 1832), pp. 215–21.

[23] Alexander W. Kingsley, *Eothen or Tales of Travel brought Home from the East* (New York, 1876), pp. 1–2.

[24] A. Schütte, *Ungarn und der Ungarische Unabhängigkeitskrieg* (2 vols.; Leipzig, 1850), I, 26–27.

[25] Tkalac, pp. 113–15.

[26] Vaniček, IV, 176.

employments did not involve fighting, but closer at home, on the Bosnian frontier, small war was endemic. Ottoman power had declined and no longer constituted a danger, but this also encouraged the free, warlike, and fanatic Moslem peasantry of northern Bosnia, organized until 1835 as a counterpart to the military border, and also called the *krajina*, to engage in frequent plunder raids into Austrian territory.[27] And if these raids were now primarily for loot and plunder and not for conquest, they were every bit as pernicious as the great *gazis* that once had poured across the frontier in the name of the sultan and the cause of Islam. During the French occupations, Marmont's energetic reprisals had chastened the Bosnians and they had kept the peace for several years. But in 1813 they renewed their incursions with a raid on Cetin, and during the next years their raids became more frequent and caused considerable damage in the Ogulin, Ottoschatz, and Banal regiments.[28] Austrian counteraction was based on a directive dating back to 1807 that authorized reprisals against clearly identified raider bases only, and this in practice was difficult because the entire population of northern Bosnia supported the raids.[29] Finally, in August, 1819, the Croatian command ordered a major reprisal action and destroyed a raider base at Ostrovica. After this there was a period of comparative quiet. Minor incidents and occasional brigandage across the frontier line continued, but the Austrian government now regarded the Porte as an element of stability and legitimacy and wanted to avoid adding to its troubles by large-scale action in Bosnia. Therefore the Hofkriegsrat directed that all provocations should be avoided and that, if at all possible, frontier incidents be settled

[27] On the Bosnian krajina, see Nedim Filipović, "Pogled na osmanski feudalizam," *Godišnjak BH*, 4 (1952) 5–146, and Hamdija Kreševljaković, "Kapetanije i kapetani u Bosni i Hercegovini," *ibid.*, 2 (1950), 89–141. Also miscellaneous "Kundschafts-Berichte aus Bosnien," 1823–25, DAZ Banska gkda. F-3.

[28] Vaniček, III, 303–5; IV, 175–77; Franz Bach, *Otočaner Regimentsgeschichte* (Karlstadt, 1853), pp. 201–2. There were rumors that French agents were behind the raids. Report from Peterwardein, Oct. 23, 1813, DAZ Banska gkda. F-3.

[29] Reprisal instructions, Dec. 7, 1807, Archduke Ludwig to FML Gyulay, Banal Gkdo., DAZ Banska gkda. F-3. Also Theodor v. Sosnosky, *Die Balkanpolitik Österreich-Ungarns seit 1866* (2 vols.; Stuttgart, 1913), I, 129–31. The best account of the military operations is Friedrich Spigl, *Repressaliengefechte an der kroatisch-türkischen Grenze in der Zeit von 1809–1845* (Vienna, 1882), passim.

by negotiation.[30] The Porte, regardless of its undertakings, however, was quite powerless to enforce its will in Bosnia, and as soon as regular troops were withdrawn, incursions into Austrian territory started again.[31] In May, 1831, after a particularly damaging raid deep into the Szluin Regiment, Feldmarschall Leutnant Count Liebenberg, commanding in Zagreb, ordered a major reprisal with several battalions. A number of villages were destroyed and some cattle recovered. This kept the border quiet for some years.[32]

The next major incident occurred in June, 1834 when a party of over two thousand Bosnians tried to surprise the fort at Cetin but were driven off, plundering the environs during their retreat. The Croatian command wanted to stage a reprisal, but Hofkriegsrat instructions limited action to hot pursuit. This was only partially successful, though a flying column under Major General Rukavina recovered most of the plunder carried off by the raiders. The following year small-scale fighting continued along the entire Banal and Karlstadt borders. The largest engagement took place on June 10 at Tržac where four battalions of Likaner and Oguliner under Rukavina beat back a large force of Bosnians.[33] But by October the Bosnians reappeared in force. This time Rukavina answered with a reprisal raid and burned the Bosnian village of Kladuš. During this action a young officer, Captain Jelačić of the 2d Banal Regiment, distinguished himself.[34] Still another serious engagement was fought in the summer of 1836 when, after suffering a number of raids, Feldmarschall Leutnant Baron Waldstätten, commanding the Croatian Border, in person led a force against Izačić and destroyed it. Casualties were high this time. The Austrian losses were 140 killed or severely wounded; enemy casualties were estimated at 500.[35]

After this there were no important incidents until 1845.

---

[30] Report from FML Lielienberg, Zagreb, to HKR, April 23, forwarded by the HKR to the Staatskanzlei, KA HKR Präs. 1830-454, and the instructions (copy) from the HKR to Lielienberg, Vienna, April 30, 1830, *ibid.*, 477.

[31] Sosnosky, p. 131.

[32] *Ibid.*, pp. 132–33.

[33] Spigl, pp. 36–38.

[34] A somewhat embroidered account in M. Hartley, *The Man who saved Austria: The Life and Times of Baron Jellačić* (London, 1912), pp. 67–68. This is in part based on Jelačić's own report of this action, Kladuš, Oct. 20, 1835 (draft), in Arhiv JAZU, Jelačić Papers, Q-2.

[35] Vjekoslav Klaić, *Geschichte Bosniens* (Leipzig, 1885), pp. 448–52.

During this period a more energetic Porte was trying to reestablish its authority in Bosnia and to break the power of the local feudal nobility. There was resistance and the province was in a state of intermittent civil war. In general Vienna favored the sultan against the rebels, and when government forces were hard pressed, they often were allowed to take refuge in the border.[36] This caused much ill will, and when the rebels threatened pursuit into Austrian territory, the Croatian Border command alerted its forces.[37] The tense situation exploded into violence in July, 1845, when some Bosnians shot a boy on the Austrian side of the frontier, and demands for handing over the guilty parties remained unanswered. The impetuous Jelačić, now colonel of the 2d Banal, decided to make an example, and without approval crossed the frontier with eight companies on July 9 and partially destroyed the Bosnian stronghold Pozvid.[38] This action, out of all proportion to the provocation, annoyed the Turkish government as much as the rebels and caused a major concentration of Turkish regulars as well as rebel troops. On the Austrian side, the first and second battalions of the Karlstadt regiments, as well as the third and fourth battalions of the Ogulin and Szluin Regiments, were mobilized and the populace alerted.[39]

But as neither the Turkish nor the Austrian government wanted an involvement the matter was settled by negotiations. Vienna, however, was perturbed by Jelačić's impetuosity and there was also severe criticism about his handling of the tactical aspects of the battle.[40] Directives were issued that in future

[36] Instructions from the Croat. Gkdo., Zagreb, to all brigades, March 9, 1836, DAZ Zagr. gkda. F-55.

[37] FML Auersperg, Croat. Gkdo., Zagreb, to Brigadier Kempen, Petrinja, concerning treatment of Turkish officials and rebel reaction, June 8, 1845, DAZ Varia, Brigada Petrinja, fold. 1. Also mobilization orders, Zagreb, June 12, 1845, *ibid.*, and instructions from Auersperg to Kempen to concentrate his forces near the frontier, June 16, 1845, *ibid.*

[38] Action report, Jelačić to Kempen, Pozvid, July 9, 1845, *ibid.* Final report, giving reasons for action taken (draft), Jelačić to Kempen, July 13, 1845, Arhiv JAZU, Jelačić Papers, Q-14, 1 and 4. See also Jelačić's letter to the Austrian historian Joseph Scheiger, relating his experiences at Pozvid, in Ivan Bojničić, ed., "Dva Jelačićeva pisma o okrasajima na hrvatsko-turskoj granici. Prilog životopisu Jelačića," *VZA*, 13 (1911), 193–201.

[39] Auersperg warns Kempen about Turkish troop concentrations, Zagreb, July 12, 1845, DAZ Varia, Brigada Petrinja, fold. 1.

[40] On the negotiations with the Turks see the reports from Dahlen, July 17–21, 1845, *ibid.* For criticism of Jelačić's tactics see Anton Springer, *Geschichte Österreichs seit dem Wiener Frieden 1809* (2 vols.; Leipzig, 1863–65), I, 278–79, and the defense by Hartley, p. 97.

overall command on the cordon in Croatia should be in the hands of a general officer and on July 12 Major General Franz Baron Dahlen was appointed to command all troops on the Croatian cordon line. Dahlen promptly issued orders restricting the right of regimental officers to initiate reprisals.[41]

The last major incident took place in February, 1846. Fighting at the frontier interchange Prosceni-Kamen, where over one hundred Bosnians were killed by the Grenzer guards, was answered by a raid into the Ogulin Regiment.[42] The Austrian authorities concentrated a very strong force, over twenty thousand men, but took no further action. Trouble loomed in Hungary and the Hofskriegsrat needed to have its hands free.

Even as the Grenzer assumed greater importance within the Austrian military establishment, the economy of the Croatian regiments continued to stagnate. Accounts by both native and foreign observers, and these became much more numerous during this period, as well as the official records, all agree that government continued to be directed toward one end: to maintain the greatest possible number of troops at the least expense. "Far from seeking to elevate the condition of the inhabitants," commented one French military observer, "the government fears that this might reduce their military qualities."[43] Therefore, the authorities did their utmost to maintain an almost exclusive agricultural economy in the regiments.[44] But improvements in public security, prolonged periods of peace, and advances in public health all contributed to a rapid population increase matched neither by increased land allotments nor by any proportionate rise in productivity. In fact, there was a decrease in the number of livestock in relation to population, and the bureaucratic administration of forests and grazing lands, held as common property under state control, was much resented.[45]

---

[41] Dahlen's directive to all regiments, Aug. 9, 1845, DAZ Varia, Brigada Petrinja, fold. 1.

[42] Report from Prosičeni-Kamen, Feb. 3, 1846, *ibid.* Mobilization orders, Feb. 6, 1846, *ibid.*

[43] M. de Terrason, "Essai sur l'organisation des Frontières Militaires et Régiments Frontières de l'Autriche," AHG Recon. Autriche, 1599.

[44] André Blanc, *La Croatie Occidentale* (Paris, 1957), pp. 198–233, 246–47.

[45] Fran Urbanić, "Prilozi gospodarskomu razvoju hrv.-slav. Krajine u 19. vijeku," *Rad*, 144 (1900), 115–16; Ognieslav M. Utiešenović, *Die Militärgrenze und die Verfassung Eine Studie über den Ursprung und das Wesen der Militärgrenzinstitution und die Stellung derselben zur Landesverfassung* (Vienna, 1861), pp. 48–49.

Agricultural methods, too, remained extremely primitive. In 1825, Pidoll v. Quintenbach, a Hofkriegsrat official, reported that over one-half of the households did not own an iron plow and that crop yields in the regiments were far below the norms achieved in civil Croatia.[46]

In the eyes of many observers the retardation of agriculture was due to the zadruge, which, so they claimed, acted as impediments to private initiative and better farming. An English traveler wrote that the system, perhaps useful in earlier times, had "developed all the evils of Communism to such an extent, that if the most ardent French Communist were to reside for a few weeks on the Croatian frontier he would be undeceived."[47] Indeed, there were at this time a great number of Grenzer petitions asking for permission to dissolve their zadruge, and our English traveler noted that "ninety-nine officers out of a hundred think that Communism ought to be abolished."[48] The Hofkriegsrat, however, regarded the zadruge, or as they were styled Hauskommunionen, as the foundation on which the manpower potential of the regiments rested and usually denied all petitions asking for their dissolution. But the result was considerable deprivation and often acute want, especially in the Karlstadt regiments that farmed the poorest soil. Here the margin of existence was paper thin and crop failure, or even a bad harvest, meant hunger and near famine. After the crop failure in 1816, there were a few fair years, but harvests were poor in 1825, 1830, 1834, 1836, and 1840.[49] There existed government magazines providing some relief, but aid was given grudgingly and commanding officers were advised to restrict aid to the very neediest families.[50]

At the same time the authorities continued to oppose any expansion of trade and industry that might diminish the hold of the zadruge on the Grenzer.[51] The several Militär Communi-

[46] "Relation des Hofr. v. Pidoll über seine i. Jahre 1825 vorgenommene Bereisung der slawonischen u. croatischen Mil.-Gränze," KA HKR Kanz. Arch. VII-369.

[47] A. A. Paton, *Highlands and Islands of the Adriatic, including Dalmatia, Croatia, and the southern Provinces of the Austrian Empire* (2 vols.; London, 1849), II, 176.

[48] Miscellaneous Grenzer petitions, DAZ Zagr. gkda. F-55 (1836), and F-86 (1845-46); Paton, II, 177-78.

[49] Bach, pp. 297-99.

[50] HKR to Croat. Gkdo., Vienna, Sept. 6, 1836, DAZ Zagr. gkda. F-55.

[51] Blanc, pp. 246-47.

täten, isolated in a hostile and non-productive environment, failed to grow. Ivanić, for example, still had less than five hundred inhabitants in 1819, and the other townships in the Karlstadt and Banal Borders were equally retarded.[52] By contrast, Karlstadt itself, which was transferred to civil Croatia in 1796, was described as bustling and prosperous.[53] Within the regiments, except for a few absolutely indispensable trades, all occupations other than agriculture were discouraged. "There exist on this frontier," another French observer reported in 1818, "no factories, no machines, no industry. There is hardly any noise but the occasional discharge of firearms."[54] This description, of course, was too severe. There were some cottage industries and a few artisans. But during the first half of the nineteenth century there was but one craftsman to every 173 inhabitants in the Croatian Military Border, compared to one to every 79 inhabitants in civil Croatia.[55]

Also in the period after 1815 there was an increasing volume of complaints about the conduct of Grenzer officers, native as well as foreign. Service in the Grenzer regiments was not considered prestigious, and Vienna was only too glad to forget the military border as long as frontier incidents were few and returns regular.[56] Promotion in the border service was slow and the duties arduous. For the regimental officers there were the long weeks spent on the cordon, and the cold winter nights out on patrol waiting to intercept a smuggler's convoy or to ambush a band of intruders from Bosnia. But here there was at least the excitement of occasional action. Routine service with the troops in their home districts, on the other hand, was dull and boring. "The day of the officer of the frontier begins at four or five o'clock in the morning," a sympathetic observer related, "and from one duty to another he is occupied till mid-

[52] Johann v. Csaplovics, *Slavonien und zum Theil Croatien* (2 vols.; Pest, 1819), I, 92; Glina and Petrinja described in Therese v. Artner, *Briefe über ein Theil von Croatien und Italien an Caroline Pichler* (Pest, 1830), pp. 29, 40–43. Ogulin is described in M. Magdić, *Topografija i povijest Ogulin* (Zagreb, 1926), pp. 249–50, and also in Carl Nagy, *Neueste statistisch-geographische Beschreibung des Königreichs Ungarn, Croatien, Slavonien, und der ungarischen Militär-grenze* (Leipzig, 1832), p. 490.

[53] Paton, II, 181-85, and Blanc, p. 269.

[54] Felix de Beaujour, *Voyage militaire dans l'empire Ottoman* (2 vols.; Paris, 1829), I, p. 427.

[55] Rudolf Bićanić, *Doba manufakture u Hrvatskoj i Slavoniji, 1750–1860* (Zagreb, 1951), pp. 78–79.

[56] Hartley, p. 92; Springer, II, 278.

day when he dines; he finishes his business again at six or seven."[57]

Officers exercised almost total and absolute control over all aspects of the life of their subordinates, and this in turn led to a variety of abuses.[58] When in 1818 Emperor Francis visited the regiments, he was shocked by the great number of Grenzer petitions requesting relief from the "arbitrary and cruel behavior, the frequent abuses, and the general misconduct of their officers."[59] Investigation revealed that many of the complaints were well founded. Officers had Grenzer labor for private purposes; they had maltreated their men and meted out harsh sentences without due process. The Hofkriegsrat cashiered one officer and severely reprimanded others. In addition officers were warned against future abuses. Especially the Hofkriegsrat remonstrated against the practice of forcing Grenzer to spend their clothing allowances with certain favored merchants. In 1820, too, corporal punishment was made subject to stricter regulation.[60]

A particularly unpleasant abuse of official power was the misuse of young Grenzer women. Life for the officers was often lonely and, except for the larger stations, officers lived in small groups or alone and had to "ride an hour or two" to see a brother officer.[61] Such conditions often led to abuses, and in 1841 a memorial from the Petrinja Brigade asked that marriage restrictions be eased because "celibate officers lead an isolated and hard life that, without the solace of a family, may easily lead them to drink and immorality."[62] Such conduct even affected senior officers. In the 1820's Colonel Knöhr of the Szluin Regiment for years kept a harem of four to six girls, restocked at regular intervals with young women from his regiment.[63] Other officers were guilty of similar behavior, and one French observer estimated that it would take years for the morale of

[57] Paton, II, 112–13.

[58] This was realized by some Austrian officials in the HKR. See for instance Carl Frhr. Pidoll zu Quintenbach, *Einige Worte über die russischen Militär-Kolonien im Vergleiche mit der k.k. österreichischen Militär-Grenze mit allgemeinen Betrachtungen darüber* (Vienna, 1847), pp. 74–75.

[59] Report of investigation, with enclosures, KA HKR 1820, B-1-55/68.

[60] Vaniček, III, 314–17.

[61] Paton, II, 155.

[62] Memorial to Gen. Count Nugent from the Petrinja Brigade, Aug. 17, 1841, in DAZ Varia Brigada Petrinja, fold. 1.

[63] Tkalać, pp. 247–48.

the Karlstadt regiments to recover.[64] How such abuses could persist is explained in a report of 1832 that complains about the "venality and misconduct among the military judges on the border."[65]

These conditions also explain the frequent desertions and the growing Grenzer dissatisfaction with their military status. Some deserters and their families vanished into Turkish territory, whereas others joined the bands of brigands infesting the hills of the Karlstadt regiments. In 1820 the Hofkriegsrat asked for an investigation and was told that desertions were due to poverty, friction within the zadruge, and dislike of military discipline. The report continued, however, that there were only 174 deserters, 47 of whom had surrendered, and 20 of whom had been caught by patrols. Moreover, asserted the report, many of the depredations ascribed to deserters actually were committed by Bosnian intruders.[66] The Hofkriegsrat continued to be disturbed by the desertions and in 1829 decreed exemplary punishments for all unauthorized absences.[67] But the punishment could not cure the wilting morale and the growing resentment against the military regime. By 1830 a confidential report conceded that "general unrest and dissatisfaction were the main causes for the constant emigration and escapes into Turkish territory" and that the basic cause was the "unfortunate condition of the inhabitants, their absolute lack of any prosperity."[68] A similar opinion was expressed two years later by Colonel Vlasić, then commander of the Szluin Regiment. "On the Banal and Karlstadt Borders," the colonel wrote, "religion, morals, education, and culture lack in comparison with other civilized countries." For this Colonel Vlasić blamed the dispersed settlement and the onerous military obligations. Moreover, the Karlstadt and Banal regiments carried a much

[64] Lt. Col. de Courtigis, in 1845, AHG Recon. Autriche, 1601. The abuses continued into the 1860's as reported by Georges Perrot, "L'Autriche d'autrefois. Les confins militaires et leur legislation," *RDM*, 84 (1869), 69. Similar incidents were reported from the Slavonian regiments, Spiridion Jovics, *Ethnographisches Gemählde der serbisch-slawonischen Militärgrenze* (Vienna, 1835), p. 140.

[65] HKR memorandum (draft), KA Mém. XXIII-74.

[66] Report from FML Radivojević, Zagreb, Feb. 11, 1820, KA HKR 1820, B-1-13/14.

[67] KA Mém. XXIII-74.

[68] "Bemerkungen über den Zustand und die Verfassung der Militär-Grenze," a confidential report to Metternich by A. Huszár, Pressburg, Oct. 28, 1830, KA Mém. XXII-84.

heavier load than other parts of the border. This, the report concluded, had created a general aversion against the military regime.[69]

Thus by 1840 Vienna was not unaware of the conditions on the Croatian Military Border, but by this time the authorities were preoccupied with the rising tide of South Slav nationalism penetrating, albeit slowly, into the regiments. During the first decade of the century the Serb national rising had attracted ardent sympathy and support, and this in turn had revived the old apprehensions about the attachment of the Orthodox, or non-Uniat Greeks as they were called in the official communications. In 1813 Karadjordje, deserted a second time by his Russian allies, fled across the Danube to seek asylum on Austrian soil, but leadership had then fallen to the astute Miloš Obrenović, who in 1815 started a second revolt. After the assassination of Karadjordje in 1817, Miloš became the unquestioned leader of the Serbs and shrewdly taking advantage of the international situation secured autonomy for his country in 1830.

During the fifteen years of the second Serb revolt and its attendant disturbances in Bosnia, Austria again remained neutral. In 1816 directives went out to all border commands to repress Serb propaganda, and standing orders were issued to watch for Serb attempts to subvert the loyalty of the Grenzer.[70] Above all, the military were suspicious of the Orthodox Church, and the seminary at Plaški near Karlstadt was denounced as a center of indoctrinating Grenzer youths with Serb nationalism.[71] As a result, though there was no return to the practices of Charles VI and Maria Theresa, the Orthodox clergy were placed under severe restrictions. In 1823 the Hofkriegsrat even considered substituting a German for the old Slavonic catechism then in use,[72] and in 1837, when the Serb national

[69] Memorial, Zagreb, Nov. 21, 1832, to FM Count Hardegg, HKR KA Mém. XXIII-74.

[70] HKR circular to all commands, Vienna, Apr. 14, 1816, in Aleksa Ivić, ed., *Arhivska gradja o srpskim i hrvatskim književnim i kulturnim radnicima, Zbornik IJK*, 3 (Belgrade, 1931), 90.

[71] See the report from B. Kopitar, censor, Vienna, Jan. 24, 1826, and the report of the investigation, FML Radivojević to the HKR, Zagreb, Aug. 29, 1826, *ibid.*, pp. 93–96.

[72] Vaniček, IV, 159–61; on the projected introduction of a German catechism see FM Bellegarde to FZM Gyulay, Vienna, Feb. 6, 1823, DAZ Banska gkda. F-3.

congress wanted to discuss questions of national interest, the military authorities ruled all such topics out of order.[73] Apprehensions concerning the Orthodox continued in 1839–41 when there were renewed allegations that the Serbs were engaged in subversive activities.[74] After the accession of Patriarch Joseph Rajačić, coming from a Grenzer family in the Ogulin Regiment and considered loyal to the dynasty, the government was reassured about the attachment of the Orthodox Grenzer.[75]

If Vienna felt somewhat easier about the Orthodox Grenzer, new complications arose from civil Croatia. By the end of the 1830's Illyrian propaganda from civil Croatia began to penetrate into the regiments and rapidly became a major concern of the authorities. The Illyrian movement was partly a legacy of the French Revolution and partly the result of ancient Croat grievances against Hungary. Although civil Croatia had generally welcomed the restoration of Austrian rule, there existed considerable sentiment for the creation of an autonomous South Slav state, and in 1814 the estates of Croatia bravely petitioned the emperor for the establishment of a greater Croatian kingdom. After some hesitation, and largely due to Metternich who wished to attach the Catholic Croats closer to the Habsburg, a new Kingdom of Illyria was proclaimed in August, 1816. The new creation, however, comprising civil Croatia, parts of Istria, Carniola, Carinthia, and Goricia, with its capital at Ljubljana, did not include Dalmatia or the Croatian Military Border.[76] Moreover, it aroused strong Hungarian opposition, and as a result it was dissolved in 1822 and Croatia restored to its old relationship with the Hungarian crown. The same year the separate Banal Border command was dissolved. These developments aggrieved the Croatian estates, and when the Sabor finally was allowed to meet in 1825, it immediately renewed its

[73] Rupert v. Schumacher, *Des Reiches Hofzaun* (3d ed.; Darmstadt, 1942), p. 258.

[74] Gustav Roloff, ed., "Fürst Metternich über die slawische und magyarische Gefahr im Jahre 1839," *MIÖG*, 52 (1938), 69–70. Also the allegations of Orthodox connections with Russia in the report of the Information Bureau to Police-minister Sedlnitzky, in Gyula Miskolczy, *A horvát kérdés története es iromanyai a rendi állam korában* (2 vols.; Budapest, 1927–28), I, 590–91.

[75] Schwicker, *Geschichte der österreichischen Militärgrenze* (Vienna, 1883), p. 306.

[76] Arthur G. Haas, *Metternich, Reorganization and Nationality, 1813–1818*, (Wiesbaden, 1963), pp. 19–21, 98–101.

demands for the dissolution of the military border. Vienna, of course, refused.[77]

At this time Croatian aspirations had very little appeal for the Grenzer. Recruited for generations from the same families and the same communities and endowed with privileges that raised them well above the serfs of civil Croatia, the Grenzer opposed all Croatian suggestions to end the separate military administration. Within the next few decades Grenzer attitudes were modified by changes in the nature of Croatian nationalism. Traditionally Croatian claims had been based on the historic-political unity of the kingdom and on the special rights of the privileged estates. But in the wake of the French occupation groups of nobles, clergy, and even the small bourgeoisie began to take an interest in the Slavic tongues and to develop a new Croatian nationalism on the basis of common language, customs, and traditions. A similar development of philological-ethnographic nationalism also took place in Hungary. Here nationalist groups wanted to make the Magyar language paramount in the lands of the crown of St. Stephen and the diet of 1832–36 enacted laws making Hungarian the authoritative text of all laws. This move was bitterly opposed by the Croatian delegation which regarded this as the opening wedge for an attack upon their national privileges. To be sure, the Croatian delegates did not at this time champion Croatian but clung to the medieval Latin as the official language. Their stand strengthened national sentiments at home.[78]

The spokesman of the new Croatian nationalism, generally called Illyrianism, was Ljudevit Gaj, who in 1831 settled in Zagreb. At first the movement was largely cultural, but it soon acquired a political program. In 1831 Count Janko Drašković launched political Illyrianism with his famous *Disertacija*, which demanded the union of Croatia, Slavonia, and Dalmatia with the Slovene areas of Carniola, Carinthia, and Styria, and the return of the Croatian Military Border to the control of the enlarged Triune Kingdom.[79] In 1836 Drašković presented

[77] Utiešenović, p. 26.

[78] Josef Matl, "Der Panslawismus als politische Idee in Südosteuropa im 19. und 20. Jahrhundert," *Schriften der Südosteuropa Gesellschaft*, 2 (Munich, 1961), 300–314. On the language conflict see George Barany, "The Hungarian Diet of 1839–40 and the Fate of Széchenyi's Middle Course," *SR*, 22 (1963), 286–94.

[79] Matl, pp. 310–11; Janko Drašković, *Disertacija iliti razgovor, darovan gospodi poklisarom zakonskim i buducem zakonotvorcem kraljevina naših za*

his ideas to the Sabor. Although this assembly by and large was still dominated by the feudal nobility, above all concerned to preserve its position and privileges, Drašković received considerable support when he called for representatives from the regiments to attend the sessions. Due to conservative opposition within the Sabor, from the Hungarian chancery, and from official Vienna, nothing came of this proposal, which was repeated in 1845.[80]

Meanwhile, Drašković and his ideas were promptly denounced by the Magyars and their friends as Russian-inspired and subversive.[81] For the moment, however, Metternich in Vienna decided to take no action "concerning the extremely delicate situation in Croatia."[82] During the next few years, Hungarian nationalists became more demanding and the diet of 1839–40 replaced Latin with Hungarian as the administrative language. In addition, the diet asserted that all indigenous troops, including the Grenzer, should wear the Hungarian national cockade, use the Hungarian language, and be commanded by Hungarian officers.[83] The language struggle now turned very bitter. There were threats and counterthreats, and early in 1841 Hungarian papers called for an "iron hand" and the use of troops to enforce language unity.[84] Thus the battle lines were clearly drawn and even the Croatian nobility, which would have preferred merely to defend its own privileges, was forced to choose between Magyarization and a wider Croatian national movement. Some nobles did indeed join the Hungarian camp, but many others chose Illyrianism. This development tended to eliminate some of the differences between the Grenzer and the estates of civil Croatia, which now began to think in terms of a common front against the Magyars.

In Vienna the government was divided. Baron Kolowrat,

budući dijetu ugarsku odaslanem, držan po jednom starom domorocu kraljevinah ovih (Karlovac, 1832), pp. 12–17.

[80] Springer, II, 114, and documents in Miskolczy, *Horvát kérdés*, II, 338–39.

[81] Report of Moyses Istvan, police agent and censor, Zagreb, Dec. 16, 1838, *ibid.*, pp. 574–76.

[82] Vote of the ministerial conference, Vienna, July 22, 1836, *ibid.*, pp. 553–55.

[83] Barany, pp. 297–98, and also Julius (Gyula) Miskolczy, *Ungarn in der Habsburger Monarchie* ("Wiener Historische Studien"), V (Vienna, 1959), pp. 82–83.

[84] Hermann Wendel, *Der Kampf der Südslawen um Freiheit und Einheit* (Frankfurt, 1925), pp. 190–91, and Hanns Schlitter, *Ungarn* in *Aus Österreichs Vormärz* (4 vols.; Zurich–Leipzig–Wien, 1920), III, 4.

the interior minister, advocated in March, 1841, that the government should use Slav nationalism to counter Hungarian revolutionary tendencies. Since the office of Ban happened to be vacant at this time, Kolowrat proposed the appointment of a strong military figure to give leadership and cohesion to the Slav movement.[85] For his part, Metternich, though suspicious of the Magyars, was more afraid of the new Slav movement, and Georg Haulik, the Catholic bishop of Zagreb was appointed as interim Ban. Two years later, increasingly disturbed about the possible repercussions of Illyrianism on the loyalty of the Grenzer, the chancellor managed to have General Franz Baron Haller, a nobleman of Hungarian birth and safely conservative convictions, installed as Ban with instructions to contain the Illyrians.[86]

Metternich's apprehensions were intensified by continued reports from Croatia alleging close ties between the Illyrians and Russia and asserting that the movement made particular progress among the Grenzer.[87] The government became concerned about the allegiance of the Grenzer and in November, 1842, an imperial directive ordered that "all necessary steps be taken to keep the border free of political intrigues."[88] In January, 1843, there followed a special investigation. The results appeared to be satisfactory and allayed suspicion. After receiving reports from Field Marshal Auersperg, then commanding in Zagreb, the ministers felt reassured that the Grenzer "because of their special status and because of their gratitude for their special privileges were immune to the blandishments of parties."[89]

Under these circumstances Metternich was willing to take a second look at the Croatian national movement. He continued to worry about the alleged connections with Russia and in 1843 forbade the use of the name Illyrian, but no real effort was made to suppress Gaj's movement and the government looked with

[85] Proposal by Kolowrat, May 20, 1840, Miskolczy, *Horvát kérdés*, I, 592–93.

[86] Julius Miskolczy, "Metternich und die ungarischen Stände," *MÖStA*, 12 (1959), 252–53.

[87] Among others March, 1842; October 26, 1844, Miskolczy, *Horvát kérdés*, I, 603–10, and II, 238–46.

[88] Emperor Ferdinand to Gen. Hardegg, Pres. HKR, Vienna, November, 1842, Miskolczy, *Horvát kérdés*, II, 31.

[89] Hardegg's report to the Staatskonferenz, Vienna, Feb. 13, 1843, *ibid.*, pp. 38–43.

some favor on Slav cultural manifestations.[90] Moreover, Metternich was not unaware, as he wrote to a trusted friend in the summer of 1843, that "Croatian affairs place a strong weapon into the hands of the government if it knows how to use this instrument."[91] When there was renewed agitation in Hungary during the diet of 1843–44, a senior Austrian official concluded that "should it ever be necessary to use force in Hungary, the enthusiasm of the ever-ready Grenzer regiments insures victory for the government."[92]

But then, to everyone's surprise, Metternich chose to relieve tensions by making concessions to the Magyars. In January, 1845, an imperial rescript announced that in the future Hungarian would be the only language used in the diet, although the Croatian delegates were allowed to use Latin for another six years. This action was much resented in Croatia and soon Count Haller was unable to maintain public order.[93] Suspected by the Magyarones as too Croatian and detested by the Illyrians as a Hungarian, he lost the confidence of the population. On July 28, 1846, the election for a new *Vicegespan* in Zagreb led to rioting, and the next day regular troops of an Italian line regiment had to be called out to restore order. There were some two dozen killed or wounded.[94] In the aftermath Haller had to resign and Bishop Haulik returned as interim Ban. When the Sabor opened in September, 1845, the Illyrians appeared in greater strength and again there were calls for the incorporation of the Grenzer regiments.[95]

But, as conditions in Hungary steadily became more revolutionary, the government continued to count on the loyalty of the Grenzer. Vienna was aware of the resentment against the military regime and the dissatisfaction with the economic conditions, but as long as serfdom continued to exist in the Habsburg lands, Grenzer status was preferable. As one intelligence report from Croatia put it, the majority of the Grenzer

---

[90] Schlitter, III, 73, 149–55.
[91] Friedrich Walter, "Die Wiener Südostpolitik im Spiegel der Geschichte der zentralen Verwaltung," in F. Walter and H. Steinacker, *Die Nationalitätenfrage im alten Ungarn und die Südostpolitik Wiens* (Munich, 1959), p. 25.
[93] Franz Count Hartig, section chief in the Staatsrath, Vienna, Nov. 17, 1843, Miskolczy, *Horvát kérdés*, II, 72–74.
[93] Report from FM Ban Haller, Zagreb, July 29, 1845, *ibid.*, pp. 303–5.
[94] Springer, II, 114.
[95] Police report, Zagreb, April 17, 1847, Miskolczy, *Horvát kérdés*, II, 542.

supported the Illyrian party, but they also considered it the
government party. Moreover, continued the report, the Grenzer were proud of their status "as personal vassals of His Majesty the Emperor, and regard themselves superior to the subjects
in provincial Croatia."[96] The government's confidence was
even more justified in the case of the regimental officers. "Nothing can exceed their loyalty," an English observer stated in
1847.[97] Therefore, the Grenzer were considered absolutely reliable, and the use of the army for internal police purposes
being a standard procedure, they were repeatedly alerted in
Hungary.[98]

By the end of 1847 tensions were rising in the Habsburg Empire and there were doubts about the loyalty of the regular
army in the face of national insurrections. The Hofkriegsrat
therefore began an ambitious program of transferring units
out of their ethnic areas. Early in 1848, as part of this relocation, four out of eight Italian infantry regiments were moved
from Italy to German Austria or Hungary and replaced by
Grenzer battalions.[99] Thus, as the pre-March era drew to its
end, the Grenzer were still regarded as highly reliable and efficient troops. Yet, there remained the question of how they
would react once serfdom was abolished in the Hungarian
Croatian lands.

[96] Report of Count Hardegg, Pres. HKR to Staatskonferenz, Vienna, Feb.
13, 1843, *ibid.*, 39–40.
[97] Paton, II, 174.
[98] Alert order for Grenzer regts. KA HKR Präs. 1846-626; Springer, II,
136–37.
[99] Kiszling, "Das Nationalitätenproblem in Habsburgs Wehrmacht," p. 82.

8

—.—.—.—.—

THE CROATIAN MILITARY
BORDER AND HUNGARY:
1848–59

The revolutionary events of 1848–49 were a watershed in the history of the Croatian Military Border. In March and April of 1848 the Grenzer put aside their reservations about Croatian aspirations and joined with the Illyrians to demand the incorporation of the regiments into a resurrected Triune Kingdom. After that the elevation of Colonel Jelačić to the post of Ban, and the general resentments against the claims of Magyar supremacy emanating from Budapest, overcame these nationalist and revolutionary tendencies. Instead, the Grenzer reverted to their traditional military allegiance and contributed substantial forces to the fight against Hungary. They also showed that the settlement of 1807 had not permanently appeased their discontents and they demanded, and received, assurances of new and more liberal arrangements. When their expectations were disappointed in the general reaction that followed the defeat of the revolutions of 1848, the Grenzer became a blunted and much less reliable instrument of Habsburg policy.

When the great wave of revolutions rolled over the Austrian Empire in March, 1848, the Hungarian diet in Budapest promptly forced through a liberal constitution and abolished feudal rights and burdens in all the lands of St. Stephen's crown. While Croatians asserted that only the Sabor was competent to pass such a law for Croatia, the measure was put into effect by the peasants who promptly refused to render feudal services and was supported by the provisional national assembly hastily assembled in Zagreb.[1] At the outset, this assembly appeared primarily directed against the existing imperial structure. Dominated by the Illyrians, it demanded the convocation of a Croatian-Slavonian-Dalmatian Sabor, the incorporation of the Croatian and Slavonian regiments into the Triune kingdom, and the recall of the Grenzer from Italy.[2] Disaffection promptly spread to the military border, where the outward calm of the last few years was deceptive. In the Szluin Regiment there was open agitation for the complete abolition of the military regime, while elsewhere the Grenzer demanded reductions in their military duties and abolition of economic restrictions, above all freedom to dissolve the zadruge.[3] Feldmarschall Leutnant Auersperg was forced to temporize and recommended to Vienna that for the time being all labor service be suspended and military duties reduced to a minimum.[4]

These developments provided the background for the sudden elevation of Colonel Jelačić of the 2d Banal Regiment to the office of Ban on March 23, and within two weeks to Feldmarschall Leutnant and commanding general in Croatia and its military border. The immediate initiative for this move came from a group of Croatian conservatives, mainly highly placed officials in church and state who favored a strong stand against Hungary, but considered the rest of the Illyrian program as altogether too radical. They hoped that a conservative but popular Ban might divert national sentiments into safer channels, and Jelačić appeared as a "providential mediator," acceptable to all.[5] His fierce anti-Magyar sentiments and his patriotic fervor recommended him to the Illyrians, and like many professional soldiers he had little sympathy for revolution and was bound by his family and long service to the cause of the dynasty. His name was first suggested to Kolowrat, who temporarily had replaced Metternich at the head of affairs, by Baron Kulmer, *Obergespan* of the Zagreb comitat and since early March liaison man for the Croatian conservatives in Vi-

---

[1] Rudolf Bićanić, "Oslobodenje kmetova u Hrvatskoj godine 1848," *Djelo*, 1 (1948), 198–200.

[2] The Croatian manifesto of March 25, 1848 (copy), KA HKR 1848, B-99-25.

[3] FML Auersperg, Zagreb, March 30, 1848, KA KM Präs. CK 1848-860.

[4] Zagreb, April 4, 1848, KA KM Präs. MK 1848-129.

[5] The term used by Josef Redlich, *Das österreichische Staats und Reichsproblem* (2 vols.; Vienna, 1920–26), I, 215.

enna. But Jelačić was also endorsed by an Illyrian delegation that had arrived in the capital to plead for the creation of an autonomous South Slav state and was supported by influential circles at court.[6] The decisive consideration, however, was his influence and prestige with the border troops that at this point constituted one of the most important elements of the Austrian army. "Austria will have to reconquer Hungary," Kulmer told the Ban on March 30, "and therefore you must at all costs retain the loyalty of the military border."[7]

The new Hungarian government, which at this time was negotiating about the powers of a "responsible" ministry in Budapest, also realized the importance of the Grenzer. Under pressure, the Austrian government was forced to concede the division of the armed forces under the control of separate Austrian and Hungarian war ministries. The exact status of the border regiments was not determined, but the Hungarians were convinced that they were included in their jurisdiction. The Budapest diet promptly proclaimed the regiments part of Hungary and allotted them a small number of deputies in the future Hungarian parliament.[8] These arrangements were incorporated in the famous "March Laws" and sanctioned on April 11 by Emperor Ferdinand.[9]

But the Vienna war ministry, successor to the Hofkriegsrat that unlike many other government agencies never lost its grip, ignored the new order and continued its control over the military borders. And in Zagreb, Jelačić in his dual capacity as Ban and commander of the border, refused to recognize the competence of the Budapest government. On April 19, he instructed all Croatian officials to sever contacts with Hungary,

[6] The appointment of Jelačić is still hotly disputed. I have followed Rudolf Kiszling, *Revolution im Kaiserthum Österreich* (2 vols.; Vienna, 1948), I, 78–82, and Julius Miskolczy, *Ungarn in der Habsburger Monarchie* ("Wiener Historische Studien"), V (Vienna, 1959), 85–86. In a more recent Marxist interpretation, Vaso Bogdanov maintains that Jelačić, of relative low military rank and belonging to the lesser gentry, was selected to attract the support of the revolutionary masses. *Historija političkih stranaka u Hrvatskoj* (Zagreb, 1958), pp. 307–17.

[7] Kulmer to Jelačić, Vienna, March 30, 1848, Arhiv JAZU, Jelačić Papers, D-I-1.

[8] Hungary proper had 277 delegates; Croatia 18; the entire Military Border 21; and Transylvania 69. Heinrich Marczali, *Ungarische Verfassungsgeschichte* (Tübingen, 1910), p. 143.

[9] William H. Stiles, *Austria in 1848–49* (2 vols.; New York, 1852), II, 55–56, and Anton Springer, *Geschichte Oesterreichs seit dem Wiener Frieden 1809* (2 vols.; Leipzig, 1863–65), II, 272–73.

and on April 27 he personally refused to accept instructions from the Hungarian war ministry.[10] He placed the third battalions on a war footing, and on May 2, alleging the threat of Turkish invasion and internal disorder, he proclaimed martial law throughout Croatia.[11] Upon his request, the new Austrian war minister, Baron Baillet de Latour, authorized mobilization of the fourth battalions and arranged for the transfer of military stores from army depots in Styria to Croatia.[12]

Clearly the Hungarian government could not tolerate such open defiance and it protested to the emperor who at this point was still hoping for an accommodation with Budapest. On May 7, therefore, an imperial edict announced that all troops stationed in Hungary-Croatia, including the military borders, were subject to the authority of the Hungarian war ministry.[13] Budapest promptly appointed Feldmarschall Leutnant Hrabowsky, commanding the Slavonian-Syrmian Border, as royal commissioner to restore the authority of the government against the Ban and to supersede him in command of the Grenzer.[14] But Hrabowsky lacked power to enforce his mandate and Jelačić refused to yield. The Ban even ignored a second imperial communication, dated May 29 to halt all preparations for the convocation of the Sabor scheduled for early June, and complained to Latour that Hrabowsky's appointment was prejudicial to Grenzer discipline.[15] Jelačić was encouraged in his obdurate stand by word from Kulmer that "Hrabowsky has not transferred any of your legal powers to him."[16] In the meantime, the Ban began to regroup his forces, normally deployed toward the Bosnian frontier along the Croatian-Hungarian boundary on the Drava.[17] When Budapest protested, the Ban insisted that these moves were purely defensive, though by

[10] Jelačić's report, Zagreb, April 27, 1848, KA KM Präs. MK 1848-857.

[11] Declaration of martial law (copy), DAZ Varia, bgda. Petrinja, F-2.

[12] Jelačić to Latour, Zagreb, May 10, 1848, Arhiv JAZU, Jelačić Papers, C-V-4.

[13] Edict printed in F.A. Nordstein, *Geschichte der Wiener Revolution* (Leipzig, 1850), pp. 131–33.

[14] Kiszling, *Revolution*, I, 82, and Stiles, II, 61–63.

[15] Jelačić to Latour, Zagreb, May 10, 1848, Arhiv JAZU, Jelačić Papers, C-V-1.

[16] Kulmer to Jelačić, Vienna, May 17, 1848, in Josip Matasović, "Kulmerova pisma banu Jelačiću 1848," *Narodna Starina*, 13 (1935), 153–54.

[17] Movement orders, May 27 and June 10, 1848, DAZ Varia bgda. Petrinja, F-2.

early June the Grenzer concentrations far outnumbered Hungarian troops on the other side of the river.[18]

The position of the Hungarian government was further complicated by a full-scale insurrection in the Slavonian-Syrmian Border. By the middle of May the Serbs of southern Hungary had declared their independence from Budapest and proclaimed the establishment of an autonomous Vojvodina. Their national congress elected Stefan Šuplikac, a grizzled Grenzer colonel serving with the Ogulin battalions in Italy, as *vojvoda*. In his absence, power was to be held by the conservative Patriarch Rajačić and a newly constituted Serb provisional authority, the *Glavni Odbor*. The immediate result was considerable confusion, since there now existed no less than three competing authorities. There was the Odbor in Karlovci, Hrabowsky at Peterwardein, who still considered himself the duly appointed commander of the Slavonian and Croatian regiments, and finally there was Jelačić attempting to extend his power over the Slavonian Grenzer. At the outset, the Odbor was primarily supported by the Serb civilian element at Karlovci and Novi Sad (Neusatz), and the Grenzer, especially the officers, found it difficult to obey an irregularly constituted body.[19] Eventually, the Brod and Gradiska Regiments subordinated themselves to the Ban, whereas the Peterwardein Regiment and the Czaikisten rallied to the Odbor.[20]

In Zagreb, meanwhile, delegates assembled for the formal opening of the Sabor on June 5. Despite the fact that the conservatives were much stronger than in the preceding national assembly, the Illyrians gained two important concessions. A deputation from the Vojvodina was invited to attend, and Jelačić was forced to concede Grenzer representation, each regiment being allowed to send four delegates.[21] During the sessions of the Sabor there emerged considerable differences between conservatives and Illyrians, especially concerning the nature

[18] Intelligence report on Hungarian dispositions, Arhiv JAZU, Jelačić Papers, F-II-1.

[19] Reports on the events in the Peterwardein Regiment, by Col. Daniel U. Rastić, Vinkovci, Aug. 3, 1848, KA KM Präs. MK 1848-4240.

[20] Orders to the Brod and Gradiska regiments (draft), Aug. 7, 1848, Arhiv JAZU, Jelačić Papers, C-XVI-1.

[21] Springer, II, 436, and the Jelačić-Latour correspondence concerning the election of Grenzer delegates. Zagreb, April 27, and Vienna, May 2, 1848, KA KM Präs. MK 1848-857.

and degree of cooperation with the Serbs. Animosity toward Hungary, so it appeared, was the only unquestioned fact of Croatian politics. Nonetheless, the differences were patched up temporarily and the Sabor voted to send a joint Croat-Serb delegation to submit the demands of the South Slavs to the emperor.[22]

But in Innsbruck, where the court had moved from revolutionary Vienna, the delegation had already been preceded by the Hungarian prime minister, Count Batthyany, who hoped to bring Croatia back to obedience by a direct appeal to the emperor. On June 10 he obtained the famous imperial decree deposing Jelačić. Hrabowsky was reconfirmed and Latour was sharply reminded that all communications with the military border were to be channeled through Budapest.[23] Batthyany placed great faith in the efficacy of this document, but time for constitutional maneuvers was running out. By the middle of June the Austrian army had begun to master the revolution. Radetzky had resumed the offensive in Italy, and Windischgrätz had smashed the revolution in Prague. A definitely military party was emerging, determined to save the empire and centralized government, if necessary against the wishes of the emperor. Support of Austria's position in Italy became the touchstone of loyalty.[24] The military tried to obtain definite commitments from the Hungarians, but this the Budapest government was unwilling to do. Jelačić, however, gave immediate proof of his earnest intentions. News of the revolutionary events at home had led to unrest and even to attempted mass desertions among the Grenzer battalions in Italy.[25] On June 20 Jelačić issued a proclamation calling on the Grenzer in Radetzky's army to fight for the preservation of the state and the dynasty and assured them that "we feel ourselves strong enough to protect your homesteads and guard our national interests."[26] This proclamation earned Jelačić the solid support of the army command, and from Vienna Kulmer reported that "everybody

[22] Stiles, II, 380–81.
[23] The decree printed in Nordstein, pp. 166–73. Considered a forgery by some writers, it is now generally accepted as genuine. Kiszling, *Revolution*, I, 163–65.
[24] Oskar Regele, *Feldmarschall Radetzky: Sein Leben, Leistung, und Erbe* (Vienna, 1957), p. 360.
[25] On Grenzer unrest see Radetzky to Jelačić, Verona, June 23, 1848, Arhiv JAZU, Jelačić Papers, E-VII-3.
[26] Proclamation in Nordstein, pp. 191–92.

here is in your favor. The June 10 decree is null and void because it was not countersigned by any of the ministers."[27]

News of the edict aroused a wave of indignation in the Sabor and brought a temporary closing of the ranks. At the same time, the deposition of Jelačić prompted renewed demands for the immediate incorporation of the military border. And now that serfdom was ended, the Grenzer avidly supported this step.[28] Despite the Ban's opposition, the Sabor passed legislation that shifted control of the regiments from Vienna to Zagreb, provided for Grenzer participation in the political affairs of the kingdom, and abolished all economic restrictions. In addition, the Sabor once again asserted Croatia's claim to the Slavonian regiments.[29] At this point it appeared possible that Jelačić was losing control over the Grenzer, but then news arrived that Hrabowsky, evidently taking the June 10 decree at face value, had attacked Karlovci and that general fighting had broken out in southern Hungary.[30] Dissensions disappeared as the Sabor resolved in favor of immediate armed aid to the Serbs. "The bullets are cast, the muskets cleaned, packs are ready, and blades sharpened," declared one Grenzer delegate, and "we are prepared to march whenever the Ban commands."[31] But Jelačić refused to be rushed into hasty action. He recognized the problem of how to combine regular and popular warfare without precipitating revolutions in Croatia and Slavonia themselves. He did utilize the opportune emergency to obtain far-reaching powers from the Sabor and to suspend all legislation concerning the military border "until the restoration of peace." Then, on July 9, he prorogued the assembly indefinitely.[32]

There was one more attempt to mediate between Hungary and Croatia. Toward the end of July the popular Archduke Johann, acting as regent in the absence of the emperor, summoned Batthyany and Jelačić for a face-to-face meeting in

[27] Kulmer to Jelačić, Vienna, June 27, 1848, Arhiv JAZU, Jelačić Papers, D-I-3.

[28] Redlich, II, 215.

[29] Resolutions and decrees of the Sabor concerning the Military Border in Stephan Pejaković, *Aktenstücke zur Geschichte des kroatisch-slawonischen Landtages und der nationalen Bewegung vom Jahre 1848* (Vienna, 1861), pp. 52–68. Also Ognieslav M. Utiešenović, *Die Militärgrenze und die Verfassung. Eine Studie über den Ursprung und das Wesen der Militärgrenzinstitution und die Stellung derselben zur Landesverfassung* (Vienna, 1861), pp. 131–51.

[30] Hrabowsky's report of the action, KA FA 1848, Hrabowsky, VI-57.

[31] Cited in Springer, II, 442.

[32] Kiszling, *Revolution*, I, 165.

Vienna. But the encounter was fruitless.[33] After spending several days in Vienna to complete his arrangements with Latour, Jelačić returned to Croatia to find that during his absence unrest in the regiments had assumed serious proportions. The Grenzer were disappointed with the suspension of the various reforms and before his departure the Ban had already been forced to issue stern orders against all agitation.[34] But Budapest had taken advantage of the situation and issued decrees granting the Grenzer complete and unconditional possession of their land, the right to choose their occupations, the free election of their magistrates, and political representation.[35] These promises had special appeal in the Brod and Gradiska Regiments, and to counteract these developments, Jelačić was forced to issue a general order conceding, in principle, the right to dissolve the zadruge, the freedom of occupation, and relief from the labor obligations.[36] In addition, the popular Ban made a quick tour of the disaffected areas and by mid-August tranquility was restored.[37]

Meanwhile, Jelačić steadily continued to augment his forces. Volunteer units were raised in civil Croatia and the fifth battalions of the regiments were called out.[38] Every man that could be spared was withdrawn from the Turkish frontier and by early September fifty thousand men were under arms — twenty-two infantry battalions, thirty-three cavalry squadrons, and eighty-one light guns.[39] Grenzer formed the bulk of the infantry and artillery. In general they were reserves of indifferent quality, though the arrival of two first-line battalions of the Ottoschatz Regiment, released from service in Italy after the capitulation of Pesciera, provided welcome stiffening.[40] The cavalry included several squadrons of regular dragoons ordered in from Styria, but for the most part it consisted of Croatian

[33] Ferdinand Hauptmann, "Banus Jellačić und Feldmarschall Fürst Windisch-Grätz," *SOF*, 15 (1956), 373–74.

[34] Orders to the Brod and Gradiska Regiments, Arhiv JAZU, Jelačić Papers, C-VI-13.

[35] Hermann Wendel, *Der Kampf der Südslawen um Freiheit und Einheit* (Frankfurt, 1925), p. 237.

[36] Decree, Aug. 6, 1848, in Pejaković, pp. 111–14.

[37] Kiszling, *Revolution*, I, 221.

[38] Orders to Brgdr. Kempen, July 11 and Aug. 27, 1848, DAZ, Varia bgda. Petrinja F-2.

[39] Strength return, Sept., 1848, Arhiv JAZU, Jelačić Papers, F-II-3.

[40] Franz Bach, *Otočaner Regimentsgeschichte* (Karlstadt, 1853), pp. 226–32.

volunteers, *Banderialhusaren*, poorly trained and mounted.[41] Overall, the Croatian forces were short on heavy artillery, percussion muskets, and field equipment. Of the Grenzer only about half were armed and equipped on the regulation pattern; the rest assembled in their national costumes, bearing whatever arms could be procured — flintlocks, shotguns, even pikes.[42] Under instructions from Latour, military depots in Styria hastily forwarded additional supplies, and the administration and staff work was much improved when a number of senior staff officers who happened to be "on leave" in Croatia joined the Ban's field headquarters northeast of Warasdin.[43] Funds to pay and rations for the troops remained a major problem for the "Croatian-Slavonian Army," as it now was styled. Budapest, understandably, refused to release funds, but in July Latour managed to persuade his civilian colleagues in Vienna to advance money to Jelačić.[44] By the end of August funds were low again and Kulmer as well as Latour made arrangements to forward substantial sums.[45]

As the summer wore on, the Ban was under heavy pressure to take the offensive. In the Vojvodina, following a short armistice, fighting erupted again, and while the Serbs, led by Austrian "volunteer" officers and reinforced by volunteers from across the Danube, were holding their own, they demanded more active support from Croatia. On July 31 Patriarch Rajačić sent a stiff note to Jelačić demanding action,[46] and from Vienna Kulmer urged the immediate invasion of Hungary.[47] But Jelačić was reluctant to take such an irrevocable step without clear orders from above. But for the moment the imperial government was unwilling to invade Hungary, although negotiations with Budapest were leading nowhere. By late August, however, court and government circles favoring a more active course were gaining ground. The court returned to Vienna and even the liberal Austrian cabinet was beginning to regret the

---

[41] Jelačić to Latour (draft of a letter requesting regular cavalry), Zagreb, Aug. 21, 1848, Arhiv JAZU, Jelačić Papers, C-V-2.

[42] Situation report, Zagreb, Sept. 9, 1848, KA FA 1848, Jellachich, IX-15.

[43] Jelačić to Latour, Zagreb, Sept. 3, 1848, *ibid.*, IX-3.

[44] Redlich, I, Pt. 2, p. 50.

[45] Kulmer to Jelačić, Vienna, Sept. 8 and 9, 1848, assuring him that heavy artillery, stores, and money were on the way. Arhiv JAZU, Jelačić Papers, D-I-23.

[46] Rajačić to Jelačić, Karlovci, July 31, 1848, Arhiv JAZU, *ibid.*, E-VII-6/1.

[47] Kulmer to Jelačić, Vienna, Aug. 14, 1848, *ibid.*, D-I-7.

extensive concessions made to Hungary in the spring. Under the influence of the centralist-minded Minister of Justice Alexander Bach, the government decided on August 29 to reintroduce centralization in the financial and military affairs of the Habsburg monarchy. Hungary, which since mid-July was organizing a purely Hungarian army, was told to cease military preparations and the military borders were to revert officially to the control of the Vienna war ministry.[48] Hungarian protests were dismissed, and on September 4 the emperor gave further proof of the changed situation and formally reinstated Jelačić in all his offices.[49]

By this time the advocates of armed intervention had daily grown more impatient with the Ban. On August 28 Kulmer warned Jelačić that confidence in him was rapidly declining and that only the actual invasion of Hungary would restore it. And in that case, asserted Kulmer, "you will receive imperial sanction."[50] A few days later Kulmer insisted that "the highest circles in Vienna expect, hope, and desire that you will not stop until you have entered Budapest. Therefore, good friend, advance!"[51] Finally, on September 4, Kulmer advised that immediate invasion was necessary to forestall a possible reconciliation between Vienna and Budapest.[52] Although Jelačić still would have preferred to wait for a direct imperial command, he decided to act. His troops were getting restive, the Serbs were growing most difficult, and the Hungarian forces daily more numerous. The imperial letter restoring him to office had to serve as his mandate. On September 8 he issued movement orders, and on September 11 his advance guard crossed the Drava without encountering any resistance.[53]

The invasion proved a disappointment. At first, to be sure, there was little resistance. The regular army units in Hungary were caught in a conflict of loyalties. Generally, the enlisted men of Hungarian nationality, including the Szekler of the Transylvanian Grenzer regiments, stood with the Budapest

---

[48] Springer, I, 493–95; Kiszling, *Revolution*, I, 236–38.

[49] Ferdinand to Jelačić, Schönbrunn, Sept. 4, 1848, KA FA 1848, Jellachich, IX-7 1/2. The imperial letter also printed in Stiles, II, 397–98.

[50] Kulmer to Jelačić, Vienna, Aug. 27, 1848, Arhiv JAZU, Jelačić Papers, D-I-13.

[51] Kulmer to Jelačić, Vienna, Sept. 12, 1848, *ibid.*, D-I-17.

[52] Kulmer to Jelačić, Vienna, Sept. 4, 1848, *ibid.*, D-I-22.

[53] Springer, II, 460–61; report, evening Sept. 11, 1848, KA FA 1848, Jellachich, IX-16.

government, but the officers were divided.[54] Some declared for the national government, others joined the Ban, and still others, like the commandant of Fortress Esseg (Osijek) declared themselves neutral.[55] The Hungarian forces slowly fell back on Budapest where the Batthyany ministry resigned on September 12 and the fiery Kossuth was hard at work organizing national resistance. But as the Ban advanced deeper into the country his difficulties mounted and the illusion that this campaign was going to be a walk-over was soon dispelled. The Croatian troops, especially the fifth battalions, revealed a most deplorable lack of discipline and looted, robbed, and not infrequently murdered the unfortunate villagers on the route of march. As a result the villages were soon deserted, while the aroused peasants joined the national guard, cut off stragglers, and hovered on the lines of communication.[56] At the same time, the spectacle of actual civil war had caused second thoughts in Vienna. The radicals were openly hostile to the Croatian intervention and the cautious Prime Minister Wessenberg found it expedient to disavow all connections with Jelačić.[57] Even Latour lost heart and in reply to a request from Jelačić for a direct order to the regular officers in the Hungarian forces to cease resistance, informed the Ban on September 19 that as a constitutional minister his hands were tied by the wishes of the cabinet.[58]

On September 29, finally, came the first serious encounter with Hungarian national troops, drawn up to defend their capital at Pakozd-Velencze. The battle actually was indecisive, but Jelačić, always more a political general than a first-rate field commander, lost his nerve. Under the cover of a three-day armistice he ordered the fifth battalions back to Croatia, and then, abandoning his dreams of conquest, he retreated northward with the remainder of his badly disorganized forces.[59]

[54] The German line regiments in Hungary joined the Ban. On the attitude of the officers see Rudolf Kiszling, "Das Nationalitätenproblem in Habsburgs Wehrmacht 1848–1918," *DR*, 4 (1959), 83–84; also the report, undated, KA, KM Präs. 1848-5823; and the letter Jelačić to Count Téléky (draft), Warasdin, Sept. 10, 1848, Arhiv JAZU, Jelačić Papers, C-XXVII-1, 2.

[55] Springer, II, 528–29.

[56] *Ibid.*, pp. 532–33; Bach, pp. 238–39, and A. Schütte, *Ungarn und der Ungarische Unabhängigkeitskrieg* (2 vols.; Leipzig, 1850), II, 127–29, 137–40.

[57] Kiszling, *Revolution*, I, 227.

[58] Latour to Jelačić, Vienna, Sept. 19, 1848, Arhiv JAZU, Jelačić Papers, E-VII-1.

[59] Battle reports, KA FA 1848, Jellachich, IX-148, 149, 150, and 151. Evaluation of the battle in Kiszling, *Revolution*, I, 226.

The Ban was saved from total disaster by the Hungarian failure to press pursuit and by a sudden change in the political picture. On the day of the battle, Count Lamberg, who in a last effort to restore peace in Hungary had been appointed imperial plenipotentiary, was murdered by a mob in Pest. The imperial government answered the event with a decree of October 4, naming the Ban commissioner for all the lands of the Hungarian crown.[60] News of this appointment, which finally gave him the emperor's public blessing, reached Jelačić on October 7, followed the next day by dispatches that a radical revolution had broken out in Vienna, that Latour had been murdered, and that the court had fled the city.[61] This development allowed Jelačić to proclaim that he deliberately had diverted his forces north to save the emperor.[62]

Brave words however could not hide the fact that the intervention had failed. Even while Jelačić was moving north, the right wing of his army under Major General Roth, which was to have united with the main body outside Budapest, found itself cut off by Hungarian troops and forced to capitulate, seven thousand strong, on October 6.[63] The fifth battalions, too, found the retreat difficult and only managed to extricate themselves with heavy casualties.[64] Jelačić crossed the Austrian frontier on October 9 and the next day he appeared before Vienna where his forces, some twenty-five thousand men, were joined by imperial units withdrawn from the city.[65] The Ban favored taking the city by coup, but Prince Windischgrätz, who had assumed command of all Austrian forces except those serving under Radetzky, sent orders to wait until he and his army arrived from Bohemia.[66] In the interlude, the Vienna revolutionaries tried to negotiate with Jelačić but were rebuffed.[67] There was no fighting and for a while the Grenzer were able to visit the taverns in town and to return freely to their camp.[68]

[60] Copy in KA FA 1848, Jellachich, X-7-1/4a.
[61] Kulmer to Jelačić, Oct. 2 and 6, 1848, Arhiv JAZU, Jelačić Papers, E-VII-13, 14.
[62] Jelačić's proclamation "On the march from the Drava to Vienna," *ibid.,* C-I-1.
[63] Schütte, II, 141.
[64] Bach, p. 235.
[65] R. John Rath, *The Viennese Revolution of 1848* (Austin, 1957), p. 335.
[66] Hauptmann, pp. 382–83.
[67] Rath, pp. 335–36; correspondence between Jelačić and parliament in Nordstein, pp. 285–88.
[68] Hauptmann, pp. 382–83.

Then on October 21, Windischgrätz appeared and preparations were made to storm the city. The actual assault began on October 28, with the Grenzer assigned the Prater-Landstrasse sector. They carried their objectives, but their record was marred by indiscriminate looting and plundering.[69] Fighting continued for several days, but after a Hungarian relief column was repulsed at Schwechat on October 30, resistance collapsed and the city capitulated.

Vienna was occupied and placed under martial law. The Grenzer made their formal entry on November 1, and the Ban, with his colorful Seressaner bodyguard, established his headquarters in the Palais Beatrix on the Landstrasse. Although publicly acclaimed a hero, Windischgrätz did not regard the Ban highly and Jelačić was lucky to retain a subordinate command.[70] His immediate concern was to restore the discipline and morale of his troops. On November 4 Jelačić issued orders that the familes of twenty-seven deserters from the Lika Regiment were to be expelled from the country.[71] Morale was not improved when news arrived the next day that the Bosnians had taken advantage of the absence of troops and had raided into the Ogulin Regiment.[72] The raid, however, was repulsed by homeguards, and on express orders from the Ban, mobilization of additional troops for field service continued.[73]

The conquest of Vienna emboldened the Austrian absolutists. On November 21 the elderly Wessenberg was succeeded as prime minister by Prince Schwarzenberg, and on December 2 Emperor Ferdinand abdicated in favor of his nephew Francis Joseph. The constituent assembly was removed from Vienna and relocated at Kremsier, a small Moravian town, where shorn of any real power it continued its deliberations. Meanwhile, the government proceeded with its main task — the subjugation of Hungary. In the winter of 1848 Windischgrätz advanced into Hungary and occupied Budapest, but the

[69] Croatian ordre de bataille, Oct. 27, 1848, KA FA 1848, Jellachich, IX-211, 212. For the Grenzer excesses, see Rath, p. 353. All troops, however, Germans, Bohemians, and Galicians, were equally guilty, but it was the Grenzer who were later exclusively blamed. Springer, II, 576.

[70] Kiszling, *Revolution*, I, 227.

[71] Order, Vienna, Nov. 4, as published Zagreb, Nov. 10, 1848, DAZ, Zagr. gkda. F-96.

[72] Reports of Turkish incursions, Oct.–Nov., 1848, *ibid.*, Varia bgda. Petrinja, F-2.

[73] Orders, Dec. 5, 1848, by FZM Dahlen, establishing 6th battalions in all regiments. *Ibid.*

Hungarian army was not defeated and withdrew to reform in the Debreczen area. In early April the Hungarians counter-attacked and forced Windischgrätz to evacuate the country. Jelačić, who had commanded the 1st Corps during the advance, covered the retreat, and then, his force, restored to independent status as the Southern Army, moved to the Bačka to protect Croatia and the Vojvodina against a Hungarian offensive.[74]

Throughout the winter and early spring Jelačić had to contend with growing unrest in Croatia. There was suspicion that the suspension of the Sabor had been a deliberate move to frustrate nationalist aims. The Illyrians regained strength and Jelačić confessed to Kulmer that agitation in "Croatia and the Military Border give me more trouble than the command of my army."[75] The suspicions of the nationalists were in fact well founded. The Schwarzenberg cabinet was determined to create a unitary, centralized Austrian state and on March 4, brushing aside a constitution drafted by the Kremsier assembly, it handed down a new constitution designed to end once and for all the troublesome historic rights of the various lands.[76] Loyal Croatia was treated no better than rebellious Hungary. Although Croatia and Vojvodina were separated from the Hungarian crown and made directly dependent on Vienna, the constitution disappointed nationalist aspirations. Croatia received certain additional territories — Rijeka, the Medjumurje district, and the three eastern comitats of Slavonia. In addition, the Brod and Gradiska regiments were formally combined with the Croatian-Slavonian Military Border. Dalmatia, however, remained separated from Croatia and the acquisition of the Slavonian comitats, predominantly Serb, embittered relations with the Vojvodina.[77] And finally, "the most ardent demand of Croatian nationalism,"[78] the union of the military border with civil Croatia was denied by the new constitution which stated that "the Military Border and all its inhabitants constitute an integral part of the imperial army."[79] On March 9 Kulmer com-

---

[74] Kiszling, *Revolution*, II, 56.

[75] Cited in Joseph A. Frhr. v. Helfert, *Die Geschichte Österreichs vom Ausgange des Wiener Oktober-Aufstandes 1848* (6 vols.; Prague and Leipzig, 1869–76), III, 177.

[76] Adolph Schwarzenberg, *Prince Felix zu Schwarzenberg, Prime Minister of Austria, 1848–1852* (New York, 1946), pp. 50, 62.

[77] Rudolf Kiszling, *Die Kroaten* (Graz-Cologne, 1956), pp. 57–58.

[78] Characterized thus by Redlich, II, 215.

[79] Printed in Utiešenović, pp. 53–54.

mented to Jelačić that "most probably our radicals will make a lot of noise about the separate status of the border . . . but this will quiet down once the Grenzer demonstrate their preference for military status." [80] Kulmer, however, misjudged the temper of the border. The Grenzer were deeply vexed by the continuation of the old arrangements and even Jelačić was moved to protest. In the end, though, he was satisfied with the imperial assurance that the Grenzer would participate in "all the concessions made to our other peoples." [81] It appears that the Ban did not at first support the new arrangement wholeheartedly, because in April Kulmer chided him for his attitude. "I understand," wrote Kulmer, "that you are supposed to have made statements favoring the incorporations of the border. Of course, I do not believe this, but it is regrettable that such rumors should even get started." [82]

For the next few months, from May to August, 1849, Jelačić devoted himself to the command of his army, which he led with indifferent success in southern Hungary. He was not only outnumbered, but also outgeneraled by the enemy,[83] and it was a sign of his decreased influence that in May Radetzky bluntly refused his request for the release of seven Grenzer battalions from Italy for service in Hungary.[84] At the same time, relations between Jelačić and Feldmarschall Leutnant Baron Haynau, who had taken command of operations in Hungary, were extremely poor and the Ban was often left in complete ignorance of the intentions of the supreme command.[85] Russian intervention finally brought about victory for the Austrians and the last Hungarian army capitulated on August 13, 1849.

The military border received little support for its services. The promised benefits materialized in the new *Grundgesetz* of May 7, 1850, which made some economic concessions but preserved the military character of the institution and its subordi-

[80] Kulmer to Jelačić, Vienna, March 9, 1849, Arhiv JAZU, Jelačić Papers, D-II-22.

[81] Franz Joseph to Jelačić, Schönbrunn, March 31, 1849, in Utiešenović, pp. 151–52.

[82] Kulmer to Jelačić, Vienna, March 9, 1849, Arhiv JAZU, Jelačić Papers, D-II-24.

[83] Kiszling, *Revolution*, II, 11, 56.

[84] Radetzky's memorandum, Milan, May 25, 1849, KA MKSM 1849-206.

[85] Friedrich Walter, "Von Windischgrätz über Welden zu Haynau," in Walter and Harold Steinacker, *Die Nationalitätenfrage im alten Ungarn und die Südostpolitik Wiens* (Munich, 1959), pp. 121–22.

nation to the war ministry.[86] Landholdings now became actual and inheritable Grenzer property and occupational restrictions were lifted, but all able-bodied men remained permanently enrolled as soldiers, military justice was maintained, and the regiments continued as the exclusive administrative units. The new law disappointed the Grenzer, who had hoped for substantial relief from their military burdens. That Austria had nothing more to offer to her loyal Grenzer was considered a breach of faith; unrest, disaffection, and a marked deterioration in morale followed. This was so evident that Jelačić was forced to warn the Grenzer that they had "bought peace at a heavy price and had the right to enjoy it." But, continued the Ban, agitation threatened the new rights and only "firm attachment to lawful authority can realize these much deserved benefits."[87]

The status of the Croatian-Slavonian Military Border was not improved when on December 31, 1851, an imperial patent abolished the 1849 constitution and inaugurated a period of neo-absolutist government. The new regime regarded all national aspirations, including the South Slav, with profound distrust. "South Slav nationalism," one officer wrote, "hides dangerous tendencies behind the mask of outward loyalty."[88] Therefore, the authorities suppressed all nationalist agitation, whether it originated in Zagreb, Belgrade, or Budapest, and embarked on a policy of Germanization that negated the limited concessions made in the new Grundgesetz.[89] Although the law provided that the native language was to be used in the administration, the courts, and the schools, German was in fact used throughout. At the same time, the military authorities placed obstacles in the way of economic improvement, especially to prevent dissolution of the zadruge.[90]

But such measures could not halt the decay of the traditional border society; they could only aggravate the economic circum-

[86] The *Grenz Grundgesetz* of 1850 printed conveniently in Utiešenović, pp. 153–59.

[87] Proclamation (copy), Vienna, July 20, 1850, DAZ Varia bgda. Petrinja, F-2.

[88] FML Adolph v. Schütte to FZM Haynau, Temesvar, Jan. 13, 1850, in Aleksa Ivić, *Arhivska gradja o srpskim i hrvatskim književnim i kulturnim radnicima*, *Zbornik IJK*, 3 (Belgrade, 1931), 160–61.

[89] Instructions from Schwarzenberg to Jelačić concerning supervision of Serb General Kničanin, visiting the Croatian-Slavonian Border, KA KM Präs. (secret), 1850-6343; Wendel, p. 287.

[90] A. Klein, "Militär-Statistische Beschreibung der k.k. Grenzländer," *ÖMZ*, 12 (1871), 130–33.

stances and the political discontent. Economically the situation of the Grenzer improved little in the period following the revolution of 1848. Agricultural production remained far behind civil Croatia.[91] Banditry continued to flourish in the Lika and Banal regiments and poverty was general.[92] A French military observer wrote that the government was aware of the situation and wanted to raise the prosperity of the population, but at the same time it also wanted to preserve the military framework and these two aims were incompatible.[93] And an English traveler concluded that "improvement is impossible under the present system."[94] The advance of capitalism and the economic changes in the rest of the Austrian monarchy could not be stopped at the boundaries of the military border. In 1858 the Austrian ministry of finance and economics requested the dissolution of the border institution, but Emperor Francis Joseph refused.[95] He did, however, reestablish the separate corps of administrative officers which had been dissolved in 1851.[96]

The efforts to keep the regiments uncontaminated by the spirit of nationalism, isolated from the new economic currents, and under exclusive military control were part of the general Austrian experiment in centralized absolute government and no longer dictated by any special considerations about the fighting potential of the Grenzer. Indeed, the military border establishment was no longer considered a serious military factor. As a leading Austrian military historian put it: "The failure of Jelačić's offensive against the Hungarian capital was a turning point in the evaluation of the Croatian-Slavonian troops. They had been overrated."[97] And in the 1850's the organiza-

---

[91] In 1864 the grain production in the regiments was only one-half that of civil Croatia. L. Katus, "Hauptzüge der kapitalistischen Entwicklung der Landwirtschaft in den südslawischen Gebieten der Österreichisch-Ungarischen Monarchie," in V. Sandor and P. Hanak, eds., *Studien zur Geschichte der Österreichisch-Ungarischen Monarchie* (Budapest, 1961), pp. 131–32.

[92] Reports concerning banditry, including raising the bounty for the capture of bandits and the proclamation of martial law in the 2d Banal, Zagreb, Oct. 15, 1854, KA MKSM 1854-3890, and KA KM Präs. 1854, 184 and 1117.

[93] Capt. M. de Chaulieu, 1863, AHG Recon. Autriche 1805, pp. 63–64.

[94] George A. Spottiswoode, "A tour in civil and military Croatia, and part of Hungary," in Frederick Galton, *Vacation tourists and notes in 1860* (London, 1861), p. 91.

[95] Schwicker, *Geschichte der österreichischen Militärgrenze*, pp. 390–92.

[96] The administrative training institute in Graz had also been dissolved in 1851. The new "Organisierungs-Statut für die Militär-Grenz-Verwaltungs-Branche," May 11, 1858, in KA Schriftgut, F-42.

[97] Kiszling, *Revolution*, I, 227; Springer, II, 578.

tion, training, and equipment of the Grenzer units was unsuitable against troops of the major western powers. In 1853 the Grenzer were mobilized to demonstrate against the Porte, and in the next year contingents from the Croatian-Slavonian regiments took part in the Austrian concentration against Russia.[98] On both occasions, however, the Grenzer manifested open disaffection which caused serious apprehension for the high command.[99]

During these years Croatia was effectively administered by foreign officials and Ban Jelačić began to have less and less influence. He commanded the Grenzer in 1853, but soon thereafter he began to show signs of the mental decline that clouded his last years. As his influence failed, the Grenzer became more and more restive, and when he died in 1859, Croatia as well as the military border had become completely estranged from Vienna.

[98] Franz Vaniček, *Specialgeschichte der Militärgrenze* (4 vols.; Vienna, 1875), IV, 382–83.

[99] "Geschichte des serbisch-banatischen Armeecorps," MS, vol. 36, KA Schriftgut, pp. 87–90, 131–32, 136–37.

9

—ᐧ—ᐧ—ᐧ—ᐧ—

TOWARD DISSOLUTION OF THE MILITARY BORDER: 1859–71

The troubled years of neo-absolutism in the Austrian Empire were interrupted by war in 1859. During this brief conflict the disappointing performance of Austria's army illustrated the empire's internal weaknesses. Austrian strategy was hampered by constant fears of internal revolt, while on the battlefield there was a marked hesitation to employ the new open-order tactics, made necessary by the increased performance of rifled arms, because the high command feared mass desertions of non-German troops. Therefore, the Austrian army was unable to exploit its superior Lorenz rifle, and because the generals did not trust their soldiers to fight in open order, they continued to have them advance in close formations, with flags flying and drums beating, and to rely on the massed bayonet charge.[1] The results were poor and the performance of troops mediocre. "Suppressed classes and peoples," one Austrian staff officer remarked bitterly, "do not furnish very enthusiastic soldiers."[2]

The same considerations affected the Grenzer regiments from the Croatian-Slavonian Border. Their combat effectiveness declined, though it remains an open question whether this was primarily the result of the upsurge of nationalism, or the result of antiquated methods and leadership. Throughout

[1] Hans Delbrück and others, *Geschichte der Kriegskunst im Rahmen der politischen Geschichte* (7 vols.; Berlin, 1900–1937), V, 229–30, 342, 425–28. See, however, the indignant denial in Heinrich v. Srbik, *Aus Österreichs Vergangenheit* (Salzburg, 1949), pp. 130–31.

[2] Eduard Ritter Bartels v. Bartberg, *Der Krieg im Jahre Jahre 1859. Nach offiziellen Quellen nicht offiziell bearbeitet* (Bamberg, 1894), p. 261.

the Italian campaign the authorities were worried about the possible effects of enemy propaganda on the disaffected Grenzer and they also took extensive precautions against a South Slav rising in Dalmatia, Croatia, and the military border. And when the imperial government was forced to concede a greater degree of political freedom after the lost war, it found the Grenzer closely aligned with opposition South Slav nationalists.

Early in 1859 Austrian relations with the Kingdom of Sardinia became progressively more embittered until in April Austria blundered into war, facing not only the Sardinians but also the well equipped and competently led French army. Although the Austrians had been concentrating troops in northern Italy since the beginning of the year, they missed an excellent, though brief, opportunity of dealing with the Sardinians before their allies arrived in force. The ten regiments of the Croatian-Slavonian Border mobilized in March and moved without incident to Italy in April.[3] Only the first and second battalions took the field, however; the third battalions remained at home to guard the frontier. The Lika, Ottoschatz, Ogulin, Szluin, Warasdin-Kreutz, Gradiska, and 2d Banal battalions joined the field army and fought at Montebello, Magenta, and Solferino. The Warasdin–St. Georg, Brod, and 1st Banal units formed part of the strategic reserve and were on guard in the rear areas. In addition, the various Seressaner units were formed into light mounted cavalry, but the war was over before they left their home stations.[4]

This time the fighting spirit of the Grenzer came under severe criticism. According to one critic the enlisted men were only brave "when they were stealing chickens, and exhibited an extraordinary concern for their safety during battle," while the officers were extremely phlegmatic, "partly due to the national character and partly because they had no national feelings and only a small measure of dynastic loyalty."[5] Perhaps this was too drastic an accusation, but in 1860 the war ministry did order an investigation into the conduct of certain Grenzer officers alleged to have been "faint-hearted, timorous, and con-

[3] FML Šokčević to FML Archduke Wilhelm, Zagreb, April 13, 1859, KA KM 1859-1433.

[4] Alphons v. Wrede, *Geschichte der k. und k. Wehrmacht*, Supplementary volumes to *MKA* (5 vols.; Vienna, 1893–1903), III, 803; V, 257–298.

[5] Bartels v. Bartberg quoted in Delbrück, V, 352–53.

fused" during the campaign.[6] Even more serious, however, were rising doubts about the overall reliability of the Grenzer.

During the war Cavour, as well as Napoleon III, entertained various plans to exploit national unrest in the Habsburg Empire. From Turin, the exiled Louis Kossuth was scheming to raise another great insurrection in Hungary. Croatia and the Grenzer played a prominent part in these plans. Despite the memories of 1848 there was a definite rapprochement between the Hungarian exiles and South Slav nationalists, disappointed with the treatment they had received. As early as 1851 Kossuth appealed to the Grenzer to rise against the Germanizing policies of the centralist regime,[7] and when war was coming closer he received encouragement and aid from Cavour.[8] In early 1859 Kossuth formed a Hungarian legion and with the aid of Eugen Kvaternik, a Croatian extremist, schemes were laid to induce Grenzer to desert and join this unit. This enterprise, to be sure, had only limited success. But there were wider ramifications. In the spring and early summer of 1859 Louis Napoleon had plans for a landing on the Dalmatian coast, to be supported by a rising in Croatia and on the military border, followed by a link-up with the Hungarians and a march on Vienna. In the end, however, Louis Napoleon decided to conclude an early armistice with Austria and merely used the Hungarian-Croatian threat to frighten the Austrians.[9]

The spectre of insurrection had indeed caused jitters in Vienna. Regular troops were diverted to Croatia and coastal defenses strengthened.[10] An English traveler noted that Croatia, as far inland as Karlstadt, had been placed in a state of defense and that the "mountains swarmed with soldiers."[11] At the same

[6] KM to Gkdo. Agram, Vienna, Apr. 29, 1869, DAZ Zagr. gkda. F-202. See also the file of action reports, investigations, and recommendations for 1859 in *ibid.*, Varia, bgda. Petrinja, F-3.

[7] Copy of leaflets found in the Banal regiments, with covering letter to Jelačić, Petrinja, Feb. 8, 1851, *ibid.*, F-2.

[8] For Cavour's plans see Angelo Tamborra, *Cavour e i Balcani* (Turin, 1958), pp. 212–20. Also Eugen Kvaternik, *La Croatie et la confédération Italienne* (Paris, 1859).

[9] Ernst Birke, *Frankreich und Ostmitteleuropa im 19. Jahrhundert* (Cologne-Graz, 1960), pp. 216–17.

[10] For troop movements and coastal fortifications, see KA KM Präs. 1859, 1841, 1845, 1900, and 2199.

[11] George A. Spottiswoode, "A tour in civil and military Croatia, and part of Hungary," in Frederick Galton, *Vacation tourists and notes in 1860* (London, 1861), pp. 83–85.

time, a number of preventive arrests were made and the scare continued into the next year when the war ministry alerted the Croatian-Slavonian command against subversive designs to disrupt the monarchy.[12] On August 31, 1860, a personal order from Francis Joseph advised the new Ban, Feldmarschall Leutnant Joseph Baron Šokčević, to arrest all suspects and to send them to Fortress Josephstadt for internment.[13] But the Austrian authorities were careful not to antagonize the Grenzer and issued instructions that returned prisoners of war who had joined the Hungarian legion should not be prosecuted.[14] Also in 1861 a "Commission to alleviate conditions on the Military Border," sat in Vienna. Its aims, however, were moderate and in the end it merely recommended restrictions on corporal punishment and minor reductions in taxes and salt prices.[15]

Such small concessions, however, could no longer satisfy the smoldering resentments of the Grenzer. One lasting result of the events from 1849 to 1860 was that it had brought the Grenzer of the Croatian-Slavonian Border and the nationalist politicians of civil Croatia closer together. This combination, with the profound shift in Grenzer attitudes, was strikingly revealed in 1861 when the February Patent once more permitted a session of the Sabor. Under the provisions of the patent the various diets functioned only as electoral colleges for the extended imperial council, the *gesammten Reichsrat*, to be set up in Vienna, but the session provided an opportunity for Croatian protests against the central authorities. When the house assembled in April, 1861, the delegates divided into three major groupings. The strongest faction was the National Liberals (*narodna liberalna stranka*), who regarded Vienna and Budapest with almost equal distrust. They were opposed by the Unionists or Magyarones, who desired a closer union with Hungary. Uncomfortably situated between the two opposing groups were the Independ-

[12] KM to Gkdo. Agram, March 4, 1860, DAZ Zagr. gkda. F 200-202.

[13] Francis Joseph to the military commanders in Transylvania, Vojvodina, Croatia, and the Military Border, (secret), Vienna, Aug. 31, 1860, KA MKSM 1860-3463. Jelačić died on May 19, 1859. He was temporarily succeeded by Count Coronini-Cronberg, who, however, in the face of mounting difficulties, resigned in June, 1860, *ibid.*, 1860-2401. The emperor then appointed FML Šokčević, Jelačić's former aide, *ibid.*, 1860-2403.

[14] KM to all commands, Vienna, Aug. 23, 1859, DAZ Zagr. gkda. F-193.

[15] Protocol of the commission, Vienna, Nov. 16–Dec. 21, 1861, with enclosures, KA Schriftgut F-25. Imperial decision on the proposals made by the commission, Vienna, April 19, 1862, KA MKSM 1862-49-6.

ents, who tended to look toward Vienna. Finally, there were the ultra-Croat followers of the fiery Ante Starčević and the deputies from the Croatian-Slavonian Border regiments.[16]

The imperial government had been most reluctant to concede representation of the Grenzer and then only with the provision that their deputies were to limit themselves to participation in the election of delegates to the imperial council. Any discussion of the military status of the border was specifically prohibited.[17] Attempts to do just that were overruled by the Ban acting on specific instructions from Vienna. The Grenzer, however, still retained an almost childlike confidence in the "good emperor who opposed the just demands of his soldiers because he was misinformed," and so they sent a delegation to Vienna to present their grievances to the monarch in person. What occurred during the audience is not a matter of record, but it appears that the delegation was curtly dismissed.[18] Such treatment failed to encourage the Grenzer to identify their interests with those of the central government. On their return the Grenzer delegates joined the nationalists and on August 5, 1861, furnished the decisive margin of votes against Croatian participation in the imperial council. Exasperated, the Ban now declared that the mandates of the Grenzer deputies had expired and despite protests by the Sabor ordered them to rejoin their regiments.[19] In Vienna the war ministry was much alarmed by this unprecedented defection of the Grenzer. Orders went out to keep the former deputies under close supervision and to transfer all native officers suspected of nationalist leanings.[20]

[16] Vaso Bogdanov, "Uloga Vojne Krajine i njenih zastupnika u Hrv. Saboru 1861," *Zbornik HIJA*, 3 (1960), 59–214, is the most complete account based on the journals of the assembly. Cf. Martin Polić, *Parlamentarna povjest kraljevine Hrvatske, Slavonije, i Dalmacije* (2 vols.; Zagreb, 1899–1900), I, 93–106.

[17] Messages on this subject exchanged between Vienna and Zagreb, including code telegrams in KA KM Präs. 1861-2248, and KA MKSM 1861-1692, and 1842.

[18] On the question of the delegation see Šokčević's message, Zagreb, July 20, KA KM Präs. 1861-337, and the telegram from Vienna, July 27, *ibid.*, 3401.

[19] Šokčević's report, Zagreb, Aug. 6, 1861, *ibid.*, 3566, and also KA KM Präs. 1861-3867.

[20] Imperial instructions, April 3, 1862, KA MKSM 1862-49-5, and KA KM Präs. 1862-2100. The report on the loyalty of Col. Petar Preradović, Zagreb, Nov. 12, 1862, is indicative of the fears of the administration. "Colonel Preradović," wrote Šokčević, "shares the opinion of the extremists that the Croatian nation has been suppressed . . . and it is in the interest of

But the purge misfired when several of the most active officers resigned and took service in Serbia from where they continued and even intensified their agitation.

For years the growing Serb national state had enlisted sympathy and support among the Grenzer, especially in the Orthodox regiments. Although the national movement on the border became divided by two centers of attraction, one in Zagreb and the other in Belgrade, there always had been a good deal of common feeling between Catholic and Orthodox Grenzer. Then, too, the events of 1848 also had created considerable sentiment for South Slav cooperation in civil Croatia and Serbia which cut across divisive religious loyalties. Moreover, an opportunity for national cooperation lay close at hand in Bosnia, where a Christian Slav population simmered with discontent under Turkish misrule. Successful insurrection here not only would provoke Serbian intervention but also would exert almost irresistible pressure on the Grenzer to give active support. In the eyes of some South Slav nationalists such a great war of liberation might well be the first step in the creation of a South Slav state comprised of Serbia, Bosnia, and the South Slav parts of the Habsburg Empire. Rumors of such a scheme had reached Vienna as early as 1845,[21] and they aroused enough anxiety there that plans for a preventive military occupation of Bosnia were made.[22] Plans for a Bosnian insurrection were revived after 1862 by Major Antunje Orešković, one of the former Grenzer officers in the Serbian service who was organizing a revolutionary network in Bosnia with connections on the Croatian-Slavonian Border.[23] Some of his collaborators were arrested by the Austrian authorities, but attempts to seize Orešković during his surreptitious visits to Croatia failed. Sum-

the service that he should not be employed in this region." Aleksa Ivić, *Arhivska gradja o srpskim i hrvatskim književnim i kulturnim radnicima, Zbornik IJK*, 3 (Belgrade, 1931), 134–35.

[21] Col. Mayerhoffer's report, Belgrade, Jan. 26, 1845, Gyula Miskolczy, *A Horvat kérdés története es irományi a rendi állam korában* (2 vols.; Budapest, 1927–28), II, 266–67; Fran Zwitter *et al.*, *Les problèmes nationaux dans la monarchie des Habsbourgs* (Belgrade, 1960), pp. 48–49.

[22] Occupation plans, March, 1854, KA MKSM 1854-874.

[23] Šokčević's report, Feb. 11, 1862, Zagreb, KA KM Präs. 1862-592. See also Hermann Wendel, *Bismarck und Serbien im Jahre 1866* (Berlin, 1927), pp. 19–27, 58, and Johann A. Reiswitz, *Belgrad-Berlin, Berlin Belgrad, 1866–71* (Munich, 1936), pp. 64–65. For Orešković see KA Konduitenliste 1861, GIR 11, and the article by V. Belić, *Narodna enciklopedija srpsko-hrvatsko-slovenačka* (4 vols.; Zagreb, 1925–29), III, 213.

ming up the situation in 1863, Šokčević concluded that although the majority of the Grenzer were still loyal, a major upheaval in Bosnia would have the most serious repercussions on the border.[24]

That same year, however, it seemed that the political constellation in Croatia once more favored the reestablishment of the traditional close relationship between the Grenzer and Vienna. A temporary alliance between the Unionists and the National Liberals alienated the fiercely anti-Hungarian Grenzer, and during the November, 1865, session of the Sabor the border deputies joined the government-supported Independents.[25] The Sabor, despite the wishes of the government, once again went on record as demanding the abolition of the military border.

In the spring of 1866 war with Prussia and Italy threatened, and the border regiments mobilized for the last time in their long history. Mobilization was not popular on the border this time, and to the former Grenzer officers in Bosnia, especially to Orešković, the moment seemed opportune for a huge South Slav insurrection under the pretense of a war of liberation in Bosnia.[26] The conspirators had made Prussian and Italian contacts and by early spring of 1866 a variety of schemes for a South Slav rising were under active consideration in Berlin and Florence as well as in Belgrade.[27] But the orderly, if unenthusiastic, mobilization of the regiments removed the necessary cadres, and Italy and Serbia hesitated to commit themselves. In Prussia interest disappeared after the rapid victories in Bohemia eliminated prospects of protracted Austrian resistance.[28]

Chances of success for such far-fetched undertakings were in any case doubtful, but the realization that the Slavs, even the Grenzer, were no longer reliable, influenced Austrian negotiations with Hungary which had been under way since 1865. When the negotiations were brought to a successful conclusion in 1867, the new dualism was exclusively a compromise

[24] Šokčević's report, Feb. 15, 1863, KA KM Präs. 1863-537, and Andreas Kienast, *Die Legion Klapka* (Vienna, 1900), pp. 50–51.

[25] The competence of the border deputies had again been restricted by imperial order. Report of Col. Schrott, Border Dept. HKR, June 12, 1865, KA Schriftgut F-57, no. 13.

[26] Kienast, pp. 60–61, 85–86; Wendel, pp. 36–37, 74–77.

[27] *Ibid.*, pp. 44–47; Reiswitz, pp. 65–69.

[28] On the mobilization, Count Usedom, Prussian envoy in Florence to Bismarck, Apr. 28, 1866, *ibid.*, pp. 57, n. 17, and 215; Wendel, pp. 38–40, 92–99.

between the emperor and the Hungarians. The Croatians, after attempting to treat with Vienna as well as Budapest, were left to make the best terms they could with the new Hungarian government. Proving obstreperous, the Sabor was dissolved by imperial decree, and in 1868 a new house, with a manufactured Unionist majority, concluded a Hungarian-Croatian subcompromise. In this agreement, the *nagoda*, Croatia-Slavonia was defined as an integral part of the Hungarian kingdom; all decisions regarding military and financial matters were reserved to the Budapest government. Accordingly, the agreement stipulated that Hungary would work for the reincorporation of the Croatian-Slavonian Military Border into the Croatian state, a point well received by almost all factions in Zagreb.[29]

The question of the future status of the military border had already come up during the negotiations leading to the *Ausgleich*. At that time the imperial war minister, Franz Baron von John, had demanded that the central war ministry retain its exclusive jurisdiction. He had tried to gain the support of the emperor by proposing to reestablish the office of Inspector General of the Military Border that had been discontinued after 1814 and had suggested Archduke Rainer for the position.[30] But the archduke wisely declined and Count Julius Andrássy, then chief Hungarian negotiator and later first prime minister, had temporized. Hungary, he had declared, could never accept John's position in principle, but for the time being would not press the issue.[31] Andrássy, however, had remained deeply suspicious of a centralized Habsburg state. He especially distrusted the imperial military and regarded the border as "an ever-present tool for the reactionary circles in Vienna to demolish, at the first opportunity, the new state of affairs in Hungary."[32] Therefore, once the Hungarian government was actually established it moved quickly to neutralize this potential threat. In the fall of 1867, Lonyay, the Hungarian minister of finance, contended that the Grenzer customs patrols were unreliable

[29] Paragraph 65 of the *nagoda* in Robert W. Seton-Watson, *The Southern Slav Question and the Habsburg Monarchy* (London, 1911), p. 372.

[30] John's proposal, Feb. 8, 1867, and Archduke Rainer's refusal, Feb. 10, 1867, KA MKSM sep. fasc. 71/65.

[31] HHStA KZ 322, Ministerrat of Feb. 11, 1867.

[32] Eduard v. Wertheimer, *Graf Julius Andrássy: Sein Leben und seine Zeit* (3 vols.; Stuttgart, 1910–13), I, 393.

and that the service should be taken over by his ministry.[33] The military were able to repudiate this first attempt, but their victory was only temporary, and relations between the military and Budapest worsened in the following year when radical Hungarian politicians demanded the creation of a completely separate Hungarian army.[34] Though in the end this controversy too was solved by a compromise, War Minister John resigned and, during an inspection tour in Croatia, Archduke Albrecht, army inspector general, prayed at Jelačić's grave. The meaning of this demonstration was only too clear and at this point Andrássy decided personally to enter the fight for the dissolution of the border.[35]

Early in 1869 the common war ministry planned to cut and sell some thirty thousand yokes of timber in the Slavonian regimental districts and to use the proceeds for public improvements. Andrássy seized this occasion, and on February 27 he protested against this action in the council of common ministers (*Ministerrat für gemeinsame Angelegenheiten*), asserting that such a step could not be taken without the concurrence of the proper Hungarian authorities. He was promptly opposed by Count Beust, the imperial chancellor, who rejoined that the compromise had in no way diminished the common war minister's exclusive competence in the military border and that the Hungarian concern over the timber sale merely was an opening wedge to abolish the organization.[36] The chancellor was, of course, quite correct. Andrássy was resolved to press for the complete dissolution of the border, and during the imperial visit to Zagreb in March he tried to approach the monarch directly. Although on this occasion Beust adroitly managed to prevent any discussion of the issue, he changed his position soon thereafter. He needed Hungarian support, or at least acquiescence, for his foreign policy and therefore decided that it was not his duty to oppose the dissolution of the border to the bitter

[33] Lonyay's request, KA KM Präs. 1867-21-9/8, and the imperial decision to have this issue solved only in cooperation with the common war ministry, Schönbrunn, Dec. 4, 1867, *ibid.*, 1868-21-8/2.

[34] Wertheimer, I, 335–40, 366–68, and the account in Edmund v. Glaise-Horstenau, *Franz Joseph's Weggefährte: Das Leben des Generalstabschefs Grafen Beck* (Vienna, 1930), pp. 146–152.

[35] Wertheimer, I, 355, and Srbik, pp. 111–13.

[36] HHStA, KZ 479 Ministerrat f. gem. Angelegenheiten, Feb. 27, 1869. For the lengthy negotiations on the issue of the forests, see KA Schriftgut, F-28, "Verhandlungen betreffend Holzverwertung in der Militärgrenze."

end. But on the other hand, he also needed the support of the military and so he adopted a neutral position from then on.[37]

The military and the emperor, for the time being, continued to oppose the disbandment of the border. Francis Joseph's devotion to the principles of the Ausgleich could not be questioned, but on any issue affecting the common army he was quick to assert his prerogatives.[38] When in the ministerial council of May 26 Andrássy once again raised the question of the timber sale, the emperor, clearly irritated, declared with some vehemence that he was not at all sure whether the Hungarian government had the competence to concern itself with administrative affairs of the military border. Forced to counter this challenge, Andrássy acknowledged that the real and fundamental issue at stake was the future status of the Militärgrenze. Appealing to the monarch's devotion to the Hungarian settlement, Andrássy claimed that he in turn was committed by the constitution as well as by the nagoda to seek the return of the border territory to the administrative control of the crown of St. Stephen.[39]

Francis Joseph faced a most agonizing internal conflict. Andrássy pressed him to accept the disbandment of the military border as a logical consequence of the Ausgleich, and the emperor recognized the force of this argument. But he considered himself primarily a soldier and was reluctant to renounce the traditional ties between his dynasty and the Grenzer. Even so, Andrássy felt sure of eventual, and perhaps near, success. "I hope to return," he wrote to his wife on the eve of the next council meeting, "with a much greater success than I had originally hoped for."[40] The next morning, July 1, 1869, Andrássy returned to the attack. He repeated his arguments about the rights of the Hungarian crown and the provisions of the nagoda and capped his presentation by arguing that while the border regiments no longer had any military value, they constituted armed support for South Slav machinations.[41]

Andrássy had scored an important point when he linked the disbandment of the border to the bogey of south Slav national-

---

[37] Friedrich Graf v. Beust, *Aus drei Vierteljahrhunderten: Erinnerungen und Aufzeichnungen* (2 vols.; Stuttgart, 1887), II, 257.

[38] Glaise-Horstenau, pp. 227–28.

[39] HHStA, KZ 479, Ministerrat f. gem. Angelegenheiten, May 26, 1869.

[40] Wertheimer, I, 398.

[41] HHStA, KZ 1937, Ministerrat f. gem. Angelegenheiten, July 1, 1869.

ism. In Croatia, nationalist resentment against the imposed Unionist regime, as well as dissatisfaction with the nagoda, had reversed attitudes toward the border. Elements of the National Liberals and, of course, the followers of Starčević, who had never accepted the nagoda, charged that the demilitarization of the border was a sellout to Budapest and that the Ban and the Sabor were but corrupt Magyar tools.[42] When the Unionist Ban, Baron Rauch, stung by accusations of personal dishonesty suppressed the opposition paper, the *Pozor*, it moved first to Vienna and then to Sisak (Sissek) on the military border. From there, under the benevolent eyes of the military administration and styled *Zatočnik* (Exile), it continued to engage in violent anti-Unionist and anti-Hungarian polemics. Financial interests in Budapest, the paper alleged, schemed to defraud the Grenzer of their last valuable property, the communal forests.[43] Similar arguments were voiced in a number of anonymous pamphlets, which attacked the proposed disbandment and accused the Hungarian government of cruelly oppressing the Croatian nation. One such piece, *Die Militärgrenz-Frage und der österreichisch-ungarische Constitutionalismus*, compared the border to the suffering Christ about to be sacrificed on the Hungarian cross.[44] Despite this extravagant hyperbole, or perhaps because of it, "many of the half-educated Grenzer regarded this pamphlet as their Bible."[45] Since Vienna no less than Budapest was convinced that South Slav nationalism was largely Moscow-inspired and designed to disrupt the Dual Monarchy, Croatian efforts to maintain the distinct character of the military border in opposition to the Unionist regime were taken as evidence of subversive intentions.[46]

[42] An exposition of the Croatian nationalist grievances in L. v. Südland, *Die Südslawische Frage und der Weltkrieg* (1st ed.; Venna, 1918), pp. 443–46.

[43] Polić, II, 7–8, and Gilbert in der Maur, *Die Jugoslawen einst und jetzt* (2 vols.; Leipzig, 1936), I, 50–51. For Grenzer attitudes, see Reiswitz, p. 176; Wertheimer, I, 412, and the reports KA MKSM 1869-49-5/3, and KA KM 1869-10A-28/4.

[44] Published in 1869 in Vienna by O. Utiešenović, a former official of the Croatian-Slavonian chancery, dismissed because of his nationalist activities. See also Daniel Grivčić (pseud.), *Gegenwart und Zukunft der k. k. Militärgrenze* (Vienna, 1869), pp. 1–3.

[45] Mollinary to Kuhn, Zagreb, May 1870, KA KM Präs. 1870-15-11/2.

[46] For a general discussion of Austro-Hungarian fears about Pan-Slavism and Russia, see Arthur J. May, *The Habsburg Monarchy 1867–1913* (Cambridge, Mass., 1951), pp. 98–101; Theodor v. Sosnosky, *Die Balkanpolitik Österreich-Ungarns seit 1866* (2 vols.; Stuttgart, 1913), I, 77–92, and B. H.

The spectre of South Slav irredentism reached even more menacing proportions in 1869 when the highlanders of the Krivošije (Bocche di Cattaro) in Dalmatia rebelled against the introduction of compulsory military service and successfully maintained their resistance until the Austrian government conceded their demands.[47] It became embarrassing to oppose dissolution of the military border, and on July 6, 1869, the new war minister, Baron Kuhn, submitted a memorandum to the emperor conceding the necessity for certain liberal reforms.[48] At the same time, however, the minister maintained that the continued existence of the border was a military necessity. But Andrássy had prepared a decisive move. When toward the end of July the Austro-Hungarian delegations met in Vienna to discuss an increased budget for the common army, the Hungarian delegates flatly refused to make any appropriations unless they were informed that positive steps had been taken toward dissolution of the military border.[49] A demand for such information was politely rejected by Kuhn, and on August 11 Andrássy warned the council of common ministers that the military budget was in danger. Andrássy declared, however, that Hungary, as always, was willing to compromise in the interest of the Dual Monarchy and would accept a gradual dissolution of the border.[50]

The threat to the army budget combined with the fear of South Slav nationalism forced the emperor's hand. On August 12 Andrássy had a very chilly audience, and during a reception given for the delegations that evening Francis Joseph pointedly ignored the Hungarians and conversed at length with Archduke Albrecht. This was merely a show of temper. The next morning the emperor called for Andrássy and informed him that he would approve the gradual dissolution of the military border.[51] Under these circumstances the council meeting in the afternoon was an anticlimax. Andrássy reviewed his ar-

Sumner, *Russia and the Balkans* (Oxford, 1937), pp. 126–32. For suspicions regarding Russian activities on the Military Border and for allegations regarding the Orthodox Church in Croatia-Slavonia, see the report by Col. König, KA KM Präs. 1869-35-12/7.

[47] Reiswitz, pp. 175–77, 236–37.

[48] KA MKSM 1869-49-2/9.

[49] Wertheimer, I, 395–97, and Walter Rogge, *Österreich von Világos bis zur Gegenwart* (2 vols.; Leipzig, 1872), II, 242.

[50] HHStA KZ 2581, Ministerrat f. gem. Angelegenheiten, Aug. 11, 1869.

[51] Wertheimer, I, 398–400.

guments for the dissolution of the border, "an unreliable military organization, potentially dangerous to the monarchy."[52] Beust, too, cautiously expressed himself in favor, while Kuhn argued for delay. In the end, the emperor overrode the opposition and informed the council of his decision. Dissolution was to be gradual and in stages; he would issue the necessary instructions directly to the war ministry. Having made up his mind, Francis Joseph acted with dispatch, and on August 19 he sent instructions to Kuhn ordering as a first step the dissolution of the Warasdin regiments and of two Szluiner companies in the Sichelburg enclave.[53]

Reaction to this decision varied. Hungary, of course, was highly satisfied, while Austrian politicians were displeased that Andrássy had gained his end not by negotiations through the common parliamentary institutions but by dealing directly with the emperor.[54] During the August 19 session of the delegations, the German liberal deputy, Dr. Sturm, protested against the decision and declared that at the time of the Ausgleich it had been understood that the military border would remain one of the common institutions of the monarchy.[55] On the Croatian-Slavonian Military Border the decision was received with outright hostility. On September 9 Colonel Adler of the Warasdiner-Kreutzer Regiment reported that the Grenzer were most unhappy about the demilitarization since this would end their right to purchase salt and tobacco at cost from military stores.[56] Several days later, on September 12, 1869, the military authorities found it necessary to announce that no discussion of this measure would be tolerated, that all opposition would be met by force and that the emperor would not receive any petitions or delegations on this matter.[57]

The greatest difficulties, however, came from the military themselves. Colonel Gustav König, the chief of the Military Border Department in the War Ministry, and certain other senior officers, tried to obstruct the execution of the decree.

---

[52] HHStA KZ 2583, Ministerrat f. gem. Angelegenheiten, Aug. 13, 1869.

[53] Letter to Kuhn, Ischl, Aug. 19, 1869, KA KM Präs. 1869-35-17/1. Copy in KA MKSM 1869-49-1/4.

[54] Wertheimer, I, 401–3; Rogge, II, 243.

[55] HHStA Stenogr. Prot. d. Delegation d. Reichsrates, 10th meeting, 2d Session, Aug. 19, 1869.

[56] Report, Bjelovar, Sept. 9, 1869, KA KM 1869-10A-107/3.

[57] *Ibid.*, 1869-10A-128/6.

They maintained that the question of implementation, and especially the disposition of the forests still owned in common by the regiments, should be discussed by a special Grenzer diet.[58] This idea was supported by the commanding general in Zagreb, General Prince Dietrichstein-Mensdorf, who advised that "if the dissolution of the border is to be carried out without tremendous upheavals, one must listen to the opinions of its delegates."[59] It appears that Kuhn at first favored these moves but withdrew when he learned that such plans were playing into the hands of Orešković and the Croatian national extremists hoping to promote a separatist Grenzer movement.[60] König and the Border Department continued in opposition. Although the colonel repeatedly offered his resignation, he remained in charge of the Border Department in Vienna until its dissolution at the end of 1871.[61] In the meantime, however, Kuhn, albeit reluctantly, decided that further obstruction was harmful and that dissolution should proceed in an orderly manner. It was on his recommendation that in January, 1870, Francis Joseph appointed Feldmarschall Leutnant Anton Baron Mollinary to supervise the process of demilitarization.[62]

Early that month the emperor received Mollinary and gave him explicit oral instructions. The compromise of 1867, the monarch declared, had once and for all settled the political future of the border and all agitation for a special diet or local autonomy were to be sternly suppressed. The emperor expressed his desire for the closest cooperation with the Hungarian ministry, and Andrássy's approval was obtained before Mollinary's appointment was gazetted on January 21, 1870. It appears that Mollinary, despite the emperor's mandate, still expected diffi-

[58] Glaise-Horstenau, p. 144; Wertheimer, I, 408–11. Complaints about these activities by the Hungarian minister of interior, Rajner, to Kuhn, Nov. 5 and 10, 1869, KA KM Präs. 1869-35-19/1. König's explanations, Nov. 24, 1869, *ibid.*

[59] Report, Zagreb, Nov. 12, 1869, *ibid.*, 1870-35-4/1.

[60] On Kuhn's change of position see Srbik, pp. 210–11. Personal differences between Kuhn, a brash German liberal centralist, and Archduke Albrecht, conservative and dynastic, may have also been a factor. *Ibid.*, pp. 173–75.

[61] König's demands for a Grenzer *Landtag* in his memorial of Jan., 1870, KA MKSM 1871-49-2/29, which also includes his offer of resignation, letter to Col. Beck, Feb. 7, 1871, enclosure, *ibid.*

[62] *Ibid.*, 1870-49-1/1, and KA KM Präs. 1870-35-4/1, contain the papers regarding Mollinary's appointment. Also Wertheimer, I, 410–11.

culties on the part of the military in Croatia and therefore secured the power to appoint his own chief of staff and summarily to remove all uncooperative officials from their posts.[63]

When Mollinary reached his command late in February, 1870, he found the country in turmoil. An extended inspection tour, undertaken with a strong escort to guard against the bandits infesting the hills of the Lika, revealed widespread opposition to the prospect of demilitarization. There was considerable distrust of the Unionist Sabor and unconcealed resentment against Hungary.[64] Petitions against demilitarization and for local autonomy were circulating and most of the native officers shared the opinion of the men.[65] Feeling ran especially high in the Ogulin Regiment where local leaders voiced outright demands for self-determination. Although Mollinary was horror struck by the independent tone adopted by enlisted men towards an imperial general officer, he refused to be provoked and limited himself to assure the men that "the emperor only wanted the best for his Grenzer."[66] In fact, despite the manifestations of disaffection, Mollinary rendered a somewhat optimistic report. The situation on the Croatian-Slavonian Military Border, he declared, had been misrepresented. There still existed strong elements of the traditional loyalty and the population understood the necessity for demilitarization. Mollinary assured Vienna that no armed resistance was to be expected in the regiments, but the situation, he warned, was aggravated by the inflammatory nationalist agitation in civil Croatia and the impatient diatribes of the Hungarian press demanding a faster tempo of demilitarization.[67] Kuhn repeatedly complained to Andrássy about the tone of the Hungarian press, and Andrássy in turn demanded that the war minister should discipline Grenzer officers promoting demands for "self-determination" and suppress the *Zatočnik*.[68]

[63] Anton Frhr. v. Mollinary, *Sechsundvierzig Jahre im österreichisch-ungarischen Heere* (2 vols.; Zurich, 1905), II, 203–12.

[64] *Ibid*., pp. 215–21.

[65] Mollinary to Kuhn, Zagreb, March 1, 1870, KA KM Präs. 1870-35-9/2.

[66] Mollinary, 2, 216-17; and his report, Zagreb, June 30, 1870, KA KM Präs. 1870-15-20/6.

[67] *Ibid*., and Mollinary, II, 223–25.

[68] *Ibid*., and KA MKSM 1870-49-1/3; Kuhn's memorandum of June 11, 1870, KA KM Präs. 1870-35-4/1, and Kuhn to Andrássy, Vienna, June 29, 1870, *ibid*., 35-13/3.

Matters were in this stage when the outbreak of the Franco-Prussian War interrupted the progress of demilitarization. Though the famous crown council of June 18 decided to adopt a policy of neutrality, Austro-Hungarian involvement was not totally excluded and limited military preparations were undertaken.[69] These caused serious misgivings on the border and late in July the *Zatočnik* came out with an editorial calling on the Grenzer to utilize the Dual Monarchy's involvement in foreign war for the realization of their national aspirations.[70] The response of the military to this flagrantly subversive act was surprising. On August 4 Kuhn suggested in the council of ministers that the foreign situation and the threatening attitude of the Grenzer demanded a temporary suspension of dissolution. The reception accorded this statement demonstrated once more Hungarian fears. Andrássy declared that any delay in carrying out the dissolution of the border would be regarded as a sign of weakness, and he insisted that reports about the disaffection and the anti-Hungarian sentiments of the Grenzer were much exaggerated. All that was required was a firm hand and the suppression of subversive propaganda. This time, however, Francis Joseph, who had not abandoned all hope of profiting from the foreign situation, supported the military. The *Zatočnik*, he agreed, had been treated too leniently and should be suspended. On the other hand, the monarch declared that the danger of war required the maintenance of the full military potential and the temporary suspension of the demilitarization of the border.[71]

Whatever plans Francis Joseph had entertained for exploiting the Franco-Prussian War evaporated after Sedan, and in November, 1870, all military preparations were halted. Once dreams of foreign adventure were abandoned, the emperor tried to find solutions for the national problems besetting the Austrian half of the Dual Monarchy. Above all, he began to seek a settlement with the Czechs of Bohemia, a move that encouraged nationalist elements in Croatia who for several years had

[69] Srbik, pp. 69–78, sorts out the conflicting accounts of Andrássy, Beust, and Kuhn. Cf. Friedrich Engel-Jánosi, "Austria in the Summer of 1870," *JCEA*, 5 (1945–46), 335–53.

[70] Copy of editorial in KA KM Präs. 1870-59-1/7. According to Kuhn, Mollinary had reported that the Grenzer would resist mobilization. KA MKSM 1870-49-1/6. Mollinary later expressed the belief that Kuhn had exaggerated the situation on the Border. Mollinary, II, 233.

[71] HHStA, KZ 2782, Ministerrat f. gem. Angelegenheiten, Aug. 4, 1870.

maintained contacts with the Czech nationalist leadership.[72] The nationalists scored a considerable success early in 1871 when the ultra-Unionist Ban Rauch was forced to resign after losing a personal suit of defamation of character brought against the publisher and the editors of the *Zatočnik*.[73] When his successor Koloman Bedeković called for new elections, the nationalists gained an overwhelming victory.[74]

The *Zatočnik* affair as well as the nationalist election victory illustrated the tremendous growth of national feeling in Croatia and revealed that aversion to the Unionist regime could unite Orthodox and Catholics. Significantly, one of the *Zatočnik*'s editors was a Catholic priest, Josip Miškatović.[75] The rise of Croatian nationalism thoroughly alarmed Vienna as well as Budapest, and such fears were exacerbated by Unionist claims that the Croatian nationalists were directed by Moscow and Prague.[76] These accusations were widely believed and brought about an unexpected alliance between the military and the Magyars.

The military, and above all Kuhn, a German nationalist from Bohemia, were anxious about the concessions made to the Czechs and were willing to align themselves with the Magyars against the supposed Slav threat.[77] With regard to the military border in Croatia-Slavonia this meant that the military were ready to accelerate demilitarization. It had, in fact, never been the emperor's intent to extend concessions made to the Slavs of Austria to those in the Hungarian kingdom. He was firmly committed to the compromise of 1867, and therefore, while the Hohenwart cabinet was seeking an accommodation with the Czechs, he was quite willing to continue the dissolu-

[72] May, pp. 58-62, and Zwitter, *et al.*, pp. 103-12.

[73] Records of the *Zatočnik* affair in DAZ Politica tiskovne parnice contra Vončina-Miškatović-Mrazović, F 1-5. Actually, there were two trials. In the first, ending Jan. 8, 1871, dealing with the complaint made by Rauch, the defendants were found not guilty. In the second process the editors were charged with the publication of subversive material in the summer of 1870 and given very light sentences. Petrinja, May 12, 1871, *ibid.*, F-2, 95.

[74] In der Maur, I, 51.

[75] On this see Mollinary's reports, Zagreb, Dec. 31, 1870, and Jan. 3, 1871, KA KM Präs. 1871-59-2/1, and 59-2/2.

[76] Mirjana Gross, "Propast starounionističke stranke u svijetlu izvještaja Mirka Bogovića," *Zbornik HIJA*, 1 (1954), 224–25.

[77] On Kuhn's militant German nationalism and dislike for Slavs, see Srbik, p. 170; Glaise-Horstenau, p. 239 n 1.

tion of the military border. The subject was reviewed during February to May, 1871, by a top-level conference in Vienna and Budapest.[78] The conferees, reassured by reports from Mollinary that the situation had eased, worked in unprecedented harmony, and on June 8, 1871, the emperor signed a series of decrees that spelled out the steps terminating the Croatian-Slavonian Military Border.[79]

By 1871 the centuries-old military society of the Grenzer had indeed become an uncomfortable anachronism. Their combat effectiveness was much reduced and the introduction of compulsory military service in the Dual Monarchy in 1868 had reduced the manpower requirements of the imperial and royal armies. By this time, too, the cordon was no longer considered effective against the plague. In the middle of the nineteenth century medical opinion became divided between two schools; the contagionists who believed that the dread disease could be transmitted from man to flea and to man again, and that a cordon sanitaire was the best and most complete defense, and the non-contagionists who placed their trust in preventive inoculations.[80]

In 1857 Austria, Bavaria, and the Ottoman Empire concluded a Danube steamboat convention that excluded steamships from the quarantine regulations if there had been no case of plague in any riparian territory during the preceding twelve months. This rule was extended on December 27, 1857, by orders of the war ministry in Vienna to all land traffic, and from then on the quarantine was merely maintained to control the cattle trade.[81]

Even so, as late as 1865 new regulations for the cordon still maintained the old system of patrols and quarantine stations.[82] In 1871 Mollinary expressed the viewpoint that the cordon was useless and merely served to inhibit trade with the Turkish provinces.[83] His ideas reflected a viewpoint held by a considerable

---

[78] Mollinary, II, 225; conference protocols in KA MKSM 1871-49-2/29.

[79] KA MKSM 1871-49-2/25.

[80] Georg Sticker, *Abhandlungen aus der Seuchengeschichte und Seuchenlehre* (2 vols. in 3; Giessen, 1908–10), I, 336–51; Erna Lesky, "Die österreichische Pestfront an der k.k. Militärgrenze," *Saeculum*, 8 (1957), 102–6, disagrees and maintains that the cordon proved very effective.

[81] KA KM 1858-21 A-1/11.

[83] *Reglement für den Land-und See-Cordon der k.k. Militär-Grenze* (Vienna, 1865).

[83] Mollinary, II, 207.

majority of medical men. Moreover, maintenance of the cordon was expensive, and Hungary was unwilling to spend any money on it.[84] Therefore the sanitary establishment was also discontinued as of the end of 1871.[85]

[84] In 1870 and again in 1871 the Hungarian delegation refused to grant any appropriations for the purposes of border administration. Each time, however, they compromised and voted 200,000 florins. HHStA Stenogr. Prot. d. Delegation d. Reichsrates, 10th meeting, 3d session, Jan. 13, 1871.

[85] Sticker, pp. 329–31.

10

— . — . — . — . —

THE LAST YEARS OF THE MILITARY BORDER: 1871–81

The resolutions of June 8, 1871, signalled the actual start of the dissolution of the Croatian-Slavonian Military Border. To be sure, the process was slow and it was only in 1881 that the last remnants of the military administration were liquidated. Certain Hungarian and Croatian circles blamed the slow pace on the "military who still were able to delay implementation of this important decision," but actually there was no longer any military opposition.[1] The problem of the Croatian Military Border had moved out of the realm of military affairs and into the arena of Croatian party policies and the wider context of the nationality struggle within the Habsburg Empire.

Dissolution was to proceed in stages. As a first step the two Warasdin regiments, the Sichelburg enclave of the Szluin Regiment, the military townships of Senj and Bjelovar, as well as Fortress Ivanić and the community of Sisak, were to be handed over to civil Croatian administration.[2] The Grenzer, still liable for active military service, were enlisted in the newly established Warasdiner Line Infantry Regiment (No. 16), and the others were transferred to the reserve rolls. The towns were given the usual charters; the Sichelburg enclave was incorporated into Carniola. Actual implementation of these measures

[1] Julian (Gyula) Miskolczy, *Ungarn in der Habsburger Monarchie*, ("Wiener Historische Studien"), V, (Vienna; 1959), p. 146.

[2] The various complex provisions in *Prev. Proglas c. kr. naredba i prev. odpis o razrješenju varaždinske Krajine grada Senja i vojne občine Siska, zatim izvedbeni propisi, kojimi se utire put razrješenju ukupne vojine Krajine* (Zagreb, 1871).

was entrusted to Feldmarschall Leutnant Ferdinand Baron Rosenzweig. The transfer proceeded without incident and was completed by October, 1871.[3]

In the meantime, following the instructions laid down in June, a new administrative framework was created to operate during the transitional phase of the military border. By this time there remained only the Croatian-Slavonian regiments, the Banat units, and the Tschaikisten battalion at Titel. The Transylvanian Military Border, where the Szekler regiments had joined the Hungarian revolution, had already been dissolved in 1851.[4] Now, the Peterwardein Regiment was transferred to the Croatian-Slavonian command, with headquarters in Zagreb, and the Banat regiments as well as the Tschaikisten were assigned to Temesvar. In both commands new regional authorities, *Landesbehörden*, were organized to conduct all economic, judicial, educational, and religious affairs of the Grenzer. The Landesbehörden were nominally civilian agencies, staffed with the personnel from the former administrative branch of the border service now transferred to civil service status. For the purposes of civil administration, the nine regiments of the Croatian-Slavonian Border were divided into 31 districts and 151 communities. For the time being, however, ultimate control in civil as well as military affairs remained in the hands of the regimental commanders, responsible in turn to the commanding generals, Mollinary in Zagreb, and Feldmarschall Leutnant Scudier in Temesvar.[5]

There were also some changes in the military sphere. Although the provisions of the universal military service law of 1868 were applicable to the Grenzer, special provisions were made for the interim period. The Grenzer were to fulfill their active service obligations in their old units, which retained their traditional designations and stations. However, the number of men was drastically reduced, the cordon service discontinued, and the Seressaner transformed into a gendarmerie force.[6] These innovations were well received and on August 16, Mol-

[3] Anton Frhr. v. Mollinary, *Sechsundvierzig Jahr im österreichisch-ungarischen Heere* (2 vols.; Zurich, 1905), II, 229–32.

[4] Joseph Wolf, "Die Banater Militärgrenze, ihre Auflösung und Einverleibung in das Königreich Ungarn," unpublished diss., University of Graz, 1947.

[5] Mollinary, II, 226–27, 238–39.

[6] Mollinary to all regiments concerning implementation of KM Präs. 1871-1937, Zagreb, June 24, 1871, DAZ Varia bgda. Petrinja F-4.

linary informed Andrássy that he was convinced that demilitarization would proceed without any trouble.[7] But Mollinary was wrong. A political storm, with grave repercussions on the military border, was brewing in Croatia.

Although the nationalists had forced the resignation of the Unionist Ban Rauch, his successor, Koloman Bedeković, tried to keep his party in power by any and all means.[8] The nationalists had gained a clear mandate in the elections for a new Sabor; fifty-one out of sixty-five seats, but the Ban tried to delay the convocation of the house. In September, 1871, enraged by these manipulations and encouraged by developments in Bohemia where Vienna was still striving to come to an accommodation with the Czechs, a group of Croatian nationalist delegates issued a manifesto denouncing the nagoda.[9] This assertion of Croatian independence, together with the demands of the Czech controlled Prague diet, which would have elevated Bohemia to an equal position with Hungary within the monarchy, aroused fierce Austro-Hungarian and Magyar opposition.[10] While the emperor was still debating what he ought to do, an uprising occurred on the military border.

On October 8, 1871, Mollinary received alarming intelligence about subversive activities in the Ogulin Regiment.[11] Before he took any action, however, news arrived early the next day that a revolt actually was under way at Rakovica.[12] The main instigators were two Croatian nationalist fanatics, members of Ante Starčević's Party of Right, Eugen Kvaternik and Ljudevit Bach, editor of the party's journal *Hvatska*.[13] These men had gained the support of the former Sergeant Radé Cuić and a number of enlisted men. On the morning of October 9, they seized the local armory and proclaimed the es-

[7] Cited in Eduard v. Wertheimer, *Graf Julius Andrássy: Sein Leben und seine Zeit* (3 vols.; Stuttgart, 1910–13), I, 412.

[8] Mirjana Gross, "Propast starounionističke stranke u svijetlu izvještaja Mirka Bogovića," *Zbornik HIJA*, 1, (1954), 224–25.

[9] L. v. Südland, *Die Südslawische Frage und der Weltkrieg* (1st ed.; Vienna, 1918), p. 447.

[10] Arthur J. May, *The Hapsburg Monarchy, 1867–1913* (Cambridge, Mass., 1951), pp. 60–61.

[11] Mollinary reports to Kuhn that he has just received word of trouble in the Ogulin Regiment, Zagreb, Oct. 8, 1871, KA KM Präs. 1871-52-16/6.

[12] Mollinary to Kuhn (code telegram), Zagreb, Oct. 9, 1871, *ibid.*, 1871-52-16/1.

[13] Mollinary to Kuhn (code telegram), Zagreb, Oct. 10, 1871, *ibid.*, 1871-52-16/2.

tablishment of an independent Croatia with a provisional government and a national army. They called on all Croatians to rally against the "Swabian dogs" who had sold the country to the Magyars and hinted that aid from France and other powers could be expected.[14] But the rebels failed to gain any significant support. Not a single officer joined the insurrectionists, and in all only the local company and a few firebrands from civil Croatia rallied to the standard of rebellion.[15]

Even so, Mollinary was at first quite alarmed. He immediately proclaimed martial law and alerted all Grenzer regiments in Croatia. He believed that such extensive precautions were necessary in view of the "dubious sentiments shown by some of the troops and the population." [16] But his fears were baseless. The vast majority of the Grenzer remained loyal and moved against the rebels even before receiving Mollinary's instructions. On October 12, troops of the Ogulin and Ottoschatz Regiments encountered the rebel forces and defeated them decisively. Kvaternik and Bach were killed, and Cuić fled into the hills with a price on his head. In all there were about a dozen casualties among the insurgents. The government forces took 63 prisoners and captured 194 rifles.[17] Rakovica was occupied the next day without a fight and a hastily convened court martial meted out swift punishment.[18] Eleven Grenzer were executed,[19] and patrols were out scouring the hills bringing in more prisoners.[20] By October 20, Mollinary, convinced that a salutary impression had been made on the malcontents, lifted martial law though arrests and trials continued for the re-

[14] Insurrectionist manifesto, Rakovica, Oct. 8, 1871, enclosure to Mollinary's report of Oct. 16, 1871, *ibid.*, 1871-52-16/24.

[15] Mollinary's final report, Zagreb, Oct. 25, 1871, *ibid.*, 1871-52-16/37.

[16] His view in code telegram of Oct. 10, 1871, *ibid.*, 1871-52-16/2.

[17] Mollinary to Kuhn (code telegram), Zagreb, Oct. 13, 1871, *ibid.*, 1871-52-16/17. There is some uncertainty how Kvaternik and Bach met their end. On Oct. 12, Mollinary reported that the two were killed during the fighting, but on Oct. 17 he wrote that the rebels themselves had shot their leaders. *Ibid.*, 1871-52-16/7, 13, and 25. It appears most likely that they were taken prisoner and shot on the spot by orders of Major Rasić of the Ogulin Regiment.

[18] DAZ Rak. buna, F-1, contains the records of the courts-martial. Major Petar Medić, Ogulin Regiment, was the chief judge.

[19] Report of executions, Lt. Col. Kukulj to Mollinary, Rakovica Oct. 16, *ibid.*, 935. Sentences had to be carried out by shooting since no gallows were available.

[20] Reports of arrests, *ibid.*, 1101, 1002, 1089, and 1096. Cuić was arrested on Nov. 1, 1871, by a patrol of the Ogulin Regiment. *Ibid.*, 1114.

mainder of the year.[21] In his final report, however, Mollinary noted with much pride that the revolt had been put down by Grenzer forces alone. This proved that there was still a great reservoir of loyalty toward the state.[22]

Unrealistic in its conception and execution, the revolt nonetheless had important consequences. It became a prime argument for those circles opposed to any accommodation with the Slavs of the empire. Andrássy, already apprehensive that the Dual Monarchy was about to be "handed over to the Slavs," denounced the rising as part of a monstrous Pan-Slav conspiracy, involving South Slav agitators, Czech propaganda, "a secret Russian society and the French International."[23] For the benefit of Vienna he painted a horrifying picture of a Croatia in revolt, followed by risings in the Vojvodina, in Dalmatia, and Bohemia. When the minister, supported by the military and his ever-loyal Unionist tools in Croatia, charged that the policies of the Hohenwart cabinet had encouraged these Pan-Slav machinations, Francis Joseph abandoned the idea of conciliating the Czechs and dismissed the cabinet.[24]

In Croatia and on the border, the fiasco of Rakovica, for the time being, broke the strength of the national extremists. There were allegations that the revolt had been masterminded from Hungary to discredit the nationalists, and the news about the fall of the Hohenwart ministry came as a heavy blow.[25] The Unionists gained new heart and renewed their offensive against the nationalist opposition. As early as October, 1871, they had charged that the real backers of the revolt were to be found in the nationalist camp, and during the winter they published a

[21] Report of the investigating commission, Krslje, Nov. 16, 1871, to Mollinary, *ibid.*, 1279.

[22] Mollinary to Kuhn, Zagreb, Oct. 25, 1871, KA KM Präs. 1871-52-16/37. Also his report Oct. 17, *ibid.*, 1871-52-16/25.

[23] Wertheimer, I, 583–84. This idea was given support by Mollinary's allegations in his code telegram, Zagreb, Oct. 15, 1871, *ibid.*, 1871-52-16/15, which alleged that the Party of the Right had been in touch with the French who had demanded that Starčević instead of Kvaternik lead the rising. Mollinary also reported on alleged connections with the Czechs, Nov. 6, 1871, *ibid.*, 1871-52-16/38. There were indeed some tentative connections between Croat and Czech nationalists, notably between J. V. Frič and Kvaternik who met the latter in Zagreb and during his exile in Paris. I am obliged to Professor Stanley Z. Pech of the University of British Columbia for information on this last point.

[24] Friedrich Graf v. Beust, *Aus drei Vierteljahrhunderten: Erinnerungen und Aufzeichnungen* (2 vols.; Stuttgart, 1887), II, 497–513.

[25] Mollinary's report, Zagreb, Nov. 1, 1871, KA KM Präs. 1871-52-16/39.

number of documents alleging that the leaders of the nationalist opposition, including Bishop Strossmayer and the historian Rački, had treasonable communications with the exiled Kossuth, the Czechs, and Moscow.[26] The nationalists countered with charges that the documents were blatant falsifications, but, keeping in mind the debacle of the *Zatočnik* process, the Ban did not dare to bring the matter to trial. Bedeković, however, was clearly unequal to his job and resigned early in 1872. New elections for the Sabor were called which, despite the most flagrant government interference, resulted once again in a nationist victory.[27] This brought affairs to an impasse. For a while, since no one acceptable to Vienna, Budapest, and the Sabor could be found to fill the position of Ban, there was talk about appointing Mollinary royal commissioner, but nothing came of this.[28] In the end, Landes Finanz Direktor Vakanović, a colorless bureaucrat, was named as interim administrator, but in late 1873, the nationalist poet Ivan Mažuranić assumed the office.[29]

In the meantime, the dissolution of the military border continued. On June 9, 1872, imperial edicts ended the last vestiges of the special status in the Banat regiments and the Tschaikisten battalion. These were dissolved and their territory incorporated into the Hungarian state.[30] In Croatia-Slavonia, however, matters proceeded more slowly. On August 1, 1873, the civil and military administration of the regiments were completely separated. Educational, judicial, and religious matters were handed over to the Sabor; the thirty-one administrative districts were abolished and six new comitats were created. At the same time, an imperial edict formally disbanded the last Grenzer regiments, effective October 1, 1873. Officers were transferred to the regular army, the reserves, or retired; enlisted Grenzer were either assigned to four newly established regiments of the line (Nos. 53, 70, 78, and 79) or transferred to the reserves. Thus on

---

[26] Ban Bedeković to Mollinary, Zagreb, Oct. 12, 1871, DAZ Rak. buna, F-1, 937. Also the letter from Dr. Mrazović to Bishop Strossmayer, Nov. 7, 1871, Arhiv JAZU, Mrazović-Strossmayer Correspondence, XI-20. Gilbert in der Maur, *Die Jugoslawen einst und jetzt* (2 vols.; Leipzig, 1936), I, 52, and B. H. Sumner, *Russia and the Balkans* (Oxford, 1937), pp. 130–31.

[27] Mollinary, II, 272.

[28] *Ibid.*, II, 274–75, 277–78.

[29] In der Maur, I, 53–54.

[30] Alphons v. Wrede, *Geschichte der K. und K. Wehrmacht*, Supplementary volumes to *MKA* (5 vols.; Vienna, 1893–1930), V, 252–53.

October 1, 1873, the military history of the Grenzer came to an end.[31]

The only remaining task was to wind up economic affairs. For this purpose there remained the Landesbehörden, which, although restricted in competence to the administration of the regimental landed properties, still constituted an essentially military organization under the control of Mollinary, recently promoted to Feldzeugmeister. Continuation of this military authority aroused grave misgivings in Croatia. In 1874 a number of nationalist deputies charged in the Sabor that this constituted a plot to prevent the final transfer of the former regimental districts to Croatia, and in July Ban Mažuranić sent a note to Mollinary inquiring about the exact date of the final handover.[32] Mollinary answered sharply that the emperor had not yet made his final decision and also complained to Colonel Beck, head of the emperor's military chancery, that Croatian allegations were baseless and that the real reason that the Sabor demanded an end to the quasimilitary administration was that its efficiency highlighted Croatian incompetence.[33] On the other hand, the Hungarians by this time were quite willing to delay the final demilitarization of the Croatian-Slavonian regiments. The main reason for this change of position was political. With the nationalists in power in Croatia, the Hungarians were eager to keep the number of deputies Croatia could send to the Hungarian parliament down.[34] Mollinary was caught in the middle, and his relations with the civil authorities, both in Zagreb and in Budapest, deteriorated rapidly.

After 1873 the remaining problems on the Croatian-Slavonian Military Border were partially economic and partially political. Neither of them could be solved alone, and Mollinary's attempt to do just that ended in his forced resignation. To be sure, Mollinary, a narrowly *kaisertreu* officer, was perhaps not the best man for the task. On the other hand, the problems involved not only the backward economic state of the regimental districts, but also the precarious relationships between Zagreb

[31] *Ibid.*, pp. 253–54; Mollinary, II, 253–55, and the documents in KA MKSM 1873 Sep. Fasc. 81/42.

[32] M. Turković, *Die Geschichte der ehemaligen croatisch-slawonischen Militärgrenze* (Sušak, 1936), pp. 82–83.

[33] Mažuranić-Mollinary correspondence in KA MKSM 1874-49-2/7; Mollinary to Beck, KA MKSM 1874-57-2/5.

[34] Mollinary, II, 273–74.

and Budapest, and the constant fears of Pan-Slavism, which were fanned anew by an insurrection in neighboring Bosnia, and were beyond solution in the framework of the Dual Monarchy. During the final years of the military administration, there were great efforts to improve the economic and cultural circumstances of the Grenzer that had remained well below the level of the other provinces of the empire. This was not so readily apparent in the Warasdin and Slavonian districts, always the most prosperous, but in western Croatia, especially in the Lika, Szluin, Ogulin, and Ottoschatz districts there prevailed "ignorance, superstition, brutality, even barbarism." [35] There were few schools, and only one institution beyond the elementary level, at Karlstadt. Only 33 per cent of the boys and 25 per cent of the girls attended schools of any kind. Over 75 per cent of the population were illiterate.[36] Agriculture had remained retarded and by 1870 the level of productivity had not risen above that achieved at the beginning of the century, despite the continual rise in population.[37] This in part explained the low state of public safety in these regions. After two hundred years of military government, it was still necessary for Mollinary to take a strong escort on his first tour of inspection and to take the most drastic measures to maintain a modicum of security.[38]

Under Mollinary's direction the Landesbehörde began a much needed program of school reform. These efforts, however, were hampered by a patent lack of interest on the part of the Budapest government, indifference in the highest Austrian circles, and "little help, but much interference," from the Croatian authorities.[39] Above all, the military border suffered from a lack of capital to make the necessary improvements. To be sure, since 1868 free commerce had been allowed in the regi-

---

[35] Georges Perrot, "L'Autriche d'autrefois. Les confins militaires et leur legislation," *RDM*, 84 (1869), 65–69. B. Panković, *Die Militärgrenzfrage in ihrer Beziehung zur orientalischen Frage* (Vienna, 1865), pp. 27–29.

[36] Franz Vaniček, *Specialgeschichte der Militärgrenze* (4 vols.; Vienna, 1875), IV, 504–25; Schwicker, *Geschichte der österreichischen Militärgrenze* (Vienna-Teschen, 1883), p. 360.

[37] L. Katus, "Hauptzüge der kapitalistischen Entwicklung der Landwirtschaft in den südslawischen Gebieten der Österreichisch-Ungarischen Monarchie," in V. Sandor and P. Hanak, eds., *Studien zur Geschichte der Österreichisch-Ungarischen Monarchie* (Budapest, 1961), p. 132; Imbro Tkalac, *Uspomene iz Hrvatske* (Zagreb, 1945), p. 53.

[38] Mollinary, II, 219–21.

[39] *Ibid.*, II, 270–73, 240–41.

ments and after 1870 permission to dissolve the zadruge had been granted freely, but capital was needed to carry out substantial public works, especially in communications.[40] For this purpose the war ministry planned to utilize part of the income from the very extensive state forests on the military border. Use of these forests, the so-called *Waldservituten*, was one of the ancient and cherished rights of the Grenzer. Traditionally they had permitted woodcutting and grazing rights in these extensive tracts, and they were extremely concerned not to lose these privileges. The government found a simple, though not altogether satisfactory, solution. The forests were divided into two parts. One part, amounting to 493,000 yokes was taken over by the government; the other part, 752,000 yokes, was made the property of the respective regiments. Within each regiment all communities formed a property commune, *Vermögensgemeinde* or *imovna opcina*, that, under the guidance of the authorities, was to administer the communal woods. There were, however, certain difficulties because the available amount of forest land differed in each regiment and did not correlate with population density. Even so, the government, eager to get this problem off its hands chose the simplest way and distributed the forest lands to each individual regiment.[41]

The military administration also tried to safeguard the property communes against unscrupulous exploitation. To this end, the Landesbehörde entered into a contract with a Budapest syndicate for logging operations in the state forests, with the understanding that part of the profits were to provide a capital fund for the construction of a railroad into the former military border area.[42] This arrangement caused considerable trouble. At first, the syndicate tried to violate its agreement, but Mollinary went to court and obtained a judgment against the group that, since the financiers enjoyed support in governmental circles, further alienated Mollinary from Budapest. Moreover, the Hungarian government was openly opposed to the railroad project. Mollinary had enjoyed excellent relations with Andrássy, but Andrássy was now in Vienna, and the Tisza government, in office since November, 1875, refused to give any

[40] Katus, pp. 118–20, 141–42.
[41] J. Tomasevich, *Peasants, politics, and economic change in Yugoslavia* (Stanford, 1955), p. 81. On the other hand, Katus, pp. 127–29, maintains that the distribution greatly favored the large landed proprietors.
[42] Mollinary, II, 257–61.

attention to the pleas of the Grenzer for a railroad from Semlin to Sisak and then on to the Adriatic, which would have enabled that region to send its products to market.[43] Mollinary repeatedly complained to Budapest and on several occasions to Vienna, but nothing was done. When a delegation of former Grenzer journeyed to Vienna to appeal directly to the emperor, they returned empty-handed.[44] Finally, in September, 1876, a top-level conference with the emperor participating, was held in Vienna, but even this failed to change the Hungarian stand.[45] Under these circumstances, suspected in Zagreb of being pro-Magyar, and considered pro-Croatian in Budapest, Mollinary felt that his usefulness was exhausted and on June 16, 1877, requested to be relieved of his appointment.[46]

The Hungarian unwillingness to contribute to the economic development of the former military border region was motivated in part by economic considerations and in part by a revived fear of South Slav nationalism. Immediately after the Rakovica revolt, there had indeed been some relaxation of tension, and when in July, 1872, the Hungarian finance minister Kerkápoly visited the regiments in Croatia, he met with a generally cordial reception.[47] The Hungarian government, however, was desperately afraid of all South Slav national movements and by this time focussed its fears once again on the Orthodox Church.[48] Therefore, when in the following month there were difficulties over the election of a new patriarch at Karlovci, the Hungarian government interfered openly and, though without success, tried to force the election of a Magyarophile candidate.[49]

Behind the Hungarian fears there were some substantial if vague, truths. There existed among the South Slavs, especially among the Serbs of Novi Sad and in Belgrade, groups intent on making the most of any trouble among the Slavs of the Austrian and the Ottoman Empires. Vienna, as well as Budapest, were particularly concerned with the activities of the se-

[43] Katus, pp. 118–19.
[44] On the Grenzer delegation in Vienna, July, 1876, see KA MKSM 1876-34-1/5.
[45] Mollinary, II, 310–12.
[46] Request for relief from duty, Zagreb, June 16, 1877, KA MKSM 1877-34-10/2.
[47] Mollinary, II, 247–48.
[48] *Ibid.*, pp. 242–43.
[49] *Ibid.*, pp. 252–53; Sumner, p. 126.

cret Serb society *Omladina*, but they also remained suspicious of the former Grenzer areas.[50] It was remembered only too well that in the 1860's plans for a huge South Slav insurrection had hinged on Bosnia, and since 1873 there were again alarming signs of impending trouble in that province.[51]

There were substantial differences of opinion between Budapest and Vienna on how to deal with the problem. Conditions in Bosnia-Herzegovina were steadily growing worse; there had been numerous insurrections in the past, and there were clear indications that a new and formidable rising was in the offing. Indeed, since 1874, endemic guerrilla warfare was being carried on against the Turkish authorities and support, at first covertly but increasingly more open and in more substantial quantity, was being given by Serbia and by semiofficial circles in Russia.[52] Under these circumstances Austria began to consider once again whether to militarily intervene in Bosnia or even to occupy the country. There were groups in the Dual Monarchy that favored such a policy. These included many of the South Slavs who wished to bring more of their fellows into the empire that then might be transformed into a triune Austro-Hungarian-Slavic state. Even more influential were the military who argued that control of Bosnia-Herzegovina was essential for the defense of Dalmatia. The Hungarians were unwilling to see any more Slavs added to the empire, but on the other hand they were also determined that Serbia should not take over Bosnia-Herzegovina and create a large South Slav state. Therefore, Andrássy, now in charge of the Dual Monarchy's foreign policy, reluctantly agreed to go along with the military.[53]

Again, the population of the former military border assumed considerable importance. As on previous occasions, there was much sympathy with the Bosnian rebels and Mollinary received implicit instructions to sponsor anti-Serb and pro-Austrian propaganda among both the population of Croatia-Slavonia and across the frontier in Bosnia where the Catholic clergy had become the most important Austrian propaganda tool.[54] Fi-

[50] Angelo Tamborra, *Cavour e i Balcani* (Turin, 1958), pp. 166–67; Sumner, p. 129.

[51] Wertheimer, II, 260–63; Theodor v. Sosnosky, *Die Balkanpolitik Österreich-Ungarns seit 1866* (2 vols.; Stuttgart, 1913), I, 119–20.

[52] Sumner, pp. 130–31.

[53] Sosnosky, I, 141–44.

[54] Mollinary, II, 300–302.

nally, the military persuaded Emperor Francis Joseph to tour Dalmatia in the spring, an open demonstration of Austrian intentions.[55] At this point, however, Hungary suddenly became afraid of getting too deeply involved in this expansionist policy and drew back. In the end, the insurrection was supported not by Austrian but by Serbian and Montenegrin arms. On July 2, 1876, Serbia and Montenegro declared war on Turkey, and there was widespread belief that the establishment of a greater South Slav state was imminent. In Croatia-Slavonia and in the Serb areas of southern Hungary there were numerous demonstrations in favor of the South Slav cause, but the Hungarian government and public opinion were openly pro-Turkish. There were numerous arrests and Serbian newspapers were suppressed. The hunt was on for "traitors" and even Ban Mažuranić in Croatia joined the search for subversive pro-Serb elements.[56]

This was the background of the Hungarian refusal to build a railroad into the military border region and the resignation of Mollinary. Resignation was a bitter pill for Mollinary because he had been promised command in case of an Austro-Hungarian action in Bosnia-Herzegovina.[57] This coveted command, as well as the final disposition of the military border, fell to Feldmarschall Leutnant Baron Philipović, who took a much more conciliatory line on the railway question and thus was acceptable to Budapest.[58] Most immediately, however, Philipović was concerned with assembling troops for an army of occupation. Troops were concentrated in Croatia-Slavonia and in Dalmatia, but they included only six battalions of former Grenzer.[59] Due to Andrássy's reluctance, the invasion of Bosnia-Herzegovina was delayed until the Dual Monarchy had obtained an international mandate, and it was not until July 21, 1878, that advance troops crossed the Sava.[60]

The troubles and the bitter fighting attending what Andrássy had hoped would be a peaceful occupation, a military promenade, need not concern us here. Austria found herself opposed

[55] Sosnosky, I, 138–39.
[56] Robert W. Seton-Watson, *The Southern Slav Question and the Habsburg Monarchy* (London, 1911), p. 95; In der Maur, I, 54.
[57] Mollinary, II, 288.
[58] *Ibid.*, p. 261.
[59] Order of battle, Sosnosky, I, 291–94.
[60] *Ibid.*, 207–8.

not only by Turkish bands, but also by the local population, Orthodox as well as Catholic, and suffered several humiliating setbacks until the country was secured. Meanwhile, Philipović, who was considered too Slavophile, was recalled from command and returned to his position as commanding general in Zagreb.[61] Here he was once again confronted by the Sabor's demands for the immediate end of the remaining vestiges of the military regime, but with Hungarian support he stubbornly resisted. At this point Budapest probably woud have preferred a reestablishment of the military regime, but the clock could not be turned back.[62] In February, 1880, Ban Mažuranić, impatient about the delay in the final incorporation of the military border threatened to resign. But he had miscalculated. Budapest was only too happy to accept his resignation, and the Croatian nationalist cause was weakened. Even so, there was now too much pressure for the decision to be reversed. In the summer of 1880 there were some final negotiations regarding the transfer of certain funds still held by the Landesbehörde, but this was the end. Military funds were handed over to the Hungarian defense ministry, whereas civilian accounts were delivered to Zagreb.[63] Then, on August 1, 1881, the last vestiges of the military regime ended.[64] From Vienna, Emperor Francis Joseph issued a last manifesto. "Since in accordance with my manifesto of August 8, 1873, all measures have been taken to place you on equal status with all the inhabitants of my lands of the Hungarian crown, and since universal military service now has been introduced and a complete civil administration has been organized in all the former Croatian-Slavonian Border territories, I now order the incorporation of these areas with my kingdoms of Croatia and Slavonia and through these with the Hungarian crown." The emperor went on to thank the Grenzer for their loyalty to the dynasty and assured them of his ever-lasting gratitude.[65] It was the last imperial order and the end of an ancient institution.[66]

[61] Edmund v. Glaise-Horstenau, *Franz Joseph's Weggefährte: Das Leben des Generalstabschefs Grafen Beck* (Vienna, 1930), p. 211.

[62] In der Maur, I, 55.

[63] Documents in KA MKSM 1880-49-5/4.

[64] Imperial-royal ordinances regarding the final handover, Vienna, July 15, 1881, KA Schriftgut, F-42.

[65] Manifesto, Vienna, Aug. 8, 1881, KA MKSM 1881-49-5/18.

[66] Report of the final handover, war ministry to Franz Joseph, Vienna, Aug. 8, 1881, KA MKSM 1881-49-5/16.

It now only remains for us briefly to draw a balance. Apologists for Habsburg rule have portrayed the military border as a haven of order and prosperity, and its government as a happy synthesis of the best in civilian administration, local folkways, and military efficiency. The *Kaisertreue* of the Grenzer became one of the best established and most cherished legends of Habsburg historiography, and the alleged record of the military border served as a justification for a Habsburg mission in southeastern Europe.[67] As late as 1918 influential Austrian military leaders hoped to revive the institution and such suggestions appeared again after Hitler's armies had smashed the Yugoslav state.[68] Moreover, the legend also gained wide currency among critics of the Habsburgs and by historians in other countries. "There arose," wrote Oscar Jászi, "a proverbial Habsburg patriotism," and more recently Peter Sugar called the border "a professional military society imbued with a loyalty to the ruler."[69] Such appraisals, however, need reassessment because they clash with sober reality. The military border in Croatia was a stagnating society. Its constitution, a series of edicts and practices dating back to the eighteenth century, restricted personal freedoms, political rights, and economic opportunities of the population. The cumbersome administrative machinery had not succeeded in providing even a modicum of economic well being and could not even assure public order and security. Under these circumstances it was not surprising that the institution became less and less viable as the nineteenth century progressed.

Here it is instructive to consider the fate of the most important counterparts to the Austrian border, above all the Russian. Although the Militärgrenze was declining after the Napoleonic

[67] Among others Hugo Kerchnawe, *Die alte k.k. Militärgrenze* (Vienna, 1939), pp. 72–75; Rupert v. Schumacher, *Des Reiches Hofzaun: Geschichte der deutschen Militärgrenze in Südosten* (3d ed.; Darmstadt, 1942), pp. 288–91; Kurt Wessely, *Die österreichische Militärgrenze: Der Deutsche Beitrag zur Verteidigung des Abendlandes gegen die Türken* (Kitzingen 1953(?), pp. 21–23.

[68] Proposal made by GM Clam-Martinić at a conference of military governors, Sarajevo, May 13, 1918, in Bernard Stulli, "Prilozi gradji za historiju jugoslavenskog pitanja 1918 godine," *AV* 4 (1960), 283, 300, 322. For suggestions made in 1941, see the memo Lt. Col. V. Meduna, Vienna, to SS Hauptstelle Munich, Oct. 1941, KA Nachlässe, B-64-1/3.

[69] Oscar Jászi, *The Dissolution of the Habsburg Monarchy,* (Chicago, 1929), p. 57; Peter F. Sugar, "The Nature of Non-Germanic Societies under Habsburg Rule," *SR*, 22 (1963), 21.

wars, it was still much admired by foreign military experts and there were several attempts to form military establishments on the old Austrian pattern. Russia continued the Cossack organization, but also established new military colonies to augment the regular army, and France briefly experimented with military settlements to protect colonization in Algeria. These various experiments failed, however, and even the Cossacks were adversely affected by processes similar to those causing decline in the Habsburg borders.

Catherine II suppressed the restless Cossacks of the Dnieper and destroyed their organization in 1775, but farther east the Cossack settlements flourished. By 1870 there existed ten Cossack "armies," each occupying its own allotted territory, distributed along the old and new frontiers of the Russian Empire in Europe and Asia. Until the era of the Crimean War, the Cossacks, numbering some two and one-half million souls in all, formed a separate caste within the state, differentiated by well-defined rights and duties from the ordinary subjects of the empire, and contributing their distinctive contingents to the tsar's army. After the war, however, the reforms of Alexander II relaxed many of the special regulations. There was pressure from mercantile and industrial interests to exploit the natural resources of the Don and Kuban Cossack regions, and in 1867 permission was granted for non-Cossacks to own land within Cossack territories. The emancipation of the serfs in 1861 and the introduction of universal military service between 1870 and 1874 further removed many of the differences between the Cossacks and their peasant neighbors. Finally in 1883, Cossack officers and men received permission to live outside Cossack territory and to renounce Cossack status.[70] After that, especially in the Don and Kuban regions, dilution of the Cossack society was fast, but even so, special Cossack formations, known for their loyalty to the tsar and feared for their brutality, formed part of the Russian army until the October Revolution.

Also, during the first half of the nineteenth century, Russia undertook to found new military colonies. This attempt, one of the military experiments of Alexander I, begun in 1811, was interrupted by Napoleon's invasion, and resumed on an expanded scale in 1816. Alexander believed that settling soldiers

[70] W. P. Cresson, *The Cossacs* (New York, 1919), pp. 209–21; Max Jähns, *Heeresverfassungen und Völkerleben* (Berlin, 1885), pp. 68–69.

on the land would save money and improve morale since the men would have their families with them. In certain selected areas of the Ukraine and northern Russia, the peasants were placed under military command and amalgamated with troops quartered in their villages. Every conceivable aspect of the peasant-soldier's life was regimented by fourteen fat volumes of regulations published in 1826. Even the children in these villages were drilled, wore uniforms, and were enrolled in the army when they came of age. Contrary to Alexander's expectations, however, the scheme was bitterly resented, and in 1831, when regular troops had been withdrawn to fight the Polish revolt, there was a bloody insurrection against the military regime. Thereafter regulations were somewhat modified, but the system was never well accepted and the record of the peasant-soldiers during the Crimean War was poor. Moreover, the administration of these colonies proved costly and did not produce the expected savings. Therefore, as part of the reforms of Alexander II, the colonies were dissolved.[71]

During the same period the French experimented briefly with the concept of military colonies for frontier defense and colonization. From 1830 on, France was building a colonial empire and soon found that traditional European methods had little application in Algeria where, after the occupation of the coastal region, the French found themselves opposed by the warlike tribes of the interior. Marshal Marmont had highly recommended the organization of the Grenzer, and after 1840 Marshal Bugeaud, governor general and commander in chief in Algeria, recommended the establishment of military colonists to hold and pacify the region. Some small scale settlements were founded, but no permanent organization emerged. Nonetheless, until the 1870's the Austrian military border institution and its possible adaptation in the French colonies was the subject of repeated staff studies.[72]

[71] Carl Frhr. v. Pidoll zu Quintenbach, *Einige Worte über die russischen Militär-Kolonien im Vergleiche mit der k.k. österreichischen Militär-Grenze und mit allegemeinen Betrachtungen darüber* (Vienna, 1847), pp. 7–24; John S. Curtiss, *The Russian Army Under Nicholas I, 1825–1855* (Durham, N.C., 1965), pp. 8–9, 265–67, 277–86.

[72] Auguste F. L. W. Marmont, *Voyage de Monsieur le Maréchal de Raguse, en Hongrie, en Transylvanie, dans la Russie méridionale, en Crimée, et sur les bords de la mer d'Azoff* (2 vols.; Brussels, 1837), I, 155, 179–81; Paul Azan, *L'Armée d'Afrique de 1830 à 1852* (Paris, 1936), passim, and AHG Recon. Autriche, 1599, 1601, and 1605.

The reason why France did not proceed further, why the Russian military colonies failed, and why even the Cossack establishment had to be modified can be found in the dynamics of nineteenth-century liberalism that opposed all closed military castes within society. As the century progressed and liberalism became politically and economically more powerful, the maintenance of military borders became increasingly difficult. This was recognized as early as 1847 by an Austrian military official who wrote that "the system is not well suited to highly developed countries."[73] Moreover, the emergence of mass armies, "universal" conscription, and a more complicated technology worked against a military establishment that produced neither competent soldiers nor productive farmers.

Similar trends also operated in the realm of the Habsburgs where the decline of the Militärgrenze was determined by a number of factors, already evident before 1848, but becoming stronger in the second half of the century. First, the decline of the Ottoman Empire and the advent of modern mass armies reduced the military value of the Grenzer. Second, in the Habsburg Empire these changes coincided with the rising tide of nationalism, of economic liberalism, and the Hungarian settlement, which together undermined the "reliability" of the border as an instrument of imperial policy. And the imperial military, though more devoted to the interests of the entire Dual Monarchy than the Hungarians, were also too suspicious of Slav nationalism to permit the continued existence of a national conscious Slavic military institution. The final crisis over the dissolution of the military border illustrated the attitudes of the Magyars and of the imperial administration toward the problem of Slav nationalism in the Habsburg Empire. It revealed the deep-rooted conflicts between the South Slavs and the ruling groups and foreshadowed the inability of the monarchy to solve this vital question.

[73] Pidoll zu Quintenbach, p. 66.

—·—·—·—·—

BIBLIOGRAPHY

NOTE ON UNPUBLISHED SOURCES AND SELECTED,
ANNOTATED BIBLIOGRAPHY

A listing of the collections and series of unpublished documentary materials used is provided in the front of the book; complete
archival citations are given in the notes. Therefore I have not repeated this list here but instead I have provided a brief discussion
of the main categories of archival information available that may
be of some use to future researchers in this subject. With the exception of a few items of private correspondence, almost all of the unpublished material is official in nature and the great bulk is in
German and written in German script. Even Ban Jelačić conducted
most of his correspondence in German.

The most important depository of materials on the military border
is the Kriegsarchiv in Vienna. Here, with a few exceptions, records
are preserved in the same manner in which they were filed by the
originating or receiving agency. In many cases the original indices
compiled for internal office use are still in use. There are considerable
gaps, however, in the papers. Because of the limited storage space
available, papers no longer required for actual administrative purposes were often discarded, although financial records, accounts,
balance sheets, and annual returns were usually preserved.

After the termination of the Inner Austrian administration, the
military border was directly supervised from Vienna and therefore
the archives of the supreme command and its agencies (*Archive der
Zentralstellen des Heeres*) are of special importance. Above all, there
are the Hofkriegsrat archives, truly an immense collection. Access
to individual papers in this collection is through a series of annual

protocol books, the *expedit* volumes for incoming and the *registratura* volumes for outgoing correspondence. Of course, to sort through all the papers relating to the military border received or issued by the Hofkriegsrat for over one hundred years, though many have been destroyed, would constitute a nearly unmanageable task. Shortcuts, however, are possible by utilizing the special collections and excerpt registers compiled for the use of various high-level commissions, such as the Militär Kommission Nostitz-Rieneck or the *Grenz* Organisierungs Kommission created by Archduke Charles.

After March, 1848, the Hofkriegsrat was superseded by the *Kriegsministerium* which continued to control the border until 1881. Records here are also spotty and in fact lean for the years 1852 to 1858 and again from 1862 to 1867. During this period, however, Emperor Franz Joseph took an increasing personal interest in military matters, and there is a great deal on border affairs in the *Archiv der Militärkanzlei des Kaisers und Königs*. Records here were filed according to various categories and incoming as well as outgoing documents, together with supporting materials, were kept together. Category 49 concerns the military border and provides a wide range of material, from the question of a pension for the widow of a Grenzer corporal to the negotiations leading to the dissolution of the institution. Moreover, probably because of the exalted nature of the office, the collection is almost entirely complete and very few items have been discarded or are otherwise missing.

There existed within the Hofkriegsrat as well as in the Kriegsministerium special military border sections, Department B and Department 10, respectively. No separate indices exist, but their records, of which relatively few have been preserved, can be approached through the regular annual indices and protocols. There does exist a special collection, the *Schriftgut betreffend die Militärgrenze*, an accumulation of various fascicles, folders, memoranda, and drafts, apparently the contents of various desk drawers and files left over from the dissolution of Department 10 in 1872. Use of this material presents certain difficulties because there are no indices, except for a brief inventory of fascicles, bound manuscript, and printed volumes. The latter conveniently include copies of the laws of 1754, 1807, and 1850, as well as the various regulations governing the Militärcommunitäten.

The *Mémoires*, serving as a catchall for a number of archival estrays, form an interesting and unique collection. In general the papers date from the later decades of the eighteenth century to the middle of the nineteenth. Here is a wide variety of reports, memoranda, and opinions on almost every conceivable subject, roughly divided into twenty-eight topical categories. Category 23 deals with the military border and includes five large manuscript volumes,

Mém. XXIII-89-93, of record excerpts dating from the establishment of the border to 1806. Other items of interest include a number of projects to alleviate the conditions of the Militärgrenze.

Finally, rivalling the Hofkriegsrat archives in scope are the *Feldakten*, which I have used rather sparingly. Dealing primarily with the conduct of military operations proper, they are of limited value for an overall history of the border. They were useful, however, for data on Grenzer performance in the field, for the operations leading to the Austrian reoccupation of the regiments ceded to France, and for the actions of the Croatian-Slavonian forces in 1848–49.

There also are papers bearing on the military border in the Haus-, Hof und Staatsarchiv. Many of these are duplicated and more easily accessible in the Kriegsarchiv, especially the reports dealing with the question of support for the Serb revolution. Also of interest are the folders dealing with the shortlived Illyrian kingdom in the period after 1814, and I have made use of the conference protocols of the council of common ministers which contain the important discussions and votes on the dissolution of the military border.

In Zagreb the two main repositories for papers dealing with the military border are the state archives, the Državni Arhiv, and the Archive of the Historical Institute of the Yugoslav Academy of Arts and Sciences. Almost all of the military papers are in the military section of the Državni Arhiv. Although there exists a brief typewritten inventory of the military collection, there exist no detailed indices. A new analytic inventory is in the process of preparation. Therefore, for this collection, I have merely given the date, the series, and the fascicle number in my notes.

The most important collection in the Državni Arhiv is the records of the *Generalkommando Agram (Zagrebačka Generalkomanda)*, over two hundred fascicles in all. As might be expected, the papers deal primarily with administrative military matters. Indeed, for the period after 1815 the series are devoid of most political material and become even more narrowly military. And for the years 1859 to 1873 the files are missing completely. There are, however, political documents in the files on the Rakovica insurrection, and almost all of the missing material can be found in the various sections of the Kriegsarchiv. Whether the disappearance of political material was accidental or deliberate is hard to determine; however, during the German occupation of Yugoslavia many documents were removed from the archive.

Papers on the brigade and regimental level are primarily restricted to the minutiae of military administration, though they sometimes contain valuable information on morale, discipline, and above all on the incidence of frontier trouble with Bosnia in the first half of

the nineteenth century. Here the most important series are those
of the Petrinja Brigade, which comprised the two Banal regiments,
followed by the various regimental archives. There are no restrictions on the use of this material.

The archive of the Historical Section of the Yugoslav Academy
contains two major series of interest to the researcher on the military border. The *Codices* contain a number of manuscripts, mainly
written by contemporary civilian observers, on conditions on the
Croatian border, dating mainly from the late eighteenth and early
nineteenth centuries. There are also a number of miscellaneous
papers on the French administration of Illyria. Perhaps of greater
importance are the Jelačić Papers (Ostavština Bana Jelačića) that,
as yet, have not been fully explored. They were used, rather selec-
tively, by Mr. Hartley for his adulatory biography of the Ban, and
more recently by Professor Vaso Bogdanov. But they still await a
thorough exploitation. In this book, they have been used extensively
for the years 1846–52, but only sparingly for the earlier period.

Materials on the French in Illyria are available both in the Archives Nationales in Paris and in the Archives de la Guerre in
Vincennes. I was not able to visit these deposits, but I am obliged
to their administrators for furnishing me with microfilms from their
collections. Although most of the documents deal with the year 1808
to 1813, the French always maintained a lively military interest in
the Grenzer regiments whose organization and development were
often considered as possible models for the expanding French colonial military establishment. In the Archives de la Guerre, the series
Reconaissances contain first-hand accounts by trained military observers for the years 1805 to 1867. In addition, a number of documents relating to the last days of the French occupation are available in the Beauharnais Archive of Princeton University.

The chief published primary sources consist of documentary collections. Unfortunately, Professor Lopašić died before he could
continue his excellent three-volume collection of *Spomenici Hrvatske Krajine* (Zagreb, 1884–89), which ends in 1747. Other collections of documents deal primarily with shorter periods or specific
incidents in the history of the military border, but they do contain
useful material. I have briefly discussed the more important items
of this kind in the bibliography. Also included in the section on
published primary materials are the various special handbooks
compiled to guide officers and administrators through the maze of
regulations governing the border establishment. Usually written by
officials of the military administration these are of considerable
value. This is not uniformly true of the books that I have classified
as "Other Contemporary Sources." These include accounts by travelers, some excellent, others rather superficial, as well as the con-

siderable number of polemical books and pamphlets dealing with the future disposition of the military border and published in Austria after the middle of the last century. These works, using history as a vehicle to advance special claims of nation, race, or mission, must be used with caution. The same warning, of course, applies to much of the secondary literature where deliberate distortions and national prejudice are only too common.

The bibliography is selective and concentrates on the military border in Croatia from 1740 to 1881. It includes a number of works on closely related topics, especially on Austrian military organization and on the problems of nationalities. It does not include, however, every title cited in the notes. Beyond this, the most important omission is secondary works in Hungarian, which I am not able to read. But I have used and included Hungarian bibliographies and source collections, because in each case a considerable amount of the material was in Latin, German, or Serbo-Croatian.

PUBLISHED PRIMARY SOURCES

Austria. *Militar Gränitz-Rechten von Ihro Kaiserl. Königl. Majestät für das Carlstädter und Varasdiner-Generalat vorgeschrieben im Jahr 1754.* Vienna, 1754.

———. *Schematismus der kaiserl. königl. Armee für das Jahr 1790.* Vienna, 1790. Appeared yearly with slightly varying titles until 1918.

———. *Grundgesetze für die Carlstädter-Warasdiner, Banal, Slavonische, und Banatische Militär-Gränze.* Vienna, 1807.

———. *Exercier-Reglement für die kaiserlich königliche Gränz-Infanterie.* Vienna, 1808.

———. *Forst-Instruction für die Grenz-Regimenter und Bataillons mit Beziehung auf das denselben untergeordnete Wald-Personale.* Vienna, 1840. A slightly changed second edition was issued in 1854.

———. *Abrichtungs-Reglement für die k.k. Linien- und Grenz-Infanterie.* Vienna, 1851.

Bartenstein, Johann C. *Kurzer Bericht von der Beschaffenheit der zerstreuten zahlreichen Illyrischen Nation in den kaiserl. königl. Erblanden.* Leipzig, 1802. Reprint of a memorandum submitted in 1761 to Joseph II.

Bergmayr, Ignaz F. *Verfassung der k.k. Militär-Gränze und Oesterreichischen Kriegsmarine.* Vienna, 1845. Useful account and commentary on the administrative practices based on the 1807 law.

———. *Handbuch zu den peinlichen Verfahren in der k.k. österreichischen Armee und in den Militaire-Gränzen.* Vienna, 1812.

Berlić, F. *Die freiwillige Theilname der Serben und Kroaten an den vier letzten österreichisch-türkischen Kriegen dargethan in einer Sammlung gleichzeitiger geschichtlicher Urkunden.* Vienna, 1854. Useful collection for the Montenegrin affair of 1788.

Bojničić, Ivan. "Dva Jelačićeva pisma o okršajima na hrvatsko-turskoj granici. Prilog životopisu bana Jelačića," *Vjesnik hrvatsko-slavonskog i dalmatinskog zemaljskog arhiva,* 13 (1911), 193–210. Letters from Jelačić to the Austrian historian Joseph Scheiger justifying his conduct during the frontier incidents of 1845 and 1846.

Boppe, P. *Document inédits sur les relations de la Serbie avec Napoléon I, 1809–14.* Paris, 1888.

Deželić, Velimir (ed.), "Kako su Francuzi g. 1813 otišli iz Karlovca," *Vjesnik hrvatsko-slavonskog i dalmatinskog zemaljskog arhiva,* 15 (1913), 198–202. A report on how the citizens of Karlstadt prevented the French from destroying the Kupa bridge.

Fiedler, Joseph. "Beiträge zur Union der Valachen in Slavonien und Syrmien," *Archiv für österreichische Geschichte,* 37 (1867), 105–45. Excellent documentary coverage on the efforts to force the Slavonian regiments to accept the Uniat rites.

Hietzinger, Carl B. v. *Statistik der Militärgränze des österreichischen Kaiserthums.* 3 vols. Vienna, 1817–23. A most useful compilation by a long-time official of the Military Border Department of the Hofkriegsrat. Although on occasion too favorable toward the administration, the data appear to be correct.

Horvat, Karlo (ed.). "Zapisci od 1752-1579. Ivana Josipovicá, župnika križevačkoga. Prilozi za povijest hrvatsku u XVIII. vijeku iz 'liber memorabilium' župe križevačke," *Starine,* 34 (1913), 305–65.

Hostinek, Josef. *Die K. u. K. Militärgrenze. Ihre Organisation und Verwaltung.* Vienna, 1861. An official handbook for the border service written by an officer in the administrative branch. Excellent source for regulations and procedures for the period 1850 to 1867.

Ivančan, Ljudevit. "Buna varaždinskog generalata i prograničnih kmetova god. 1755," *Vjesnik hrvatsko-slavonskog i dalmatinskog zemaljskog arhiva,* 4 (1902), 240–59. Still the best collection of documents on the Warasdin revolt and its aftermath.

———. "Iztraga proti buntovnim krajišnikom varaždinskoga generalata g. 1755," *Vjesnik hrvatskoslavonskog i dalmatinskog zemaljskog arhiva,* 5 (1903), 65–88.

Ivić, Aleksa. *Spisi bečkih arhiva o prvom Srpskom ustanku.* Vols. 8, 10, 11, 12 and 14 of *Zbornik za istoriju, jezik i književnost srpskog naroda.* Belgrade, 1935–39.

Jovics, Spiridion. *Ethnographisches Gemählde der slavonischen*

Militärgrenze, oder ausführliche Darstellung der Lage, Beschaffenheit und politischen Verfassung des Landes, dann der Lebensart, Sitten, Gebräuche, der geistigen Bildung und des Characters seiner Bewohner. Vienna, 1835. Written by a subordinate official, a native "son of the border," this account tends to prettify the harsh realities of Grenzer life.

Klein, A. "Militär-Statistische Beschreibung der k.k. Grenzländer," *Streffleur's österreichische militärische Zeitschrift,* 12 (1871), 123–39. The author, a captain in the judicial branch, gives a frank description of border conditions during the period of dissolution.

Krainz, Leopold M. *Die k.k. Militärgrenze und deren Grundgesetz: Eine kultur-historische Skizze.* Vienna, 1866. The title is somewhat misleading. The book is not a historical treatment but a semiofficial handbook for officers in the border service. The author was an administrative-judicial officer in the 2d Banal Regiment.

Kukuljević, Joannes. *Jura regni Croatiae, Dalmatiae et Slavoniae.* 3 vols. Zagreb, 1861-62. A useful collection of documents, including the acts of the Sabor concerning the military border.

Kušlan, D., and M. Šuhaj. *Saborski spisi sabora kraljevina Dalmacije, Hrvatske i Slavonije od. god. 1861.* 2 vols. Zagreb, 1861.

Lopašić, Radoslav (ed.). *Spomenici hrvatske krajine.* Vols. 15, 16, and 20 of *Monumenta spectantia historiam Slavorum Meridionalium.* Zagreb, 1884–89. The best collection of documentary materials on the military border up to the 1740's.

Matasović, Josip. "Kulmerova pisma banu Jelačiću 1848," *Narodna Starina,* 13 (1935), 153–54.

Matić, Tomo. "Pabirči iz arhiva Austrijske Polizeihofstelle iz godina 1797-1810," *Starine,* 46 (1956), 45–62.

Miskolczy, Gyula. *A horvát kérdés története es irományai a rendi állam korában.* 2 vols. Budapest, 1927–28. A most useful collection with much material on the influence, real or supposed, of the Illyrian movement on the Grenzer.

Nemeth, Krešimir. "Nekoliko néobjavljenih pisama iz korespondencije Kulmer-Jelačić 19, III.- 5. V. 1849," *Arhivski vjesnik,* 2 (1958), 333–59.

Pejaković, Stjepan. *Aktenstücke zur Geschichte des kroatischslawonischen Landtages und der nationalen Bewegung vom Jahre 1848.* Vienna, 1861.

Rastić, Danilo. *Regulament zadržavanja muštranja i manevre pešaka od l kolovoza 1791.* Karlovac, 1811. Croatian translation of the French infantry regulations of August 1, 1791, issued for the Grenzer in the French service.

Schwicker, Johann H. "Zur Geschichte der Kirchlichen Union in der croatischen Militärgrenze," *Archiv für österreichische Geschichte*, 52 (1875), 276–400. With important documents on attempts to force the Grenzer into the Uniat rites.

Smičiklas, T. (ed.), *Balthasar Adami Kercselich: Annuae 1748–1767*. Vol. 30 of *Monumenta spectantia historiam Slavorum Meridionalium*. Zagreb, 1901.

Sporer, Franz. *Das Forstwesen in der k.k. österreichischen Militärgrenze, oder vollständiges Forstlehrbuch für das Militär-Grenze-Forstschutzpersonal*. 3 vols. Zagreb, 1841–43.

Stopfer, Mathias. *Erläuterungen der Grundgesetze für die Carlstädter, Warasdiner, Banal, Slavonische und Banatische Militär Gränze*. Vienna, 1831.

―――. *Erläuterungen über die Militär-Gränz Verwaltung des österreichischen Kaiserthums*. Vienna, 1838.

―――. *Lehrbuch über die Militär-Gränz-Verwaltung des österreichischen Kaiserthums*. Graz, 1842. These three volumes are semiofficial compilations for the use of administrative officers in the frontier service. Beyond that they provide an interesting picture of the border as seen through the eyes of a subaltern.

Thim, Jószef. *A magyaroszági 1848-49-iki szerb fölkeles története.* 3 vols. Budapest, 1930–35. Documents on the Serb rising in the Vojvodina and the Slavonian and Banat regiments.

Trautmann, Johann Ritter v. "Übersicht der Entstehung, Verfassung und Verwaltung der österreichischen Militär-Grenze," *Österreichische militärische Zeitschrift*, No. 2 (1836), 278–93; No. 3 (1837), 67–81.

Tritschler, K. "Der österreichische Grenzoffizier nach seinen Pflichten und den hierdurch bedingten Eigenschaften," *Österreichische militärische Zeitschrift*, (1832), 323–36. The last two items are poor for historical data, but they provide an excellent picture of the attitudes and duties of administrative and line officers in the border service.

OTHER CONTEMPORARY SOURCES

Artner, Therese v. *Briefe über einen Theil von Croatien und Italien an Caroline Pichler*. Pest, 1830.

Bach, Franz. *Otočaner Regiments Geschichte. Vom Ursprung dieser Gegend, ihrer Bevölkerung und ihre Schicksale*. Karlstadt, 1853. Especially interesting for the early nineteenth century, this is a surprisingly frank account by a serving officer.

Beaujour, Félix de. *Voyage militaire dans l'empire Ottoman*. 2 vols. Paris, 1829.

"Beytrag zur Geschichte der k.k. Gränzregimenter, theils aus öffentlichen Relationen und Beschreibungen, theils aus besondern Nachrichten und Schriften zusammengezogen." Vienna, 1788. A small pamphlet primarily dealing with military exploits of the Carlstadt regiments.

Bogović, Mirko. *Politische Rückblicke im Bezug auf Kroatien.* Zagreb, 1861. Pamphlet by a prominent Unionist.

Breton, J.B.J. de la Martinière. *L'Illyrie et la Dalmatie ou moeurs et coutumes de leurs habitants.* 2 vols. Paris, 1815.

————. *Illyrien und Dalmatien oder Sitten, Gebräuche und Trachten der Illyrier und Dalmatier und ihrer Nachbarn, aus dem französischen nach Hacquet, Fortis und Cassis.* Pest, 1826.

Bright, Richard. *Travels from Vienna through Lower Hungary.* Edinburgh, 1819. The famous Dr. Bright makes some interesting observations on the military border regiments.

Caragoli: Ungarn, Militairgrenze, Slavonien, Croatien. Berlin, 1832.

Chenot, Adam. *Tractatus de peste.* Vienna, 1766.

Chopin, Jean M. *Provinces danubiennes: Bosnie, Servie, Herzégovine, Bulgarie, Slavonie, Illyrie, Croatie, Dalmatie, Montenegro, Albanie.* Paris, 1856.

Csaplovics, Johann v. *Slavonien und zum Theil Croatien.* 2 vols. Pest, 1819. Contains several of the Illyrian privileges as well as a critical account of Austrian religious policy on the Border.

————. *Neueste statistisch-geographische Beschreibung des Königreichs Ungarn, Croatien, Slavonien under der Ungarischen Militärgrenze.* Buda, 1832.

Czoernig, Karl Freiherr v. *Ethnographie der Oesterreichischen Monarchie.* 3 vols. Vienna, 1857.

Demian, Johann A. *Statistische Beschreibung der Militärgrenze.* 2 vols. Vienna, 1806. These two volumes, by a serving Austrian officer, reveal disenchantment with the military administration and severe criticism of Grenzer conduct and character.

————. *Tableau géographique et politique des royaumes de Hongrie, d'Esclavonie, et de la grande principate de Transylvanie.* 2 vols. Paris, 1809.

————. *Statistische Darstellung der Illyrischen Provinzen: Die illyrische Militär-Provinz.* Tübingen, 1810. Largely a repetition of the 1806 data, this study is disappointing for the French period.

Desboeufs, Charles (ed.). *Souvenirs du capitaine Desboeufs.* Paris, 1901. Recollections of a Napoleonic veteran concerning Marmont's reprisals in Bosnia.

Ebner, Ladislas. *Historisch statistisch topographische Beschreibung der königl. Freystadt Varasdin.* Warasdin, 1827.

Engel, Johann C. v. *Staatskunde und Geschichte von Dalmatien, Croatien, und Slawonien, nebst einigen ungedruckten Denkmälern Ungarischer Geschichte.* Halle, 1798.

Die Erlebnisse eines k.k. Offiziers im österreichisch-serbischen Armeekorps in den Jahren 1848 und 1849. Semlin, 1861.

Der Feldzug in Ungarn und Siebenbürgen im Sommer des Jahres 1849. Pest, 1850.

Fortis, Albert. *Voyage en Dalmatie*. 2 vols. Berne, 1778.

Fras, Franz Julius. *Merkwürdigheiten oder historischstatistischtopographische Beschreibung der Karlstädter Militärgrenze*. Karlstadt, 1830.

————. *Vollständige Topographie der Karlstädter Militär-Grenze mit besonderer Rücksicht auf die Beschreibung der Schlösser, Ruinen, Inskriptionen und anderen dergl. Überbleibseln für Reisende und zur Förderung der Vaterlandsliebe*. Zagreb, 1835. Not always correct for historical background, but interesting for contemporary observations.

Griselini, Francesco. *Versuch einer politischen und natürlichen Geschichte des Temeswarer Bannats in Briefen an Standespersonen und Gelehrte*. Vienna, 1780.

Grivčić, Daniel. *Gegenwart und Zukunft der k.k. Militärgrenze. Von einem Grenzer*. Vienna, 1869. A pamphlet bitterly opposing demilitarization.

Hacquet, Balthasar. *Abbildungen und Beschreibung der südwestlich und östlichen Wenden, Illyrier, und Slaven, deren geographische Ausbreitung von dem adriatischen Meere bis an den Ponto, deren Sitten, Gebräuche, Hanthierungen, Gewerbe, Religion, usw. nach einer zehnjährigen Reise und vierzigjährigen Aufenthalt in jenen Gegenden*. 2 vols. Leipzig, 1801–3.

Kohl, Johann G. *Hundert Tage auf Reisen in den österreichischen Staaten*. 4 vols. Leipzig and Dresden, 1842.

————. *Austria, Vienna, Prague, Hungary, Bohemia, the Danube, Galicia, Styria, Moravia, Bukovina, and the Military Frontier*. London, 1843. A condensation of the above. Kohl was an intelligent observer, but his German chauvinism induced him to overestimate the blessings visited by "German" discipline on the Grenzer.

Körner, Friedrich. *Vaterländische Bilder aus Ungarn und Siebenbürgen, der Woiwodina und dem Banat, Kroatien, Slavonien, der Militärgrenze, sowie Dalmatien*. 2 vols. Leipzig, 1858.

Krichel, Adalbert J. *Fussreisen durch den grössten Theil der österreichischen Staaten in den Jahren 1827, 1828, bis Ende Mai 1829, und zwar: durch Ungarn, Siebenbürgen, die Militärgrenze fast in allen Theilen*. 3 vols. Vienna, 1830–31.

Kussan, Paul. *Kurzgefasste Geschichte des Oguliner 3 National-Grenz Infantrie Regiments. Nach den gesammelten Schriften und Urkunden*. Vienna, 1852. Regimental history by a subaltern containing first hand observations on the Grenzer during the events of 1848–49.

Kvaternik, Eugen. *La Croatie et la confédération Italienne.* Paris, 1859.

————. *Das historisch-diplomatisch Verhältniss des Königreiches Kroatien zur ungarischen St. Stefanskrone.* Zagreb, 1861. Two volumes by one of the most uncompromising exponents of the national Croatian movement.

l'Homme de Courbière, Wilhelm O. R. de. *Über Verwerthung der Heereskraft zur Zeit des Friedens. Vornehmlich über Akkerbauende Truppen sowohl im allgemeinen, wie über die Einführung derselben in Preussen. Nach der Art der Truppen der k.k. Militair-Grenze und der k. Russischen Militair-Colonien.* Düsseldorf, 1854.

————. *Offenes Wort an die Staats-Finanz-und Kriegswissenschaft über Beifügung von Ackerbautruppen zum deutschen Heer auf den Staatsdomänen des Reiches.* Berlin, 1879. Two pamphlets urging the introduction of military colonies in the Prussian-German army.

Marmont, Auguste F.L.W. *Mémoires du Maréchal Marmont, Duc de Raguse.* 9 vols. Paris, 1857.

————. *Voyage de Monsieur le Maréchal, Duc de Raguse, en Hongrie, en Transylvania, dans la Russie méridionale, en Crimée, et sur les Bords de la Mer d'Azoff, à Constantinople, dans quelques parties de l'Asie-Mineure, en Syrie, en Palestine et en Égypte.* 2 vols. Brussels, 1837. Vol. 3 of the *Mémoires* contains recollections and documents relating to Marmont's command of the military border; vol. 1 of the *Voyage* compares this institution with the Russian military colonies founded by Catherine II.

Merkwürdige historische Nachrichten von dem beym jetzigen Krieg von neuen bekannt gewordenen Völkern, in welchem ihr Character, ihre Sitten, Gewohnheiten und Waffen beschrieben werden. Jena, 1743. Describes the first appearance of the Grenzer during the Silesian wars.

Mollinary, Anton Frhr. v. *Sechsundvierzig Jahre im österreichisch-ungarischen Heere, 1833–1879.* 2 vols. Zurich, 1905. A first-hand account by the next to the last commanding general of the Croatian regiments.

Nagy, Carl. *Neueste statistische-geographische Beschreibung des Königreichs Ungarn, Croatien, Slavonien und der ungarischen Militärgrenze.* Leipzig, 1832.

Nordstein, F. A. *Geschichte der Wiener Revolution.* Leipzig, 1850. Conventional liberal and pro-Hungarian, this volume contains a number of letters, edicts, etc., addressed by Emperor Ferdinand to Jelačić, as well as a detailed description of the alleged Croatian atrocities in Vienna.

Novaković, Stephani. *Dissertatio brevis ac sincera hungari auctoris de gente serbica, perperam rasciana dicta, ejusque meritis ac fatis in Hungaria, cum appendice privilegiorum eidem genti elargitorum.* Buda, 1790.

————. *Kurzgefasste Abhandlung über die Verdienste und Schicksale der serbischen oder raizischen Nation in dem Königreiche Ungarn. Von einem ungarischen Patrioten, mit einem Anhang der denselben verliehenen Privilegien.* Novi Sad, 1791.

Panković, B. *Die Militärgrenzefrage in ihrer Beziehung zur orientalischen Frage vom politischen, staatsrechtlichen, und administrativen Standpunkt beleuchtet.* Vienna, 1865. A Croatian nationalist pamphlet.

Paton, A. A. *Highlands and Islands of the Adriatic including Dalmatia, Croatia, and the southern Provinces of the Austrian Empire.* 2 vols. London, 1849. Volume 2 contains an account of conditions on the Croatian Military Border in 1847. On the whole, the author was favorably impressed by the Austrian administration and unaware of the tensions arising out of the growth of the South Slav national movement.

Pidoll zu Quintenbach, Carl Frhr. v. *Einige Worte über die Wirtschaft der Karlstädter Grenzer, den an dieser Grenze angestellten Herren Offizieren achtungsvoll gewidmet.* Vienna, 1844.

————. *Einige Worte über die russischen Militär-Kolonien im Vergleiche mit der k.k. österreichischen Militär-Grenze und mit allgemeinen Betrachtungen darüber.* Vienna, 1847. The author, a member of the Hofkriegsrat Military Border Department for over forty years, warns against abuses of the Grenzer and gives his ideas on how to improve economic conditions.

Spottiswoode, George A. "A tour in civil and military Croatia, and part of Hungary," in Sir Francis Galton, *Vacation tourists and notes of travel in 1860.* London, 1861.

Starčević, Ante. *Nekolike uspomene.* Zagreb, 1870.

Stiles, William H. *Austria in 1848–49.* 2 vols. New York, 1852. Stiles, United States chargé d'affaires in Vienna, observed some phases of the revolution at first hand. Contains an account of the Grenzer in Vienna.

Teleki von Szék, Dominik. *Reisen durch Ungern und einige angränzende Länder. Beschrieben vom Reichsgrafen Dominik Teleki von Szék.* Pest, 1805.

Tkalac, E. I. v. *Jugenderinnerungen aus Kroatien.* Leipzig, 1894.

————. *Uspomene iz Hrvatske.* Zagreb, 1945.

Utiešenović, Ognieslav M. *Die Militärgrenze und die Verfassung. Eine Studie über den Ursprung und das Wesen der Militärgrenzinstitution und die Stellung derselben zur Landesverfassung.* Vienna, 1861.

————. *Die Militärgrenz-Frage und der österreichische-ungarische Constitutionalismus.* 1869. A former official of the Croatian Court Chancery, dismissed as an "ultra-nationalist," presents the case for Croatian jurisdiction on the military border.

"Vojnička krajina. Na razkřšcu svoje proslasti i budućnosti." Sisak, 1871. Pamphlet protesting the dissolution of the Military Border.

Vukassovich, Johann D. v. "Beschreibung des Karlstädter Generalats," *Ungarisches Magazin*, 3 (1783), 432–36.

Wilkinson, James G. *Dalmatia and Montenegro with a journey to Mostar in Hercegovina.* 2 vols. London, 1848.

SECONDARY MATERIALS

"Die Sendung des österreichischen Hauptmanns Vukassevich nach Montenegro im Jahre 1788," *Osterreichische militärische Zeitschrift*, (1828), 170–93, 263–80.

Bartels v. Bartberg, Eduard. *Der Krieg im Jahre 1859. Nach offiziellen Quellen nicht offiziell bearbeitet.* Bamberg, 1894. This work contains serious charges against the conduct of the Grenzer. Equally critical of other aspects of the war, this publication led to Bartels' forced resignation from the Austrian army.

Beer, Adolf. *Die orientalische Politik Österreichs seit 1774.* Prag-Leipzig, 1883.

Bernath, Mathias. "Die Errichtung der Siebenbürgischen Militärgrenze und die Wiener Rumänenpolitik in der frühjosephinischen Zeit," *Südost-Forschungen*, 19 (1960), 164–93.

Bertling, M. *Die Kroaten und Panduren in der Mitte des XVIII. Jahrhundertes und ihre Verwendung in den Friederizianischen Kriegen.* Berlin, 1912.

Bićanić, Rudolf. "Oslobodjenje kmetova u Hrvatskoj godine 1848," *Djelo*, 1 (1948), 190–200.

————. *Doba manufakture u Hrvatskoj i Slavoniji 1750-1860.* Zagreb, 1951.

Birke, Ernest. *Frankreich und Ostmitteleuropa im 19. Jahrhundert.* Cologne-Graz, 1960.

Black, Cyril E. "Fouché in Illyria," *Journal of Central European Affairs*, 2 (1943), 386–95.

Blanc, André. "Les confins militaires croates au xix siècle," *Revue des Études Slaves*, 28 (1951), 111–28.

————. *La Croatie occidentale. Étude de géographie humaine.* Paris, 1957. A major work containing much useful material on the Karlstadt and Banal regiments. Unfortunately the author did not consult the documents in the Državni Arhiv or in the Kriegsarchiv.

Bogdanov, Vaso. *Društvene i političke borbe u Hrvatskoj 1848-49.* Zagreb, 1949.

210   Bibliography

————. *Historija političkih stranaka u hrvatskoj od prvih strana-čkih grupiranja do 1918.* Zagreb, 1958.

————. "Uloga vojne krajine i njenih zastupnika u Hrv. Saboru 1861," *Zbornik historijskog instituta Jugoslavenske Akademije,* 3 (1960), 59–214. Works by the presently most prominent Croatian historian. Authoritative and based on good sources, but heavily oriented toward economic interpretation.

Boppe, P. *La Croatie Militaire (1809–1813). Les régiments croates à la Grande Armée.* Paris, 1900. This study contains a number of interesting documents from the French archives, including the papers of Marshal Marmont deposited in Châtillon-sur-Seine.

Čulinović, Ferdo. *Seljačke bune u Hrvatskoj.* Zagreb, 1951.

Devčić, Ivan. *Hrvati i Hrvatska pod Napoleonom velikim.* Zagreb, 1905. A brief account taken mainly from Boppe.

Ferguson, Alan D. "Russian Landmilitia and Austrian Militärgrenze," *Südost-Forschungen,* 13 (1954), 137–58.

Filipovič, Nedim. "Pogled na osmanski feudalizam," *Godišnjak istoriskog društva Bosne i Hercegovine,* 4 (1952), 5-146.

Gopčević, Spiridion. *Beiträge zur neueren Kriegsgeschichte der Balkanhalbinsel.* Leipzig, 1887.

Gragge, Robert. *Preussen, Weimar, und die ungarische Königskrone.* Berlin, 1923.

Gross, Mirjana. "Propast starounionističke stranke u svijetlu izveštaja Mirka Bogovića," *Zbornik historijskog instituta Jugoslavenske Akademije,* 1 (1954), 223–49. The military border seen through the eyes of a Unionist politician shortly before and after the Rakovica rising.

Grujić, Radoslav, M. "Prilozi za istoriju seobe Srba u Rusiji," *Spomenik,* 51 (1913), 70–79.

Hartley, M. *The Man who saved Austria. The Life and Times of Baron Jellacic.* London, 1912. An interesting but uncritical book, written to please the Jellačić family.

Hauptmann, Ferdinand. "Banus Jellačić und Feldmarschall Fürst Windisch-Grätz," *Südost-Forschungen,* 15 (1956), 372–402.

Jähns, Max. *Heeresverfassungen und Völkerleben.* Berlin, 1885. Contains comparisons of the Roman, Frankish, Austrian, and Russian military colonies.

Jelavich, Charles. "Some Aspects of Serbian Religious Development in the Eighteenth Century," *Church History,* 23 (1954), 144–52.

Kemény, Gábor G., and László Katus (eds.). *Nemmagyar Népek (Nemzetiségek).* Vol. 4 of *Magyar Történeti Bibliográfia 1825–1867.* Budapest, 1959. Contains over 30,000 titles, an index of names, and a table of contents in English, French, German, Hungarian, and Russian. A most valuable compendium.

Kerchnawe, Hugo. *Die alte k.k. Militärgrenze. Ein Schutzwall Euro-*

pas. Vienna, 1939. An inaccurate and propagandist account extolling the virtues of military rule and German mission.

Kienast, Andreas. *Die Legion Klapka. Eine Episode aus dem Jahre 1866 und ihre Vorgeschichte.* Vienna, 1900. Contains information on the attempts of Orešković to raise the Grenzer against Austria.

Kiszling, Rudolf. *Die Revolution im Kaisertum Österreich 1848-1849.* 2 vols. Vienna, 1948. Highly critical of Jelačić's military abilities.

————. *Die Kroaten: Der Schicksalsweg eines Südslawenvolkes.* Graz-Cologne, 1956.

————. "Das Nationalitätenproblem im Habsburgs Wehrmacht 1848–1918," *Der Donauraum*, 4 (1959), 82–92.

————. "Die militärischen Beziehungen der Kroaten und Nordserben zu den Deutschen," *Südostdeutsche Vierteljahresblätter*, 8 (1960), 19–23.

Kostić, Lazo. *Sporni predeli Srba i Hrvata.* Chicago, 1957. Polemical assertion of the Serb character of the Croatian Military Border.

Kotasek, Edith. *Feldmarschall Graf Lacy. Ein Leben für Österreichs Heer.* Horn, 1956.

Krones, Franz X. Frhr. v. "Josef Freiherr von Simbschen und die Stellung Österreichs zur Serbischen Frage 1807–10," *Archiv für Österreichische Geschichte*, 76 (1890), 127–260.

Lendl, Egon. "Zur politischen Geographie der österreichischen Militärgrenze," *Der Donauraum*, 8 (1963), 201–14.

Lesky, Erna. "Die österreichische Pestfront an der k.k. Militärgrenze," *Saeculum*, 8 (1957), 82–106. An important article, unforunately marred by the determination to make the institution appear in the best possible light.

Magdić, M. *Topografija i povijest Ogulina.* Zagreb, 1926.

Marchal, Chevalier. "Notice sur la Croatie militaire et sur les autres provinces illyriennes sous l'empire de Napoléon," *Bullétin de l'Academie Royale des Sciences, des Lettres et des Beaux Arts de Belgique*, 15 (1848), 569–85.

McNeill, William H. *Europe's Steppe Frontier 1500-1800.* Chicago, 1964. By far best comparative study of borders in eastern and southeastern Europe.

Milleker, Felix. *Geschichte der Banater Militärgrenze, 1764–1873.* Pancevo, 1926.

Moačanin, Fedor. "Periodizacija Vojne krajine," *Historijski zbornik*, 13 (1960), 111–17.

Moačanin, Fedor. "O nekim problemima iz historije Vojne krajine I," *Historijski zbornik*, 17 (1964), 327–57.

Neustädter, Josip. *Ban Jelačić i dogadjaji u Hrvatskoj od godine 1848.* Zagreb, 1942.

Novak, Grga. *Prošlost Dalmacije.* 2 parts. Zagreb, 1944. Contains a brief description of the Venetian military frontier in Dalmatia in the eighteenth century.

Pavlović, I. "Vojna granica i srpska vojska," *Glasnik istorijskog društva,* 9 (1936), 335–46. Contributions of the Grenzer during the formation of Serbia's regular army.

Perrot, Georges. "L'Autriche d'autrefois. Les confins militaires et leur législation," *Revue des deux Mondes,* 84 (1869), 38–70.

Picot, Émile. *Les Serbes de Hongrie. Leur histoire, leurs privilèges, leur église, leur état politique et social.* Prague, 1873. An interesting, if heavily biased, account by the French consul at Temesvar.

Pisani, Paul. *La Dalmatie de 1797 à 1815.* Paris, 1893.

Pivec-Stelè, Melitta. *La Vie Économique des Provinces Illyriennes.* Paris, 1930. Excellent study based on use of the French and Yugoslav archives, together with an extensive critical bibliography.

Popović, Daka. "Statut za Hrvatsko-slavonsku i Banatsko-srpsku vojnu granicu od 7 Maja 1850 godine," *Zbornik Matice Srpske* 5 (1953), 103–11.

Preradovich, Nikolaus v. "Deutsche und Südslawen," *Südostdeutsche Vierteljahresblätter,* 8 (1960), 24–26. A descendant of the famous Croatian poet assails the legend of the proverbial imperial loyalty of the Croats.

Pribičević, Adam. *Naseljevanje Srba po Hrvatskoj i Dalmaciji.* Windsor, 1955.

Prpić, George. "French Rule in Croatia: 1806-1813," *Balkan Studies* 5 (1964), 221–76. A fine essay emphasizing reforms in civil Croatia and their effects on the rise of the Illyrian movement.

Radonić, J., and Kostić, M. *Srpske privilegije od 1690 do 1792.* Belgrade, 1954.

Reiswitz, Johann A. v. *Belgrad-Berlin, Berlin-Belgrad 1866–1871.* Munich, 1936. Together with Wendel, this work provides important background materials for the attempts to raise the military border against Austria.

Rothenberg, Gunther E. *The Austrian Military Border in Croatia: 1522-1747.* Urbana, Ill., 1960.

———. "A Note on the Kriegsarchiv Wien," *Austrian History Newsletter,* 4 (1963), 73–78.

———. "The Struggle over the Dissolution of the Croatian Military Border," *Slavic Review,* 23 (1964), 63–78.

———. "Ban Jelačić, the Croatian Military Border, and the Intervention against Hungary," *Austrian History Yearbook,* 1 (1965), 45–73.

————. "The Croatian Military Border and the Rise of Yugoslav Nationalism," *Slavonic and East European Review*, 43 (1964), 34–45.

Scheffler, J. "Die österreichische Militärgrenze," *Odalisk*, 8 (1939), 21–31.

Schmarda, Carl. *Kurzgefasste Geschichte des k.u.k. Ottočaner Infanterie-Regiments Graf Jellačić Nr. 79 und seiner Stammregimenter*. Zagreb, 1898. A short, essentially regimental history inferior to Bach.

Schumacher, Rupert v. "Das Schrifttum über die ehemalige Militärgrenze," *Deutsches Archiv für Landes und Volksforchung*, 6 (1942), 207–40. Excellent, annotated bibliography that is marred, however, by several mistakes and must therefore be used with caution.

————. *Des Reiches Hofzaun. Geschichte der deutschen Militärgrenze in Südosten*. 2d ed. Darmstadt, 1942. A national-socialist propaganda work, extolling the German contribution and the theme of blood and soil.

Schwarz, Gavro. "Prilozi k povjesti židova u Hrvatskoj u XVIII stoljecu," *Vjesnik hrvatsko-slavonskog i dalmatinskog zemaljskog arhiva*, 3 (1901), 185–94.

Schwicker, Johann H. *Geschichte der österreichischen Militärgrenze*. Vienna-Teschen, 1883. Probably the most often cited account. Unreliable for the period to 1740 and poor for the period after 1850, it provides a reasonably objective summary of the years in between.

Šidak, Jaroslav. "Značenje Rakovičke bune u Austrijskoj politici g. 1871," *Historijski pregled*, 7 (1961), 26–43.

Šišić, Ferdo. *Franjo Barun Trenck i njegovi panduri*. Zagreb, 1900.

Spigl, Friedrich. *Repressaliengefechte an der kroatisch-türkischen Grenze in der Zeit von 1809–1845*. Vienna, 1882.

Sučević, Branko P. "Razvitak 'vlaških prava' u Varaždinskom generalatu," *Historijski zbornik*, 6 (1953), 33–70. This important article places the gradual erosion of the Grenzer privileges within the general framework of the developing absolutism and centralized government.

Tamborra, Angelo. *Cavour e i Balcani*. Turin, 1958. Interesting sidelight on the attempts of Eugen Kvaternik to subvert the military border in 1858–59.

Thiel, Victor. "Die Innerösterreichische Zentralverwaltung, 1564–1749," *Archiv für österreichische Geschichte*, 105 (1916), 1–210; 111 (1930), 497–670. Excellent exposition of the relationship between Inner Austria and the Military Border.

Turković, Milan. *Die Geschichte der ehemaligen croatisch-slawonischen Militärgrenze*. Susak, 1936. The title is somewhat misleading. Treatment here is episodic, with the main emphasis given to the administration of the public forests.

————. *Iz prošlosti grada Karlovac.* Susak, 1938.

Valentić, M. "O nekim problemima Vojne Krajine u XIX stoljeću," *Historijski zbornik,* 17 (1964), 359–83.

Vaniček, Franz. *Specialgeschichte der Militärgrenze aus den Originalquellen und Quellenwerken geschöpft.* 4 vols. Vienna, 1875. The extensive treatment of the military border suffers from faulty organization and numerous mistakes and misprints. Issued under official auspices, it tends to gloss over shortcomings of the Austrian government. Nonetheless, the four volumes provide a great mass of detail not obtainable in any other printed work.

Vrbanić, Fran. "Prilozi gospodarskomu razvoju hrv.-slav. krajine u 19. vijeku," *Rad,* 144 (1900), 40–131.

Walter, Friedrich, and Harold Steinacker. *Die Nationalitätenfrage im alten Ungarn und die Südostpolitik Wiens.* Munich, 1959.

Wendel, Hermann. *Bismarck und Serbien im Jahre 1866.* Berlin, 1866. Useful supplement to Reiswitz.

Wessely, Kurt. *Die österreichische Militärgrenze. Der deutsche Beitrag zur Verteidigung des Abendlandes gegen die Türken,* Kitzingen, 1953 (?). An unfortunate postwar revival of pan-German ideology.

Wrede, Alphons Frhr. v. *Geschichte der k. u. k. Wehrmacht. Die Regimenter, Corps, Branchen und Anstalten von 1618 bis Ende des XIX Jahrhunderts.* 5 vols. in 6. Vienna, 1898–1903. Issued as special supplementary volumes to *Mitteilungen des k.k. Kriegsarchivs.* An excellent compendium of regimental history including a list of engagements in which each unit participated. Vol. 5 contains the history of the Grenzer regiments.

INDEX

215